Transforming Cybersecurity with Machine Learning

This book provides an in-depth exploration of the dynamic intersection between machine learning (ML) and cybersecurity, offering a detailed analysis of how these technologies are reshaping the security landscape. It tracks the significant progress of machine learning in the context of cybersecurity, providing insights into the latest advancements, emerging trends, and the challenges ahead. Crafted with a discerning audience in mind, this book is a valuable resource for academic researchers, industry practitioners, and students alike. It is particularly suitable for those interested in understanding the transformative role ML plays in modern cybersecurity.

Kutub Thakur, PhD, is a distinguished cybersecurity expert, educator, and researcher with extensive experience across both public and private sectors, including the United Nations, major financial institutions, utility companies, and academic institutions. He earned a PhD in computer science with a specialization in cybersecurity at Pace University in New York, an MS in electrical and computer control systems engineering at the University of Wisconsin, and a BS in computer systems technology at the City University of New York.

Al-Sakib Khan Pathan, PhD, is a professor in the Computer Science and Engineering Department at the United International University (UIU), Bangladesh. He earned a PhD in computer engineering in 2009 at Kyung Hee University, South Korea, and a BSc in computer science and information technology at the Islamic University of Technology (IUT), Bangladesh, in 2003. He has served as chair and a member at numerous top-ranked international conferences. He is currently the editor-in-chief of two journals: *International Journal of Computers and Applications* and *Journal of Cyber Security Technology*. Dr. Pathan has also edited or authored 36 books. He is a senior member of the IEEE.

Transforming Cybersecurity with Machine Learning

Kutub Thakur and Al-Sakib Khan Pathan

CRC Press
Taylor & Francis Group
Boca Raton London New York

CRC Press is an imprint of the
Taylor & Francis Group, an **Informa** business

Designed cover image: Shutterstock

First edition published 2026
by CRC Press
2385 NW Executive Center Drive, Suite 320, Boca Raton FL, 33431

and by CRC Press
4 Park Square, Milton Park, Abingdon, Oxon, OX14 4RN

CRC Press is an imprint of Taylor & Francis Group, LLC

© 2026 Kutub Thakur and Al-Sakib Khan Pathan

ISBN: 978-1-041-17167-6 (hbk)
ISBN: 978-1-041-17168-3 (pbk)
ISBN: 978-1-003-68832-7 (ebk)

DOI: 10.1201/9781003688327

Typeset in Sabon
by SPi Technologies India Pvt Ltd (Straive)

To my beloved wife, Nawshin Thakur, my precious daughter, Eyana Thakur, and my wonderful son, Ezyan Thakur—
You are my strength, my purpose, and my greatest joy.

Kutub Thakur

To my parents, Abdus Salam Khan Pathan and Delowara Khanom; my wife, Labiba Mahmud; and three daughters, Rumaysa, Rufaida, and Ruqayya

Al-Sakib Khan Pathan

Contents

Preface

First and foremost, this textbook is designed to serve as an essential resource for teaching at both the undergraduate and graduate levels. It can also be utilized as a comprehensive reference for professionals and researchers in the field.

This book provides an in-depth exploration of the dynamic intersection between machine learning (ML) and cybersecurity, offering a detailed analysis of how these technologies are reshaping the security landscape. It tracks the significant progress of machine learning in the context of cybersecurity, providing insights into the latest advancements, emerging trends, and the challenges ahead.

Crafted with a discerning audience in mind, this book could be a valuable resource for academic researchers, industry practitioners, and students alike. It is particularly suitable for those with an interest in understanding the transformative role machine learning plays in modern cybersecurity.

In a world where cybersecurity threats are constantly evolving, this book provides a well-structured introduction to the emerging technologies, their applications, and their potential to revolutionize how we protect digital assets. Readers will gain a comprehensive understanding of machine learning techniques and their application to real-world cybersecurity problems, ensuring they are well-equipped to tackle the complex challenges of the field.

With its wide-ranging appeal, this book serves as a crucial resource for graduate and undergraduate students, cybersecurity professionals, and researchers seeking to deepen their understanding of the critical intersection between machine learning and cybersecurity. It is an invaluable guide for anyone looking to navigate and contribute to this rapidly advancing domain.

ML and cybersecurity are often discussed separately in separate books. Hence, this book would give a clear overview of ML first and then show how this technology transforms the cybersecurity field. The readers can easily understand the transition of technologies and the mutual link between the two areas. For this, after providing an introduction in Chapter 1, we have made Chapter 2 somewhat lengthy with sufficient primary information so that the readers are familiar with various technical terms used in the later part of the book.

We are very grateful to Almighty Allah for giving us this time to be able to complete another project of this caliber. We also would like to sincerely thank our family members who always encourage us to excel in professional and research fields and provide their relentless support. Last but not least, thanks to Gabriella Williams, editor of Cybersecurity, Privacy and Risk, for approving this book project.

Kutub Thakur
Al-Sakib Khan Pathan

Chapter 1

An overview of the machine learning role in cybersecurity transformation

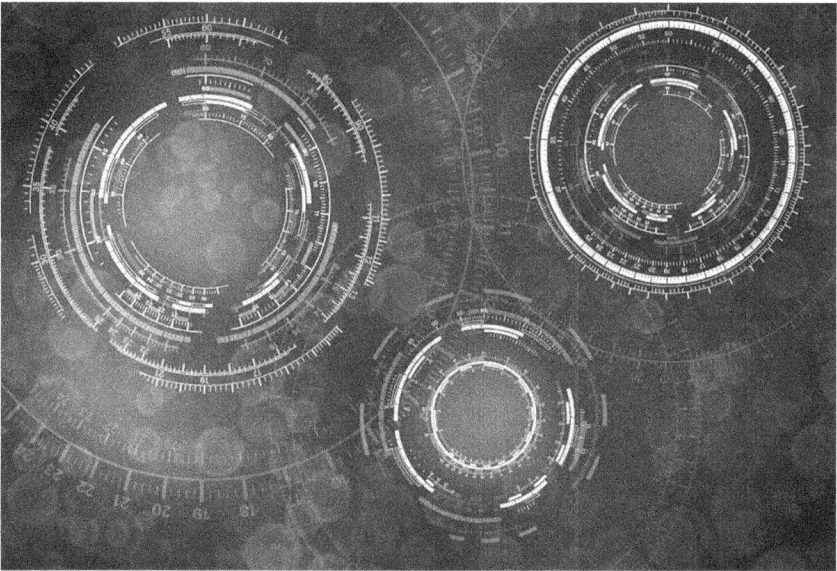

DOI: 10.1201/9781003688327-1

AN OVERVIEW OF MODERN CYBERSECURITY

The field of information technology (IT) is passing through a revolutionary phase in which it is changing its shape drastically due to unprecedented development. The emergence of modern and innovative technologies in the entire sphere of information and communication technology (ICT) is driving this change with its clear mark, especially in the areas of software development and computer programming languages. Eventually, these advancements are directly impacting the field of cybersecurity, which is one of the most important domains that plays a pivotal role not only in the smooth operations of the modern services powered by IT but also in the development of modern technologies to cater to the emerging demands as well as the needs of contemporary businesses.

Cybersecurity is constantly going through massive shifts powered by the most advanced technologies and domains of science, especially data science (DS), which is extensively used in developing the most sophisticated cybersecurity systems that can catch and fix cyber threats at multiple layers in the entire IT stack consisting of networks, endpoints, wireless routers, edge devices, websites, web applications, and other specialized software and hardware services. The main objective of cybersecurity is to protect your valuable data, software assets, and smooth operations of your IT services. In the cybersecurity or data security field, three main objectives are defined to be achieved by establishing robust cybersecurity. Those three objectives are referred to as "CIA" in short, which stands for confidentiality, integrity, and availability of personal or business data, governed under certain data regulatory rules, and maintained with full accuracy and correctness. To achieve those objectives, it considers three major components at the core of its definition, such as:[1]

- **Confidentiality** – The confidentiality of data relates to securing data or valuable digital assets from theft, unlawful access, data breach, or unintentional sharing of data with unauthorized third parties in violation of regulations.
- **Integrity** – This aspect deals with the accuracy, correctness, and consistency of the data stored or transported over the IT networks and systems.
- **Availability** – This is another objective of cybersecurity, which is to allow the data and other IT services related to your data or any other purposes to run smoothly in all conditions by averting any cyber threats through different ways. The availability of $24 \times 7 \times 365$ is required in the modern service-level standards worldwide.

The landscape of cybersecurity threats is expanding exponentially due to numerous reasons, such as increasing surface area of IT operations, exponential growth of the Internet of Things (IoT) field, huge level of automation in various walks of life and businesses, huge expansion of IT technologies, especially in the field of telecommunication and software development, and many others. The development of modern computing and storage technologies has also increased the landscape of cybersecurity threats substantially across all domains and industries worldwide. The frequency, cost, and business impact of cyber threats have increased significantly and continuously, increasing at a huge pace due to highly skilled threat actors and the use of sophisticated tools and techniques by those cybersecurity threat actors.

The average number of cybersecurity attacks recorded in 2021 was about 15.1% higher than the same in 2020.[2] The ratio of the small- and medium-sized businesses (SMBs) that have their respective cybersecurity policies in place is just around 50%, which allows the hackers a wider space to launch sophisticated cyberattacks not only against those vulnerable SMBs but also to use them as bots for launching cyberattacks on other major targets controlled under a remote control center. At the same time, the average cost of a data breach has also increased significantly. The average cost of a single global data breach in 2022 is estimated at about US $4.35 million, and the average cost of a single breach in the USA is about US $9.44 billion in 2022. The average cost in the USA was about US $9.05 in 2021.[3]

The most important sources of cybersecurity threats that have increased during the past few years include:

- Malware attacks.
- Ransomware attacks.
- Phishing and spamming attacks.
- Distributed Denial-of-Service (DDoS) attacks.
- SQL injection attacks.
- Zero-day exploit attacks.
- Man in the Middle (MitM) attacks.
- Password theft or breaking attacks.
- Cross-site scripting (XSS) attacks.

The average cost that the global industry has to pay for cybersecurity breaches or data breaches is expected to cross US $10.5 trillion by 2025 (latest prediction at the time of writing this book) from just US $3 trillion in 2015. Phishing and social engineering attacks form a huge portion of this threat landscape at about 57%, followed by stolen or compromised devices.[4] The shape of cyberattacks is also changing from random attacks to targeted ones, and a majority of the attacks are targeted toward banking and financial businesses, followed by healthcare and others. The average frequency of ransomware has increased to 11 seconds per attack in 2021, as compared to about 40 seconds per attack in 2016.

In such volatile circumstances, a highly responsive, preemptive, robust cybersecurity mechanism is highly required to cope with such a huge and ever-expanding landscape of cyber threats. The use of machine learning (ML) is being extensively adopted by hackers to evade different security measures, such as CAPTCHA and passwords. The bots used by the threat actors are trained to provide suitable responses to the security barriers, like CAPTCHA and password filling, so that they can evade those barriers and intrude into the systems. To cope with such critical steps and techniques from hackers, an effective use of machine learning (ML), artificial intelligence (AI), data analytics, and other data science techniques is very important to be deployed in the cybersecurity platforms and algorithms for generating suitable responses in time to those high-tech cyberattacks on the networks or systems. The most important components that are heavily deployed in cybersecurity for the transformation of cybersecurity landscapes include the following:[5]

- Data Science (DS).
- Machine Learning (ML).

Data has always been a very critical item in any kind of business decision, policymaking, strategy carving, or launching any activity against or for achieving certain objectives. The analysis of data to derive the most valuable information (that can be used for the solution-driven projects) has been very difficult and costly in the past. But in the modern world of technologies, it has become very easy to analyze heaps of raw data and skim for the most valuable information from those piles of raw data. In this process, machine learning has become a very pivotal instrument to collect, analyze, scan, and skim through the valuable information from a huge volume of raw data. Thus, the deployment of ML in cybersecurity has expanded the use of data science and its components.

Machine learning is basically used to understand different patterns, behaviors, frequencies, and many other parameters of activities of threat actors or hackers to devise a suitable counter policy to avoid those emerging threats in a real-time scenario. Based on the current trend, the new concept of cybersecurity data science (CDS) is emerging as a key field of IT that is designed to merge data science and cybersecurity by using the power of machine learning. In this entire area, machine learning is the core component that is helping to realize a new domain of IT, named cybersecurity data science.

The Google trends of the popularity of the three terms – cybersecurity, machine learning, and data science – are compared in the real-world global scenario, as shown in Figure 1.1.

As the figure shows, the popularity indices of those three terms were very low in the beginning, especially from 2004 through 2013–14. But after 2016, all those terms achieved a greater level of popularity simultaneously and became very complementary components to cybersecurity onwards. Why has machine learning become so crucial for the cybersecurity field? Let us try to understand.

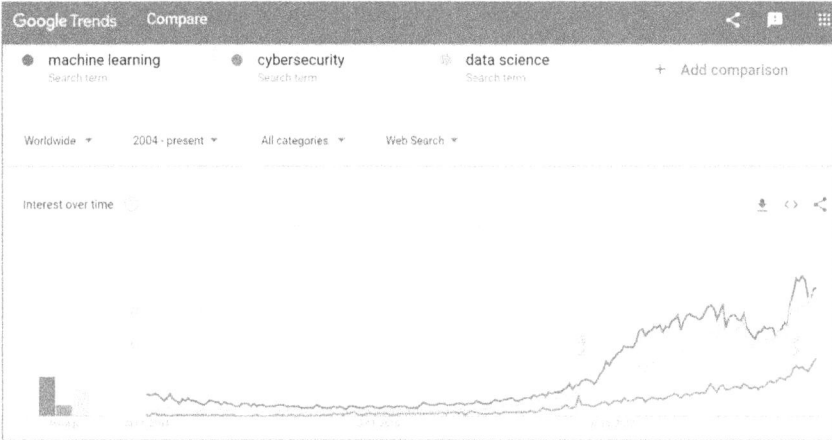

Figure 1.1 Cybersecurity, data science, and machine learning Google Trends comparison.

IMPORTANCE OF MACHINE LEARNING

The traditional ways of cybersecurity that were very popular during the last two decades have become very weak and obsolete in certain aspects because many new technologies have changed the landscape of cybersecurity threats, as well as the way to counter them in real-time environments. The speed of computing or processing power has increased multiple times, data transmission lanes have widened hugely, and many other aspects of the IT field have changed significantly. Thus, the traditional ways to cope with the cybersecurity threat were not powerful enough to counter the high-tech strategies of threat actors or hackers in this field.

An automated cybersecurity response for every emerging threat became one of the most important domains in the field of cybersecurity. Real-time response based on the previous trends and information was much needed to develop a suitable response to the emerging threats. This was not possible without the analysis of huge data created through system logs, hacker attacks, traffic behaviors, system responses, frequencies of activities, and many other such parameters of an event on the live systems. The analysis of huge data, which is also referred to as big data in modern technical terms, has become very critical to be managed and analyzed for obtaining valuable information that can help in devising a suitable response to the emerging cybersecurity threats. To understand and analyze that kind of data, machine learning was the only way out because no other processing power can carry out such a huge volume of processing tasks within a very short period of time.

To make highly intelligent cybersecurity decisions, an automated cybersecurity solution that can use the power of ML for processing data and finding valuable information is in place. The machines designed for the specific cybersecurity purposes are trained for different scenarios of past cyberattacks and related data of different events in such a way that the machine becomes *intelligent* enough to make automated decisions in case of any emerging test data in the real-world cybersecurity environment. The cybersecurity data science (CDS) powered by machine learning (ML) is normally designed to achieve:

- Processing of data related to emerging threats.
- Quantification of cyber risks.
- Developing or activating predefined counter responses automatically.
- Deployment of past intelligence or understanding of events through machine learning.

The ultimate objective of cybersecurity data science is to develop a comprehensive security solution that can replace the traditional ways of security, which may include:

- Digital access control system.
- Authentication and authorization systems.
- Encryption mechanisms.
- Antimalware tools.
- Security firewalls.

The above-mentioned traditional mechanism for cybersecurity may not be useful for the latest forms of businesses and emerging high-tech threats from highly skilled threat actors that use the most sophisticated hacking tools. The new systems that can offer robust replacement of cybersecurity provided by the traditional tools or systems are also a multi-layer approach integrated into one unified or even distributed module of security.

The main objectives and activities that a modern cybersecurity platform should perform by using the power of machine learning systems include:[5, 6]

- Classification of different types of emerging attacks, such as U2R attack, R2L attack, DoS (Denial-of-Service), DDoS (Distributed Denial-of-Service), probing attack, or anything else.
- Detection and analysis of DDoS in a software-defined environment.
- Detection of intrusion, classification, and selection of features of attacks.
- Creation of robust intrusion detection and response systems for single as well as multi-class categorization.
- Detection and evaluation of host-based anomaly.
- Reduction in the false alarms and other irrelevant alerts.
- Running malicious code to check the behavior of systems for detecting any such malicious code by analyzing and understanding the behavior of systems and services.

- Measurement and analysis of the performance of the systems, services, and devices.
- Detection and identification of different types of malware and associated risk factors.
- Scanning the entire infrastructure and software environments for any kind of vulnerabilities and anomalies
- Scanning incoming packets and other communication messages to analyze threats and create suitable and automated responses to the emerging threats.

All of the above-mentioned activities require an extensive understanding of the power in the machines so that they can make decisions about the environment and emerging threats as fast as possible. In certain cases, a real-time analysis and response would be required for certain emerging threats in mission-critical industries and business processes. This is only possible when the machines are powered with machine learning technology to learn, analyze, and decide about cybersecurity threat situations with an information-based smart decision. For achieving the above-mentioned objectives, a range of machine learning techniques is deployed in the cybersecurity systems. A few of the most important machine learning techniques are mentioned in the following list:

- Deployment of deep learning based on neural networks.
- Data clustering technique.
- Data association and analysis technique.
- Data classification technique.
- Feature engineering method.

HOW DOES IT WORK TO TRANSFORM CYBERSECURITY?

Before diving into the depths of cybersecurity transformation through machine learning, it is imperative to have a look at the changing threat surface of IT services, applications, and infrastructure. The present challenges of the cybersecurity field are driven by a wide range of components, technologies, techniques, the size of systems, sophisticated approaches adopted by threat actors, and many others. The landscape of threat has expanded manifold. The major components of the cybersecurity field that pose serious challenges for cybersecurity specialists to cope with the emerging threats in networks and services are mentioned below:

- High-tech approach and tools used by threat actors.
- An extensive increase in the number of cybersecurity attacks.
- Emerging new data, regulatory rules, and legislation.
- Exponential expansion in the IT ecosystem powered by IoT, BYOD (Bring Your Own Device), and other technologies.

- Shortage of skilled and experienced cybersecurity experts and specialists.
- The increasing cost of a single data breach worldwide.
- Ever-changing techniques and patterns of cyberattacks.
- Cyber threats being used as weapons of war in modern hybrid wars.

The number of threat actors has increased significantly due to the involvement of governments, militaries, terrorists, and other malicious actors sponsored by different actors, either covertly or overtly. The presence of a huge number of threat actors and the severity and length of the threat surface have increased significantly. The threat actors are getting smarter and smarter by adopting new types of technologies, techniques, and patterns to evade the cybersecurity measures established by security professionals and systems. According to Statista, the number of cyberattacks observed in the 4th quarter of 2020 was 125.74 million.[7] The average cost of a single data breach has gone into the millions by 2022. The cost of data breaches will continue increasing in the future, too, as per numerous projections by research organizations. The total cost of data breaches to the global industry has already gone into trillions of dollars a year. It is expected that it will cross the mark of US$10 trillion within a few more years. This huge cost of data breaches is the third largest economy in the world after the United States of America (USA) and China in 2022.

Different governments and regions are developing numerous rules and regulations for the protection of personal and business data, such as the General Data Protection Regulation (GDPR), the Personal Information Protection and Electronic Documents Act (PIPEDA), the Protection of Personal Information (POPI), the General Personal Data Protection Law (Portuguese: *Lei Geral de Proteção de Dados Pessoais*), or LGPD, and others. The field of information and communication is continuously evolving, so new regulations are expected to emerge in the market. To follow those regulations through manual and traditional security systems is not an easy task in a global market where the required cybersecurity professionals are already in short supply. The qualified, skilled, and experienced experts and specialists are required in a large number to cope with the emerging threats in the field of cybersecurity. An extended and capable cybersecurity system will be required to cope with those regulations and other policies.

Another very serious challenge that the cybersecurity field faces is the undefined boundary and location of cyber threats and hidden enemies, which may be either state or non-state actors. Many countries have their own secret army units for cyberwars, and many other countries are pursuing building cyber capacities to be used for military purposes. Thus, a huge investment is being made by state as well as non-state actors like terrorists, monetary theft-related criminals, and other criminals. They use the most advanced and sophisticated tools and technologies to exploit the vulnerabilities in the cyber systems and infrastructures. They are also using machine learning technologies in their aggressive and malicious activities to inflict substantial damage to the targets for achieving their objectives. It is very difficult for security professionals to cope with the advanced techniques employed by hackers that incorporate the most advanced machine learning technologies.

Another very important aspect of the cybersecurity surface is the extended area of modern IT networks and infrastructure powered by the Internet of Things (IoT) and the "Bring Your Own Device" (BYOD) techniques. The number of connected devices is expected to cross the 27 billion mark by 2025 from about 14.4 billion devices (endpoints) in 2022.[8] This huge network of connected devices poses numerous challenges pertaining to cybersecurity for experts. Hackers can control any device located anywhere in the world by exploiting their vulnerabilities and poor maintenance of the firmware and software applications. Those connected devices use small firmware from a large number of companies that have to patch and update the software, firmware, and applications on a regular basis. In certain cases, the concerned companies fail to develop patches to overcome the vulnerabilities in those devices and firmware applications. Hackers always try to target any new technology, service, or product to find out vulnerabilities to exploit. If they are fast enough to catch those vulnerabilities before the concerned companies release their supportive patch, they can significantly damage the entire cybersecurity ecosystem.

In such conditions, the deployment of machine learning and automation processes in cybersecurity systems is crucial to cope with the emerging threats from malicious users and hackers in the field of cybersecurity.

Cybersecurity transformation

The replacement of traditional ways of cybersecurity with the advanced, capable, efficient, and automated cybersecurity systems is referred to as the transformation of the cybersecurity ecosystem. This is possible only when the industry experts can utilize the historical and real-time data generated by the IT users, endpoints, and systems to mine out the most valuable information that can be deployed to make data-driven decisions for preventing the emerging threats automatically. This is possible through machine learning capabilities, which make a machine learn from the trends, patterns, behaviors, and other events in such a way that it can project the future actions of the adversaries or hackers easily. According to the latest research from Precedence Research Inc., the global market value of machine learning services and solutions is expected to reach US$305.62 billion by 2030 from just US$15.47 billion in 2021, with a whopping growth rate of over 39.3% CAGR (Compound Annual Growth Rate) during the projected period between 2022 and 2030. A huge part of this gigantic market size is contributed by the cybersecurity field solutions. Another research predicts that the volume of the machine learning market in the field of cybersecurity will cross the US$46.3 billion mark by 2027.[9,10]

Machine learning has a range of capabilities that can transform cyberse-curity to yield the best results in the industry, such as:

- **Learning capability** – Machine learning is the name of the technology that enables computers or machines to learn from the data fed to them in the shape of training datasets. They scan the data in the form of text, audio, video, and sensory information such as touch, smell, blow, light, and many others. It is a kind of humanlike capability of a computer machine so that it can somewhat understand, assess, evaluate, and make decisions based on the information it learns from the input data in the form of training datasets. With this capability, machine learning in the cybersecurity systems can trace the past data for different attack patterns, techniques, areas, locations, addresses, and many other components and make decisions based on the information learned from the past data. The modern machine learning algorithms and technologies are also fully capable of analyzing real-time data and responding effectively on the basis of patterns and trends in the real-time data.

- **Faster speed** – The speed of manual cybersecurity processes or traditional ways is limited to certain functionalities and would require huge efforts to catch up to the speed of the latest tools and techniques used by threat actors in the field of cybersecurity. Machine learning is powered by intelligent computers along with the huge processing capacity that offers super speed to catch up with the emerging threats by analyzing the most complicated techniques and tools used for launching cyberattacks.

- **Data mining ability** – Machine learning is capable of mining the huge piles of data for valuable information that can be utilized for building security responses or making certain policy decisions to cope with the emerging threats. ML has enabled machines to explore huge piles of data generated by a range of contributors, such as end-users, endpoints, network elements, system agents, web applications, and many others, to find out the most useful information in such a way that it can help either to avert or mitigate any emerging cybersecurity threats in the systems.

- **Automated response** – The cybersecurity systems powered by ML can generate such a suitable response to the emerging threats that they can detect by analyzing and monitoring the activities of users, system elements, and other components of the cyber environment. A range of predefined automated responses can also be activated immediately as soon as the threat from adversaries is detected.

- **Data-driven decision making** – The decision-making capability of machine learning makes it one of the most powerful technologies to be deployed in the cybersecurity domain. The right decision made based on the right information will make your system so effective and responsive that a substantial volume of threat surface can be either averted or mitigated easily.

- **Real-time response** – Machine learning technology is very capable of analyzing and responding to real-time activities on the systems or web environment. Nowadays, computing power is available in huge volumes, which can be used for machine learning algorithms to scan and analyze real-time activities and generate a suitable response to any kind of emerging cybersecurity threat in the ecosystem.
- **Huge capacity** – The capacity of machine learning is directly associated with the processing power. In the modern technological environment, computer processing power can be used in different models in such a way that it can provide you with the most reliable results in a very short period of time. This creates a large capacity of machine learning algorithms to scan, analyze, and respond to the emerging threats in this field.
- **Proactive and responsive** – Proactivity and responsiveness are two other very important parameters of machine learning due to their ability to understand and respond automatically. Machine learning technology can be very proactive and responsive for previously learned scenarios as well as future projections based on the previous understanding of the behaviors of the threat actors.
- **Cheaper and effective** – The machine learning technology is becoming cheaper and more effective in all domains of information technology, especially in the field of cybersecurity. This is the reason that many businesses are turning toward machine learning technology to deploy in their cybersecurity solutions.

Chapter 2

Machine learning (ML)

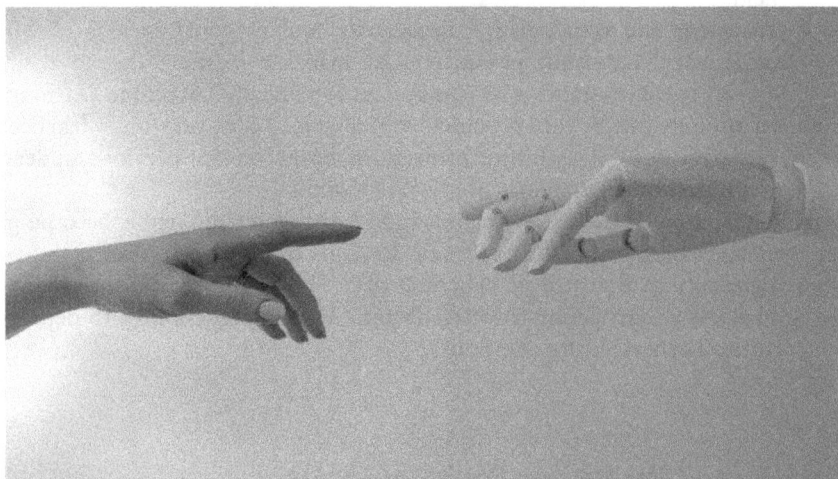

DOI: 10.1201/9781003688327-2

INTRODUCTION

Machine learning, precisely referred to as ML, is a major component of the Artificial Intelligence (AI) field. In fact, it is a subdomain of AI, which is a large field that encompasses many other technological components and scientific realms. ML is a process that is designed for machines, especially computers and software applications running on different computing machines, to behave like human beings do in learning about the events, environments, data, and other inputs that they get in their daily lives. That means machine learning mimics the learning process of the human being. The learning process consists of different stages, such as:

- Ingesting past data, structured or unstructured, as an input.
- Analyzing the input data through different types of logic defined in the learning algorithms.
- Skimming the most valuable and meaningful information from the processing of input data.
- Using valuable/meaningful information for making data-driven decisions.
- Taking automated responses based on data-driven decisions.

This entire process is governed by the learning algorithms developed for the machines to go through the learning process. In other words, machine learning is a subfield of artificial intelligence, which makes the software applications more reliable and accurate in making decisions for future predictions by learning from the historical data without being explicitly programmed to carry out an explicit function or activity.[11] In machine learning, the software applications use purpose-specific algorithms to assess the historical data of the events and make a prediction based on the trends and patterns of the past data in the shape of an output value. This is completely independent as far as the human intervention at the operational level is concerned. There are numerous examples that can explain the concept of machine learning more accurately. One of those examples is the recommendation engines installed on retail and entertainment websites that offer you numerous suggestions and recommendations of products based on your interests and your past behavior on that particular website. When you, as a client, go to the Netflix website to search for a certain movie, it shows you the most related movies and other movies that you may be interested in. This is done through a machine learning mechanism, which ingests your browsing behavior, analyzes it, and makes predictions from the information it collects by analyzing your behavior. Another example of machine learning is the spam filtering incorporated into emails, such as Gmail and other providers. Any spam email hitting your inbox is separated based on the responses to that email from different clients or the content it carries for the target audience.

Machine learning has become a vital part of all modern business activities, especially in web environments. The entire world of business is transforming into digital automation. Machine learning and other domains of artificial intelligence are the most important components in materializing automation in all business process automation and industrial automation systems. The machine learning technology has also made it possible to scan, analyze, and skim information from big data, which is expanding at an exponential pace across all domains of businesses and social activities of human societies worldwide. Machine learning can get the most valuable business information by mining huge piles of data created through system events/logs, end-user activities, and business activities across the domains of industries and societies. Businesses get deeper insight into the customer behaviors, market behaviors, future trends, and possible futuristic businesses, which allow them to develop the most suitable products for the targeted market segments and improve the customer experience on the existing services and products perfectly. The future of modern businesses will heavily depend upon business process automation and data-driven decisions for every domain of business, such as marketing, product research, sales, customer service, and many others.

The complete process of building a machine learning solution on a computer involves a few very important steps taken by the experts or data specialists. The steps are mentioned below:[11]

- Identification of the most relevant datasets and preparation for the analysis of datasets.
- Selection of a suitable machine learning algorithm that matches the requirements of the activity to be performed by the machine learning application.
- Development of a dataset analysis model based on the selected machine learning algorithms in the second step.
- The training of machine learning applications or models through test datasets and making modifications and revisions if the desired accuracy and objective are not achieved.
- Finally, commissioning of the machine learning model to generate different findings and scores on the raw input data.

Machine learning has many types based on the training models, such as supervised, unsupervised, semi-supervised, and reinforcement machine learning models, which will be discussed later. Different machine learning models are used for different purposes and applications in businesses and industries. The most common applications of machine learning models are mentioned in the following list:

- Data mining field.
- Business intelligence (BI).
- Data analytics and other forms of data science.

- Customer relationship management (CRM) applications.
- Virtual assistants and chatbots.
- Human resources information systems (HRIS).
- Driverless cars.

DATA SCIENCE, ARTIFICIAL INTELLIGENCE, AND MACHINE LEARNING

Machine learning, data science, and artificial intelligence are all interrelated domains that complement each other or are under the influence of one domain on another. The advancement in industrial and business process automation was the result of the power of these three important technologies used in software and hardware models. Let us try to find out the parallels and differences between these topics one by one.

Data science

Data science is a technology that deals with computer programming, statistics, mathematics, and social sciences simultaneously. This technology studies different processes of data analysis and maintenance, such as data collection, sorting, filtering, classifying, categorizing, and devising results useful for making information-driven decisions. It also deals with different types of data systems, forms, and formats. It uses different tools, algorithms, statistical models, principles, and systems to process the random data clusters in structured and unstructured forms.[12]

The professionals who deal with the processing of data are known as data scientists, specialists, experts, and analysts. They use different systems, which are specialized in data modeling and warehousing of exponentially growing data in all domains of business. The data modeling and warehousing systems enable the scientists to track and manage large volumes of data properly through different schemes and models. The stored data is further analyzed through different applications powered by numerous task-specific algorithms to conduct data analysis and information extraction, which is also known as valuable Business Intelligence (BI). BI is the core component that businesses are interested in while using modern technology and tools related to data science. Data science uses different steps to accomplish the task associated with the data science process management, such as:

- Definition of business problem.
- Collection of suitable data.
- Data cleaning and scrubbing.
- Exploratory analysis of data.
- Data modeling.
- Data visualization.

Data science plays a vital role in the deployment of machine learning in different ML- and AI-powered projects because machines are trained through datasets in different formats and forms of data. Without data science, the advancements in the fields of machine learning and artificial intelligence are very limited or somewhat impossible. The most important focus areas of data science are related to:

- Extracting valuable information from piles of unstructured raw data – it is like extracting a needle from a haystack.
- Cleaning and analyzing the data to make it structured for effective analysis.
- Helping businesses and industries solve business problems based on the business intelligence it gains through data analysis.
- Helping businesses in planning effective projects that can create a competitive edge over competitors.
- Focusing on perspective, descriptive, and predictive analytics to solve a range of business problems effectively.
- Implementation of a range of mathematical, statistical, big data analytics, data wrangling, and machine learning for providing accurate answers to business queries.
- Extracting information from all sizes of data volumes and types of data formats.
- Helping businesses make informed decisions based on the information extracted through multiple processes of data science.

The volume of data created in the modern environment of information technology is huge and expanding exponentially in all domains of industry. Managing and extracting useful information from those huge volumes of unstructured data is not possible through the traditional ways of data analysis based on manual statistics and low-grade analytic tools. Data science uses the most advanced technologies to handle and manage those gigantic volumes of unstructured data and provide valuable information for business decision-making. The example of a data science analytics application is shown in Figure 2.1.

Data analytics is one of the fastest-growing domains in information technology. According to a recent projection, the global market value of big data analytics will reach US \$655.55 billion by 2029 from just US \$271.83 billion in 2021, with a whopping growth rate of over 13.4% CAGR (Compound Annual Growth Rate) over the projected time period between 2022 and 2029.[14] Without data analytics, businesses would not become so competitive and information-based as they are now in the global marketplace.

Artificial intelligence (AI)

Artificial intelligence, also known as AI, is a broader field that aims at the techniques that can use logic or reasoning in machines to replicate the human brain or human intelligence. The (somewhat) imitation of the

Figure 2.1 Pictorial view of a data analytic application. (Pixabay).

capabilities of the human brain is done to learn and decide about the input data through different ways, like text, audio, video, and a range of other sensors used in the modern world to represent different characteristics, items, and senses, such as heat, light, thrust, blow, and many others. In simple words, this is the field of science that deals with the cognitive abilities of machines that mimic the human brain's capabilities. Human cognition is known as natural intelligence, and machines' cognitive capabilities are known as artificial intelligence. The main characteristics of the artificial intelligence (AI) field of technology are summarized as:[13]

- Developing systems and applications that simulate the cognitive intelligence and logical reasoning capabilities of a human brain.
- Building machines that can behave intelligently to interact with other machines, processes, or human beings.
- Creation of software applications that can handle a range of tasks, which are traditionally handled by human beings.
- Using a range of subfields such as natural language processing (NLP), neural networks (NN), machine learning (ML), deep learning (DL), and others for training the machines to think and decide automatically.
- Developing algorithms focusing on perception, planning, and predictions.

AI is a vast field that started long before the advent of modern computing systems and software programming. The concept of artificial intelligence was initially fictitious, in which the machines, mostly hardware machines, would be considered as thinking machines to replace human cognitive capabilities. That initial concept of artificial intelligence was mostly focused on robotics and industrial automation processes in manufacturing and other domains. With the passage of time and the advent of modern computing and software applications, the area of artificial intelligence has expanded significantly. It got grounded in software applications through its subdomains such as machine learning, natural language processing, deep learning, and others. Thus, the importance of artificial intelligence grew significantly. The use of artificial intelligence in a wide range of fields powered by the data sciences and machine learning is doing wonders, such as in:

- Cybersecurity industry.
- Healthcare and medicine.
- Banking and finance.
- Marketing and e-commerce.
- Driverless vehicles.
- Industrial process automation.

The future of artificial intelligence is very bright, and numerous advanced levels of robotics and AI-powered products are observed in this field. Those projects may reach the capabilities of the human brain to a certain extent or even supersede it in certain cases, leading to technological singularity. The virtual concept of future artificial intelligence-powered machines is depicted in Figure 2.2.

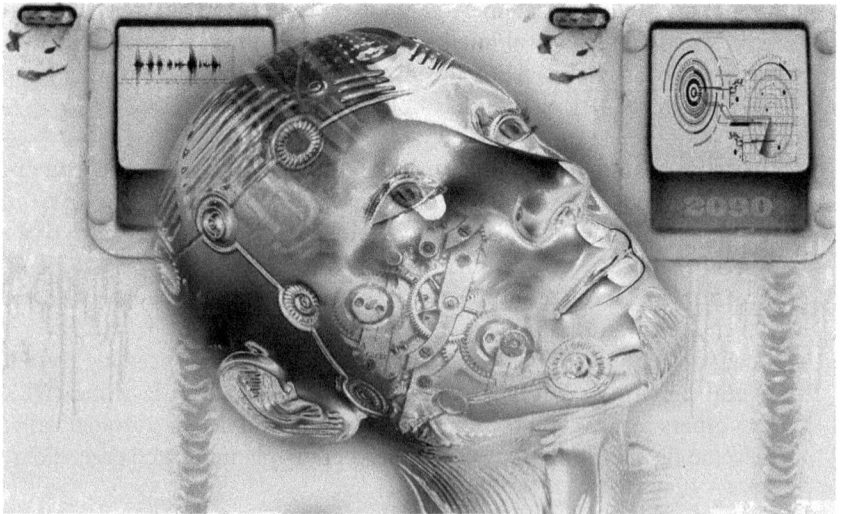

Figure 2.2 Virtual concept of an AI machine. (pixabay).

Artificial intelligence is broadly categorized into three major stages that are defined in terms of the level of intelligence in the machines. Those stages are defined in comparison with the natural intelligence levels of human beings. The three stages are:

- Artificial Narrow Intelligence (ANI).
- Artificial General Intelligence (AGI).
- Artificial Super Intelligence (ASI).

Artificial narrow intelligence, precisely referred to as ANI, is the stage of intelligence of machines in which the machines can perform the functions or activities that they are programmed or trained for. They do not have the ability to make independent decisions in different conditions and generate contemporary responses in the given situation. Narrow intelligence is also known as weak intelligence (WI). All examples of modern artificial intelligence systems, such as Siri, driverless cars, Sophia the robot, and similar systems, are types of weak intelligence. In other words, it can be said that the present-day stage of artificial intelligence is fully under the category of weak intelligence.

Artificial general intelligence, precisely referred to as AGI, is the expected level of intelligence of machines equal to the level of the human brain. Well, it may not be a real intelligence but rather a kind of synthetic intelligence that would still be programmed and influenced by human developers, who have superior intelligence that is applied based on various situations and contexts. In this level of artificial intelligence, the systems are expected to be able to understand complex problems, devise suitable solutions to those problems, and be able to (kind of) think and make decisions like the human brain does. This is the second-level stage of artificial intelligence, but no practical machine has yet been developed that can qualify for this category to think and decide like a human does! This is still a fictitious concept of artificial intelligence, and many experts believe that technology may not be able to reach this level of artificial intelligence at all. There are, however, certain scientists (very optimistic among them) who believe that this level of artificial intelligence is not far away. They think that it may be achieved within the next couple of decades or so.

Artificial super intelligence, precisely known as ASI, is the most advanced imagined level of AI, which is defined as the capabilities of the machines that would exceed the capabilities of the human brain! In other words, the idea is that the machines will supersede the thinking and decision-making capabilities of human beings, and they will even start designing and regenerating, duplicating machines at a very fast pace, and may control human capabilities. They may even start redesigning us who created the artificial intelligence systems. In reality, this is just a hypothetical idea of an artificial intelligence stage, and many AI professionals and scientists are very skeptical about machines reaching this level of intelligence by the machines.

At the same time, some scientists, like, for instance, Stephen Hawking, warned humanity about the horrors associated with the super-intelligent machines. If super-intelligent machines are created, they will be much stronger and faster than human beings because a human is a natural creation and needs periodic rest and many other life-related things to remain alive and lead a regular life. The evolution of human cells is very slow compared to the growth of technological calculations. Thus, if the machines overtake the powers of humans and use humans as a product for their own thoughts and creativity, this could be called the doomsday for human beings, and sometimes, it is referred to as the *technological singularity*.

As far as the types of artificial intelligence are concerned, there are four major types of it that are given below:[15]

- Reactive Machines Artificial Intelligence.
- Limited Memory Artificial Intelligence.
- Theory of Mind Artificial Intelligence.
- Self-Aware Artificial Intelligence.

Reactive machines artificial intelligence is the basic type of machine learning in which the machines respond to the present input data that they receive. It does not use past experience or establish any interface with the past data or learning for making the decisions. It is a very simple type of artificial intelligence that can perform only modest tasks that are predefined to be activated against the response of the present data. The example of reactive machines artificial intelligence is the IBM Chess software program that was designed to perform chess moves based on the current situation available in the game. It became successful in beating the world champion of chess, Garry Kasparov of the Russian Federation, back in 1997.

Limited memory artificial intelligence is a more advanced type of AI in which the machines use past data or experience by establishing interfaces with the past data input stored in the short memory of machines for making future decisions. In this type of artificial intelligence, the machines are trained with past data through data feeding or training datasets. They understand and differentiate different items, conditions, and environments by learning from past data and make future decisions based on that under-standing or learning. The example of this type of artificial intelligence is a *driverless car*. The machines used in driverless cars are trained for all types of environments available on roads and streets, such as moving vehicles, people, animals, signals, sidelines, lanes, and all other things that are encountered in driving. The machines learn about them, and when they encounter those items during the drive, they make decisions to make the driving experience safer and more efficient for the passengers. An example of an autonomous vehicle using this type of artificial intelligence is shown in Figure 2.3.

Figure 2.3 Autonomous vehicle – an example of a limited memory AI type. (Pixabay).

As the name implies, the theory of mind's artificial intelligence is fully focused on learning and understanding human emotions, ideologies, and beliefs. This is an advanced version of AI, which is still in the research phase and has not matured as of yet. This type of artificial intelligence is going to play a very pivotal role in mechanizing the most complex abstracts that humans conceive and act on. The abstract concept is shown in Figure 2.4.

Last but not least, self-aware artificial intelligence is the most advanced type of artificial intelligence that has not yet been materialized in the world in any shape or manifestation, but scientists are rigorously working on this type of AI. This is a type of AI in which the machines would have their own consciousness about themselves and can understand and become very well aware of their existence and future thoughts. This type of artificial intelligence can fall under the highest level of artificial intelligence category referred to as artificial super intelligence (ASI). This is the most advanced version, which may prove to be very destructive for human history, culture, creed, and existence. As noted before, many scientists, technology experts, and geniuses are very concerned about the materialization of this type of artificial intelligence, which will bring huge levels of destruction to humans and many natural processes and natural resources, or to the entire earth and universe. In fact, the entire natural ecosystem will be at stake. The abstract example of self-aware artificial intelligence is shown in Figure 2.5.

Artificial intelligence is a very vast field, which consists of numerous domains of technologies, statistics, and science. The most common fields that are part of artificial intelligence are mentioned in the following list:

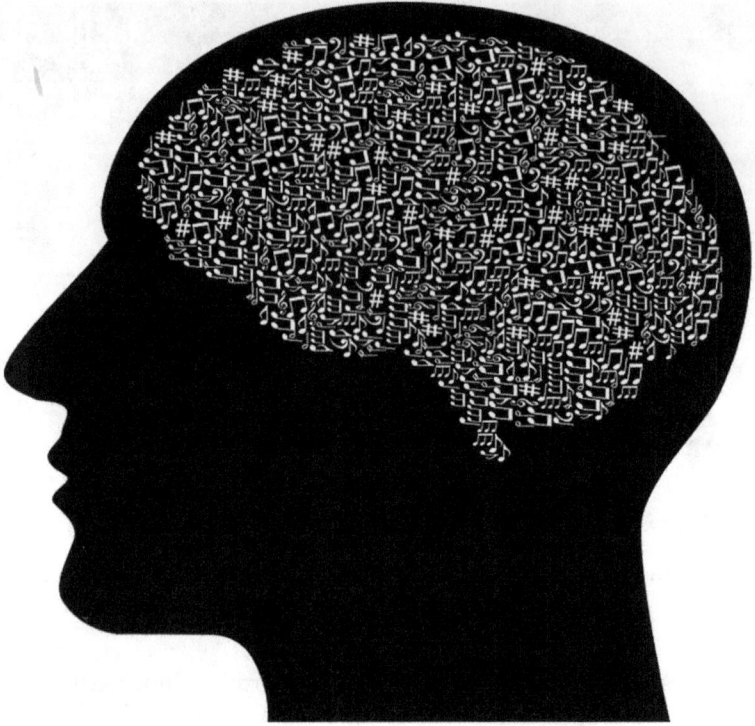

Figure 2.4 Abstract depiction of the theory of mind's artificial intelligence. (Pixabay).

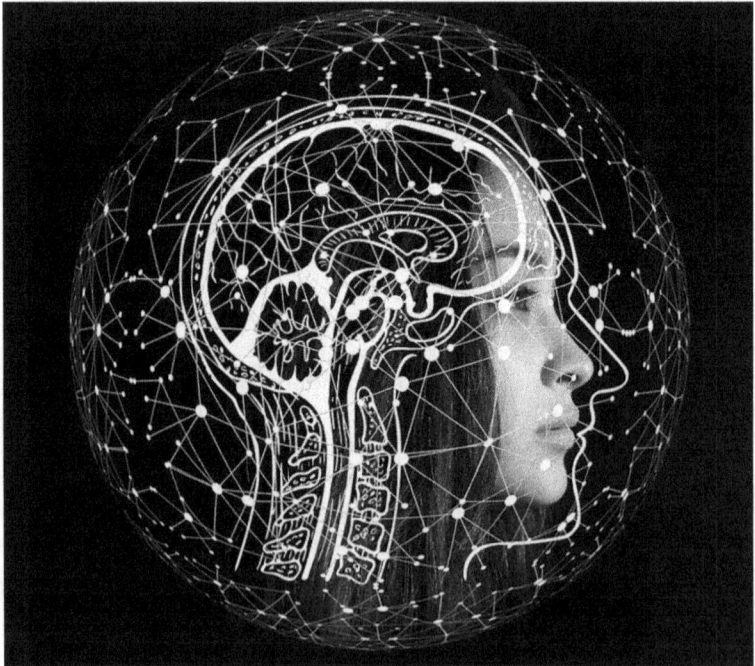

Figure 2.5 Self-aware artificial intelligence abstract example. (Pixabay).

- Machine Learning (ML).
- Neural Network or Deep Learning (NN/DL).
- Expert Systems (ES).
- Fuzzy Logic (FL).
- Natural Language Processing (NLP).

Machine learning (ML)

Machine learning, precisely referred to as ML, is a very crucial technology that is a subdomain of artificial intelligence. Although machine learning is a subdomain of artificial intelligence, in many scenarios, those terms are used interchangeably. ML is being used in all major and innovative business applications in modern businesses, such as chatbots on websites and online platforms, recommendation engines on e-commerce websites, language processing applications, translation applications, editing and proofreading applications, entertainment platforms, and much more.

Machine learning can be defined as

> The field of artificial intelligence in which the machines are made capable of performing complex tasks by developing capabilities in machines that imitate the thinking and decision power of human being. The learning of machines is based on the different types of algorithms and types of machine learning. The learning of machine in the ML takes place through input or feeding of data in different forms and formats to the machines to develop skills that resemble to human brain capabilities without any explicit computer programming.[16]

The systems that are trained under the machine learning field become able to perform the most complex tasks that require capabilities to visualize, analyze, and understand the environment or surroundings of the artificial intelligence system, and make decisions based on the understanding of the environment without any explicit programming. The development of such a level of capabilities in machines is possible only through machine learning, which is gaining strong roots in almost all fields and industries.

Training machines through the machine learning process consists of multiple steps that make a complete cycle of learning without any explicit programming to produce the desired output results. Those steps include:

- Data gathering.
- Data preparation.
- Choosing an ML model.
- Training machine.
- Evaluation of data.
- Tuning of hyper-parameters.
- Predictions.

All the steps are specialized processes governed by certain principles, regulations, and algorithms. The successful deployment of the entire process based on the above-mentioned seven (7) machine learning steps is referred to as the machine learning process.

Four (4) major types or categories of machine learning are listed below:

- Supervised machine learning.
- Unsupervised machine learning.
- Semi-supervised machine learning.
- Reinforcement machine learning.

Supervised machine learning is a type in which the algorithms developed by the data scientists use the labeled data as an input for learning, with predefined variables to analyze and evaluate for establishing correlations. The input as well as the output of the machine learning algorithm used in this type of learning is prespecified. As the name implies, it requires supervision from a human or requires human intervention for learning.

Unsupervised machine learning uses unlabeled data as input to the machine learning algorithm to train on. The machine algorithm scans and analyzes the entire data to figure out any meaningful correlation among the data without any human intervention. The input and output of this type of machine learning are predetermined.

The semi-supervised machine learning uses an algorithm that can take both labeled and unlabeled datasets as inputs. The algorithm is not bound to stick to the labeled training datasets only, but can also scan for the meaning of correlations without any human-defined intervention. This algorithm can develop an understanding of the data by predefined labels as well as independent observations.

Reinforcement machine learning is a type of machine learning in which the data scientists develop a complete set of tasks in a complete process for the algorithm to follow. The machines are taught through this process to accomplish all predefined tasks to complete the entire learning process. Every step is governed by predefined rules to provide negative or positive cues.

The machine learning functions can be categorized into three types, as mentioned and explained in the following list:

- **Descriptive function** – This machine learning algorithm explains what happened with the help of training datasets.
- **Predictive function** – This function of machine learning predicts what is going to happen in the future based on the understanding of the data.
- **Prescriptive function** – The prescriptive function determines what action should be taken based on the understanding of the system data.

There are some additional fields of machine learning that are very commonly used in the modern field of machine learning. These fields include:

- Neural networks (NN).
- Deep learning (DL).
- Natural language processing (NLP).

The details of these fields of machine learning, types, functions, steps, and models will be provided in the subsequent discussions.

A SHORT HISTORY OF MACHINE LEARNING

The traces of the initial history of machine learning can be found in mathematics, statistics, and the theory of probabilities because machine learning is governed by the algorithms that are developed on the basis of numerous mathematical, logical, and statistical formulas based on the different theories of probabilities. Thus, it can be said that the indirect relationship with the modern machine learning events and theories can be traced back to the 18th century, when the Bayes theorem was developed in the history of mathematical research. The direct relationship of scientific work that relates to the modern machine learning field can be traced back to the mid-20th century.

Both the initial and modern events pertaining to the machine learning history can be set as the following timeline:[17,18,19]

- **1763** – The mathematical research by Thomas Bayes and Richard Price that led to the definition of Bayes' theorem later in the 19th century.
- **1805** – The discovery of the least squares method by Adrien-Marie Legendre, extensively used in data fitting applications.
- **1812** – Publishing of Bayes' theorem officially by Pierre Simon Laplace. This theorem laid the foundation of probability science.
- **1913** – Discovery of Markov Chains by Andrey Markov for the analysis and assessment of a poem using this technique.
- **1943** – The invention of the first model for developing an artificial neuron that mimics the human neuron. This development lays the foundation of modern machine learning. This model was invented by Warren McCulloch and Walter Pitts.
- **1950** – The development of the Turing learning machine powered by the Turing Test. This was developed by Alan Turing.
- **1951** – Marvin Minsky and Dean Edmonds built the first neural network machine in history that could learn.
- **1952** – Arthur Samuel develops the first machine learning computer program named Machines Playing Checkers.

- **1957** – The first time in history, the development of the perceptron was announced by scientist Frank Rosenblatt.
- **1963** – Machines Playing Tic-Tac-Toe was invented with the help of boxes and beads that used a reinforcement machine learning model for this purpose. This machine learning capability was developed by Donald Michie.
- **1967** – The first time the development of the nearest neighbor machine learning algorithm was developed for mapping the routes.
- **1969** – The paper regarding the limitations of neural networks was described with proper research, which was published by Marvin Minsky and Seymour Papert.
- **1970** – The discovery of automatic differentiation (AD) was made by Seppo Linnainmaa. It performs a differentiation function on the discrete connected networks.
- **1973** – Emergence of AI Winter. In response to the Lighthill report, the British government cut funds for AI for all universities except three. This is known as the AI Winter event.
- **1979** – The development of an automatic cart named Stanford Cart, which could avoid the navigational obstacles in a room. This machine was developed by a team of students at Stanford University.
- **1979** – An artificial neural network (ANN) based on the neocognitron by Kunihiko Fukushima. This invention became the pathfinder for convolutional neural networks later on.
- **1981** – The introduction of the Explanation-Based Learning (EBL) method developed by Gerald Dejong. This algorithm was able to analyze computer data and develop a general rule to accept and discard the information based on its importance.
- **1082** – The Recurrent Neural Network was developed by John Hopfield. He popularized it as Hopfield Networks, which can serve as content-addressable memory systems.
- **1985** – An application named NetTalk was developed by Terry Sejnowski. This application could pronounce natural language words like children do.
- **1986** – The reverse of the automatic differentiation function was developed by Seppo Linnainmaa, which was named Backpropagation. It is extensively used in modern machine learning applications.
- **1989** – A new model of reinforcement learning named Q-learning was developed by Christopher Watkins for greater improvement of the feasibility and practicality of reinforcement machine learning. The release of the first machine learning software for computers, named Evolver, was made by Axcelis Inc. It was the first commercialized software program for personal computers.
- **1992** – The development of a machine playing backgammon named TD-Gammon was developed by Gerald Tesauro. This computer program would use an artificial neural network, which was trained on temporal-difference (TD) learning.

- 1995 – Random Forest and Support Vector Machine algorithms were developed by Tin Kam Ho and the team of Corinna Cortes and Vladimir Vapnik, respectively, through their own papers.
- 1997 – Garry Kasparov, the chess world champion, was defeated for the first time by a machine learning system named Deep Blue by IBM in the chess championship. In the same year, a recurrent neural network efficiency-improving machine learning-based powerful model named Long Short-Term Memory (LSTM) was invented by Sepp Hochreiter and Jurgen Schmidhuber to make recurrent neural networks more effective.
- 1998 – The first database system was developed that could recognize the handwritten text. This database was referred to as the Modified National Institute of Standards and Technology Database, precisely known as the MNIST Database, developed by the students of an American high school and the employees of the American Census Bureau under the leadership of computer scientist Yann LeCun. This machine was also able to understand both handwritten and digital presentations of digits simultaneously.
- 2002 – The first time a machine learning library was released, named the TORCH machine learning library.
- 2006 – The term "Deep Learning" was first coined by Geoffrey Hinton. This year, a machine learning-based recommendation and review system was launched by Netflix, named the Netflix Prize. It was designed for competition purposes for the customers to review, rate, and recommend manually in comparison with the automated recommendations. The first-time prize was won in 2009, three years after its launch.
- 2009 – A visual database named ImageNet was developed by Fei-Fei Li, who developed this by envisioning that without a large amount of real-world information, machine learning cannot grow at the speed that the scientists are focusing on. With the development of this huge database system for machine learning, the effectiveness and growth of machine learning have increased significantly.
- 2010 – The efficiency of Microsoft Kinect reached tracking about 20 features of a human body at a speed of 30 times per second. This opened up the arena of interacting with the computer through movements and gestures. For the first time in the history of machine learning, an online website named Kaggle was launched for machine learning competitions.
- 2011 – The human competitor of IBM Watson at Jeopardy was beaten.
- 2012 – The successful development of a neural network on YouTube to recognize a cat through unlabeled training datasets. This project was developed by Andrew Ng and Jeff Dean, the leaders of the Google Brain team.
- 2014 – Facebook launches the DeepFace application to recognize faces. It was a powerful neural network developed by Facebook, which

was able to recognize faces with as much as 97.35% accuracy and reliability. In the same year, a massive parallel machine learning platform named Sibyl was launched by Google. This platform would allow the company's employees internally to make predictions and recommendations about user behaviors through this platform, and understand the user behaviors.

- **2015** – Amazon's machine learning platform was launched. Meanwhile, Microsoft launched its toolkit for distributed machine learning for sharing and coordinating machine learning work and projects on a unified platform.
- **2015** – A warning for the human being was issued through a letter written and endorsed by Stephen Hawking, Elon Musk, and over 3000 robotics and artificial intelligence researchers and scientists.
- **2016** – The first computer Go program was launched by the Google Corporation. This program was named Google's AlphaGo. This program beats a human professional player in the chess game. Later on, this program was revised in 2017 and named AlphaGo Zero, which would allow more than one player to play.
- **1918** – The development of the machine learning-powered system "AlphaFord 1" that could predict the protein structure, named as Critical Assessment of Techniques for Protein Structure Prediction, precisely referred to as CASP.
- **2021** – Launch of "Alpha Ford 2" for the competition of critical assessment of techniques for protein structure prediction. It scored over 90% accuracy in predicting the protein structures.

The continual growth in machine learning technology, its toolkits, platforms, techniques, and use cases is being noticed in all fields of industry and business. The new trends that are revolutionizing the growth and progress in the field of machine learning include quantum artificial intelligence, automated machine learning (AutoML), multi-model machine learning, multi-objective machine learning, tiny machine learning, democratized machine learning, and many others. All these trends are heading toward highly competitive and fast-growing technological markets across all regions and verticals in the world.[20]

MAIN SUBDOMAINS OF MACHINE LEARNING

Machine learning has been evolving very fast during the past few years or decades. Therefore, more subfields and domains will arise with the advancements in the growth of this technology. The newer trends and techniques will emerge in this field to augment the progress that has been underway in recent years.

Till now, the most important subdomains that are very well-known to the scientists and domain specialists include:

- Natural language processing (NLP).
- Deep learning (DL).
- Neural networks (NN).

There are many subfields and technologies that are being used within the above-mentioned subdomains of machine learning, which will be discussed further in the upcoming topics of this book. Meanwhile, new trends in the market are also emerging that may bring forth new domains and realms in this fast-growing field of machine learning. Among those domains, quantum machine learning, automated machine learning, tiny machine learning, and multi-objective and multi-model machine learning are a few very important ones, which may lead to newer techniques, algorithms, platforms, and even new subdomains of machine learning.

Let us now have a deeper insight into the most important subdomains of the machine learning field.

Natural language processing

Natural language processing, precisely referred to as NLP, is a subset of machine learning technology or a very powerful field in artificial intelligence (AI). As the name implies, it is the artificial ability of machines to process natural language to understand the meaning of the natural language in the form of written text or spoken voice. The technical definition of natural language processing can be defined as:

> The ability or capability of a computer machine to understand the natural language spoken or written by human being and respond to the understanding of language in the same way as human does.[21]

For instance, a person speaks or writes a text to another person, who understands it and responds according to their understanding. Natural language works like that in both written and spoken formats. Exactly in the same way, the natural language processing technology enables the machines to understand natural language communication, either from other machines or from humans, in both text and written formats, and produce a corresponding response (of the understanding of that natural language interaction or communication). The response can be either in text format or in spoken voice formats. Thus, natural language processing technology establishes an automated communication and interface system between humans and machines as well as between machines and machines. A computer machine powered by natural language processing capabilities takes natural language spoken data and text through a microphone and text input, respectively. The camera scanning for taking the handwritten or other types of printed data is also used in modern natural processing applications. It is similar to the ears and eyes of a person, which are used for taking natural language data from other people in our real-world environment. The output of the natural language processing system is generated in the form of voice and text through speakers and text screens, respectively. The examples of natural language processing (NLP) that you may have encountered include chatbots, GPS voice on navigational applications in cars, guidelines on Google Maps roads, and many others.

Short history of NLP

The history of the natural language processing field can be traced back to the 1950s, when the machine learning pioneer Alan Turing proposed a test to gauge the intelligence of a machine in his research paper named "computing machinery and intelligence". It was the beginning of the first generation of natural language processing. We can divide the history of NLP into three main categories or eras: 1) Symbolic NLP, 2) Statistical NLP, and 3) Neural NLP. The first generation of NLP technology started in the 1950s and lasted till the 1990s. The second era starts in the 1990s and lasts till 2010. Finally, the third era of modern NLP started in the 2010s and continues to this day. The chronicles of NLP history are mentioned in the following list.[24]

- **1950** – Turing test by Alan Turing.
- **1954** – Georgetown experiment for automated translation of 16 sentences of the Russian language to English.
- **1960s** – The development of SHRDLU and ELIZA programs for understanding natural language through computer machines.
- **1966** – Publication of the Automatic Language Processing Advisory Committee (ALPAC) report by a team of scientists led by John R. Pierce.
- **1970s** – Numerous programs were written by different scientists and companies for converting natural language real-world data into computer-understandable structured data. The examples include MARGIE, PAM, SAM, QUALM, TaleSpin, POLITICS, PLOT UNITS, and many others. The development of the first-ever chatting bot was also developed during this period, such as the PARRY chat-bot and others.
- **1980s** – This decade marked the end of symbolic natural language processing. In the early 1990s, the statistical NLP approach hit the technological market in the field of natural language processing. The main highlights of this decade include the development and discoveries of numerous techniques, tools, and research, such as the HPSG system, the LESK Algorithm, the Racter chat-bot, the Jabberwacky chat-bot, and others.

- 1990s – This decade was a transformational decade for natural language processing technology. It evolved from symbolic NLP to statistical NLP by using the power of data analytics and statistical theories. Numerous statistical methods were incorporated into this field during this decade. The development of textual corpora and the practical implementation of machine translation were a few major highlights of this decade.
- 2000s – This era saw the development of numerous supervised and unsupervised models of machine learning. They were not so accurate and reliable, but set the tone for a bright future of the progress of natural language processing technology.
- 2010s – This decade saw another shift in the approaches of natural language processing technology. Now, the neural network approach has either replaced or complemented the statistical approach of machine learning for natural language. Numerous modules, models, approaches, and techniques have been developed to make machines understand natural language and respond properly. Unsupervised machine learning has taken new heights, especially in the field of automated driving and other domains. Advancements in many online applications for processing text as well as audio data have been made. There are numerous automated domain processes in all types of businesses that are taking place in this fast-growing technological decade in artificial intelligence.

The natural language processing field has become very important in modern businesses as well as in our social lives. With the advent of modern information technologies, the data created in the forms of text and audio on websites, business applications, process applications, communication platforms, voice communication, and many others is huge, precisely referred to as *big data* in modern terminology. This huge unstructured data contains valuable business intelligence and other information that can be used in increasing business efficiency, team productivity, effective process management, and many other areas. But, without the help of any technology (that enables understanding), it would not be possible to understand, analyze, and skim through the valuable information from such a huge volume of data. The processing of natural language is very difficult through normal rule-based software applications because of the numerous ambiguities of natural language that we speak or write. The most important ambiguities present in our natural language include the following.[22]

- Homophones and homonyms in natural language.
- Sarcasm, metaphors, and idioms.
- Irregular exceptions in sentence structures.
- Grammatical and usage exceptions.
- The ever-changing and evolving nature of language.
- Tones and emotions.

With the advent of modern techniques such as statistical models and neural networks, the importance of natural language processing has taken center stage in all domains of business, such as sales, customers, healthcare, medication, marketing, advertisement, eLearning, e-commerce, retail sales, and many others. Now, all language ambiguities can be made understandable to the machines through neural networks or deep learning techniques. Thus, the most valuable business intelligence can easily be achieved from the piles of unstructured data.

The natural language processing field can be categorized into three major eras that are listed below:[23]

- Symbolic natural language processing era (1950–1990).
- Statistical natural language processing era (1990–2010).
- Neural natural language processing era (2010–present).

In the first era of NLP, a set of rules and corresponding responses would be designed for the machines to understand the responses from the corresponding outputs. It was just a preliminary type of language understanding by machines based on a few rules and corresponding responses. This era is also known as the rule-based basic natural language processing era.

The second era of NLP was based on more sophisticated algorithms based on the machine learning concept. The availability of higher computing or processing power and advanced software applications and associated tools made it possible for large-scale processing of natural language data through machine learning algorithms powered by statistical data and applications.

The third era of NLP is the modern era of machine learning, which is based on the latest neural networks that integrate deep learning into the algorithms and define their own rules of understanding and response-building based on their own experience with the language during direct interaction, as well as during data training.

Natural language processing incorporates different scientific processes and techniques into its entire system. The techniques and processes include the following.[22]

- Different forms of computational linguistics.
- Rule-based modeling of natural language that humans speak.
- Machine learning techniques.
- Deep learning models.
- Statistical and data analysis models.

The natural language processing field consists of two major language processing phases, as mentioned below:

- Data preprocessing phase.
- Algorithm development phase.

Let us explain the above-mentioned phases of natural language processing with the help of all major methods involved in these.

Data preprocessing phase

In this phase of natural language processing, the data is cleaned and tagged in such a way that the natural language processing algorithms can easily understand the data for further processing, understanding, and creating suitable responses. This phase uses different ways for cleaning and making machine-readable data, such as:[21]

- **Tokenization** – In this method, the input data in the form of text or voice is broken into smaller parts or units to further work with, in such a way that it is easy to understand and sort out from the complex sentences.
- **Removing stop words** – In this method of cleaning the data, the most common words that are *not-so-important* in the meaning of a sentence are removed, and only the unique words on which the meaning of a sentence depends are left. By doing so, the machines can understand and process the sentences faster and more accurately.
- **Stemming and lemmatization** – This is another very important process used in the cleaning of natural language data in the form of complex sentences. This method is used to reduce the lengthy words in different formats or conjugations to the root of the word. For instance, the word "learning" will be reduced to its root word, "learn".
- **Parts of speech marking** – In this method, each main word in a sentence is tagged with the respective part of speech it belongs to. For instance, in the sentence *"John drives a beautiful car"*, the word "John" is marked as a noun, the word "drives" is tagged as a verb, the word "beautiful" is tagged as an adjective, and "car" is again tagged as a noun. Thus, complete information based on the parts of speech is provided to the machine learning algorithms that will be used for natural language processing.

Algorithm development phase

The algorithm development phase, or data processing through algorithms, is the second phase of natural language processing technology. In this phase, the most suitable algorithms are developed and fed with the cleaned NLP data achieved in the first phase to train on. The algorithms can vary from application to application based on the most commonly used categories. The most common categories of NLP algorithms are:

- **Rule-based algorithms** – The rule-based algorithms are the preliminary types of NLP algorithms that were used during the early days of this technology and are still in use in numerous applications. These algorithms are developed on the basis of grammatical and other linguistic rules implemented into the algorithm software, along with the suitable corresponding understanding or tagging. The response generated with the help of this algorithm is also in line with the predefined rules that have been fed to the computer program. This type of algorithm does not understand and respond to the emotions, sarcasm, and other feelings embedded in the natural language.

- **Machine learning-based algorithms** – The machine learning-powered algorithms are the latest category of natural language processing algorithms. These algorithms use the modern technologies that have evolved in the data science, machine learning, and artificial intelligence fields. These algorithms use statistical and neural network methods to understand and respond to the natural language input data or communication. This category of ML-based algorithms can further be classified into two subcategories.
  - **Statistical NLP algorithms** – This category uses different types of statistical models for materializing the machine learning capabilities of computers. A range of data analytics results and useful information is the core component of these NLP algorithms for processing the data.
  - **Neural network-based algorithms** – These types of algorithms use the latest technologies in the field of machine learning, such as neural networks, deep learning, representation learning, and others. These algorithms define their own rules based on the understanding and repetitive interaction with natural language communication in different forms.

To summarize, natural language processing can be classified into three categories based on the algorithms and technology advancement, such as rule-based NLP learning, statistics-based NLP learning, and neural network-based NLP learning.

The development of natural language processing algorithms is based on two major techniques, in different customized ways to ingest the natural language-based data and process it. The techniques are:

- Syntax analysis technique.
- Semantic analysis technique.

Every technique used in the NLP algorithms consists of different types of analyses that are described separately in the following sub-sections.

Syntax analysis

The arrangement and structure of a natural language sentence that makes grammatical sense for the NLP algorithms is known as syntax analysis. The syntax analysis is used by the NLP algorithms to evaluate the meaning of the sentence from a grammatical perspective. The main processes involved in this analysis include the following:

- **Parsing** – In this process, the sentence under analysis is broken into different parts of speech to make it more understandable for the algorithm from a parts-of-speech perspective. For example, in the sentence *"I practice law in a reputed agency"*, the parsing process tags "I" as a pronoun, "practice" as a verb, "law" as a noun, "in" as a preposition, the word "reputed" as an adjective, and the word "agency" as a noun.
- **Breaking sentences** – The long and complex sentences are broken for a better understanding of the paragraph in this process. For instance, the period sign indicates that the sentence has ended and a new sentence has started.
- **Segmentation of words** – Separating words in a paragraph or sentence from other words in such a way that the natural language processing algorithms can easily differentiate between each word separately. For example, any digital space or white space on a printed page can be made for the machine algorithm to understand as the border separation between two separate words.
- **Stemming** – The stemming process is used to link any word with its root word. The words are used in different forms, conjugations, moods, and degrees. The stemming process describes the root word of that particular word. For example, the drinking will be stemmed as "drink".
- **Morphological segmentation** – This process is used to break a word into smaller parts that are called morphemes. For instance, the word 'unpredictably' is segmented into different parts such as *un + predict + able + ly*.

Semantic analysis

The semantic analysis is a process to differentiate between the meanings of different, similar-looking words. The NLP algorithm uses semantic analysis as the basic tool to understand the meaning behind a particular word. It uses different subprocesses as mentioned below.

- **Disambiguation of word sense** – This sub-process is used to differentiate between similar meanings based on the context of the sentence. It allows a natural language processing algorithm to learn about the context of the content or sentence to decide the meaning of a word that has multiple meanings. For instance, consider two examples – "A friend in deed" and "a court deed". The meanings of the word "deed" in the two sentences are different based on the context or the background of the sentence.
- **Named entity recognition** – In this process or technique, the words are classified into different categories that are much broader and help the NLP algorithm to decide the correct meanings of those words.

For example, apples, mangoes, peaches, and bananas can be categorized as fruits, which is a general class of the items mentioned on this list. Thus, NLP algorithms will not get confused by those items and can easily understand them.

- **Natural language generation** – This is another very important part of semantic analysis in which the NLP algorithms can generate a report based on the information they understood from the data mining or data analysis that they conducted through different processes. It can generate a report based on the understanding of semantic analysis for posting to some public platforms, such as Twitter, or on private platforms.

NLP tools

Natural language processing technology is commonly developed and implemented through a few very important tools and platforms. The most common and very fundamental tools for developing NLP algorithms are mentioned below:

- **Natural Language Processing Toolkit (NLTK)** – It is a very powerful toolkit for the development of natural language algorithms. It is based on the Python programming language and consists of a large library covering a wide range of functions and tasks related to NLP, sub-tasks such as parsing, segmentation, lemmatization, stemming, word trimming, sentence breaking, and others. It is an open-source platform.
- **Gensim** – It is a powerful library that consists of a large number of functions, tasks, sub-tasks, processes, and related modules, extensively useful for the development of modern NLP algorithms, document indexing, and topic modeling in customized apps and algorithms.
- **Intel NLP Architect** – This is another powerful platform developed by Intel Inc. The Intel Natural Language Processing Architect deals with the deep learning machine learning approach and helps with deep learning topologies and other techniques.

Use cases of NLP

Natural language processing (NLP), especially the latest models powered by deep learning, is extensively used in multiple applications in a wide range of industries. The usage of NLP is expected to increase exponentially in the near future. According to the latest forecast (at the time of writing this book), the global market size of natural language processing technology will reach US$361.6 billion by 2030 from just US$18.6 billion in 2021, with a whopping growth of over 39.06% CAGR for the forecast period from 2022 to 2030.[24]

There are numerous use cases and practical applications of natural language processing technology in modern industries, as listed below.

- **Text extraction** – This is a use case of NLP in which the huge text can be scanned for skimming words to be used for a particular purpose, such as search engine optimization and other similar kinds of applications in the industry.
- **Speech recognition** – By this use case, any piece of voice or speech can be recognized in terms of the meaning of the speech, tone, voice, pitch, frequency, and others. The use of this capability is extensive in forensic applications.
- **Optical character recognition (OCR)** – The printed and handwritten text can be identified and understood with the help of a natural language processing application. This has paved the way for strong growth in education, remote learning, healthcare, and other fields.
- **Text classification** – The categorization of a particular type of word into a class is the most useful use case of natural language processing. This helps determine the intention of web users on any particular website for particular products.
- **Machine translation** – The translation of languages from one natural language to another natural language spoken on the earth can be accomplished through the effective use of natural language processing algorithms.
- **Natural language generation** – In this use case, the power of NLP algorithms is used to generate a report or an article based on the understanding of a large piece of text in the form of natural language. It can also be automated to publish on any public or private platforms.
- **Voice-to-text and text-to-voice conversion** – NLP algorithms are used for performing conversion of data from one format to another. It can help you convert text into voice and voice into a text transcript.

The most common examples of industrial applications of NLP-powered systems include chatbots, virtual assistants, automated navigational apps powered by GPS, recommendation engines, search engine optimization, and many more.

Deep learning

Deep learning, precisely referred to as DL, is a subdomain of machine learning and artificial intelligence. Deep learning is also known as neural organized learning and deep structured learning. As the name implies, deep learning is a type of machine learning capability that is based on deeper information about any object, entity, or information. It uses huge volumes of data to learn, improve, and adjust learning algorithms by using artificial neural networks deeply. Artificial neural networks are a layered structure of nodes similar to the complex structure of the human brain. The artificial neural network (ANN) also consists of multiple layers and nodes to process huge amounts data and learn from the data by assigning weightage at every node and forwarding the information in a logical format if the value of the information crosses the threshold value of that particular node.

In simple words, deep learning can be characterized and defined based on the points mentioned below.[25,26]

- Deep learning is a subset of machine learning (ML).
- This learning mimics the functionality of the human brain.
- It uses the concept of artificial neural networks consisting of multiple layers and nodes based on the complexity of the abstraction, with representation learning.
- Deep learning extracts features of objects/abstractions at a very high level to produce the most accurate and reliable results or outputs.
- It uses huge data to learn; thus, it is also known as a crucial component of data science.
- It uses statistics and predictive models to learn.
- It is a hierarchical model of learning based on the complexity of abstraction learning in the previous layer.
- The iteration of output information continues till an accurate result or output is not achieved and verified by a human or human-programmed system.
- The depth of a neural network is associated with the number of layers used.

In deep learning, the machines take huge amounts of real-world data to recognize objects or any other entity and produce the output, which is verified, whether it is correct or not. If the predictive output is not correct, the algorithm learns from the past experience and adjusts accordingly, and repeats the processes of learning through neural networks and predicts the output with more accuracy. It will keep understanding from every past experience and result, and keep on updating its understanding based on the huge data ingested as training datasets.

Let us understand this process from a human brain activity perspective. Say, for instance, a toddler who is not aware of a cat will need help from the parents to teach him/her. This work is accomplished by the data input to the neural network, which processes the data and tries to predict the animal. The next time, when the toddler points out the cat and says that it is a dog, the parents will say no (i.e., it is not a dog but a cat). Thus, the toddler learns from the experience that the shape he/she has noticed is a cat, not a dog. Eventually, after that, the kid will point to the cat and will say "cat". The parents will then affirm that. Thus, the learning process would be complete for recognizing a cat. Similarly, the output prediction in deep learning will be verified in terms of accuracy, and an acceptable level of accuracy will be achieved.

The deep learning field uses many learning methods in its algorithms. A few very important ones extensively used in modern deep learning are:

- Learning rate decay method.
- Dropout learning method.
- Training from scratch method.
- Transfer learning method.

There are numerous examples where deep learning is used for automated predictions through machines. A few of them are:

- Natural language processing (NLP) platforms.
- Speech recognition software apps.
- Image recognition platforms.
- Driverless vehicles.

Deep learning is the fastest-growing domain in artificial intelligence. To have a deeper dive into multiple aspects, a separate chapter is dedicated to this topic.

Neural networks

The neural network is an artificial network of nodes that mimics the neurons of a human brain. It is connected with nodes in different layers to process the input data to generate an accurate prediction based on the understanding of the input data. It is similar to the human brain structure in which the neurons are interconnected to millions of neurons to process the input data received through different senses such as eyes, ears, tongue, skin, nose, and gut feeling. The entire information is processed through a network of natural neurons to understand and estimate the tentative output based on the previous understanding of real-world scenarios and current input data.

Likewise, artificial intelligence has a very important subdomain named artificial neural networks that are designed to make the machine learn from the real-world data ingested through multiple sources such as keyboards, cameras, microphones, motion sensors, heat sensors, light, lasers, and many other sensors and rays. This learning process is based on the processing of the data through a set of nodes separated into different layers. The main layers of a neural network include:[28]

- Input layer.
- Hidden layer.
- Output layer.

The number of input and output layers is always one for each, while the number of hidden layers can be one or more than one, based on the power of the neural network. The deeper understanding of the past and real-world data is fully dependent on the number of hidden layers and the number of nodes connected to each other in different layers. Each node connected to an artificial neural network, precisely referred to as ANN, has its own specified value for reference to the other nodes in the complex network of machine learning. This is a digital and logical network; hence, the input as well as the output of a node will be just 0 or 1 or yes or no. Each node also has a specified threshold value of signal. If the signal strength crosses that threshold value, the node will pass the information to the deeper end or output layer nodes. If it is less than the specified threshold value, the node does not pass information to the next layer. The state of a node to pass the information further to the next layer in an information processing flow is called the activeness of the node or the active condition of the node. The schematic diagram of an artificial neural network is shown in Figure 2.6.

The main purpose of neural networks used in the modern machine learning or artificial intelligence field is to teach machines to learn about the environment, similar to the human brain. The network is designed in such a way that it can adjust to the understanding of the past and new data it receives from the present conditions. The output of an artificial neural network is rechecked on the basis of accuracy. If the result or the predictive output of this network is not correct or less accurate, it will be repeated and corrected automatically by the neural network till it achieves the most accurate results. Thus, the machines understand the environment and input data by adjusting the learning algorithms in such a way that they predict the correct output through computer processing of the artificial neural nodes.

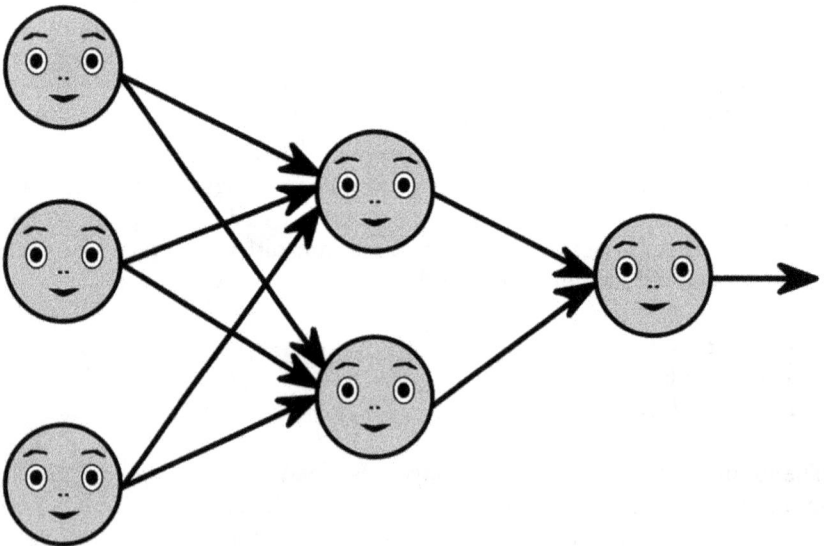

Figure 2.6 Concept of neural network nodal connection. (Pixabay).

The neural networks are extensively used in numerous business applications in the present marketplace. The most common applications and use cases of neural networks are mentioned in the following list.[27]

- Medical imaging and diagnosis.
- Marketing and behavior analysis.
- Computer vision-based applications.
- Self-driving vehicles.
- Digital authentication and security.
- Recommendation engines.

As the neural networks are evolving very fast due to the availability of huge volumes of data to ingest and learn from, new types are emerging. The most common types of artificial neural networks (ANN) are mentioned in the following list.

- Backpropagation algorithm.
- Feedforward neural network.
- Convolutional neural network.

This is a very powerful field of machine learning, which needs extra and separate space for detailed discussions. Therefore, a later chapter has been dedicated to artificial neural networks and deep learning in this book.

TYPES OF MACHINE LEARNING

Machine learning is a very complex domain that requires numerous algorithms, machine learning techniques, data processing, and other processes. Those processes are computation-intensive and data hungry to train on the machines to learn like the human brain does. Different types of machine learning are deployed to enable computing machines and systems to learn and decide in a digital environment. The most common types of machine learning used in the modern field of ML are three, and the fourth one is a hybrid type of machine learning that is formed by combining the two other types of machine learning. Four major types of machine learning are listed below:[29]

- Supervised machine learning.
- Unsupervised machine learning.
- Semi-supervised machine learning.
- Reinforcement machine learning.

The details of the above-mentioned types of machine learning are mentioned separately in the following topics, respectively.

Supervised machine learning

Supervised machine learning is one of the basic types of machine learning used in modern artificial intelligence. In this type of machine learning, the intelligent machines or systems are trained on real-world input data, which is labeled for an output. In other words, the input data in a particular training dataset is labeled with the information for generating an output. It is similar to the training imparted to a student under the supervision of a teacher. The supervised machine learning has various characteristics, like:[30,31]

- The computer model is trained through training datasets labeled for an output.
- The model is trained with a huge amount of data to help the compute system generate predictions accurately based on the labeled information in the training datasets for a long time until the system becomes able to generate accurate output.
- The main purpose of supervised training is to make compute systems able to detect the underlying patterns to recognize and map the relationship with the labeled output.
- The level of accuracy determines the level of capability of that particular system. If the compute system generates accurate results or output against the never-before-seen test data, the machine has learned from the supervised learning perfectly.
- Supervised machine learning is very useful and effective for two major categories, such as classification of data and projection/prediction of data based on different types of regression machine learning algorithms.
- In supervised learning, the labeled data is ingested by the system, which enables it to generate correct output based on the labeled information.
- In this kind of machine learning, the algorithms used for training are designed to map input variable data (x) to the output (y) variable.
- A few examples of supervised machine learning use cases include fraud detection, spam filters, risk assessment, image classification, and so on.

How does supervised machine learning work?

In supervised machine learning, the computer systems are trained with the training datasets that are labeled for the output to train on. The machine learns on the basis of the labeled input data and produces the results that are in line with the labels provided to the machine to learn about the training datasets. The process of supervised machine learning consists of a labeled training dataset, test datasets, and result accuracy monitoring. The labeled input training datasets with the entities are named accurately to train the machine to generate accurate results. Numerous labeled training datasets are fed to compute systems to learn about the features of the labeled entity and produce the result that is labeled. Once it has learned enough to generate accurate results, the test dataset is fed to check the accuracy of the results. The test datasets are labeled but not disclosed to the machine learning algorithm. The compute system generates the results based on its previous learning. If the results are accurate, the system has learned sufficiently; otherwise, more training datasets are fed to make its understanding more reliable. The entire process of the supervised machine learning workflow is shown with a schematic diagram in Figure 2.7.

In this diagram (Figure 2.7), a large number of training datasets (with proper labels on the entities containing that input data) are fed into the supervised ML training model or algorithm, which learns from the input data labeled as triangle, square, and hexagonal. The model evaluates and learns that a sketch with three sides is a triangle, a figure with four equal sides and four equal angles is a square, and a picture with six angles is called a hexagon. When the compute system is tested for accuracy, the input without labels disclosed to the algorithm is fed as a test dataset, which is never-before-seen data, to predict the test items. If it predicts that one test input is a triangle and one is a square, as shown in the figure, the results are accurate, and the machine has successfully learned from the previous training datasets that were labeled to map such things.

The entire process or workflow of supervised machine learning consists of the following major steps.[30]

- In the first step, the activity of determining the types of training datasets is accomplished.
- Once training datasets are defined, the labeling of the training datasets is done in the second step of supervised machine learning.
- The training datasets are divided into three main categories in the third step: training dataset, test dataset, and validation dataset.

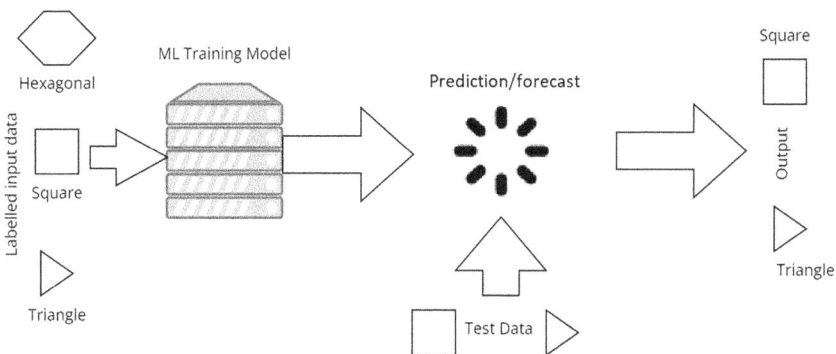

Figure 2.7 Schematic diagram of supervised machine learning.

- In this step, different and sufficient characteristics and features of training dataset items are identified in such a way that machines can easily understand the features to identify and map the features to determine the test data input for validation.
- The right algorithm for supervised machine learning is chosen, such as a decision tree, support vector machine, or other. These algorithms will be discussed in the upcoming topic and subsequent subtopics.
- In the next step, the algorithm is run on the training datasets to evaluate and understand. Sometimes, the validation datasets, which are subsets of the main training dataset, are also used for validating the learning process.
- In the final step, the accuracy of the model is checked through the test dataset. If the supervised training algorithm is capable of predicting the correct results, the model is working accurately; otherwise, the model should be trained again.

Types of supervised machine learning

The supervised machine learning algorithms can be classified into two major categories based on the output or results of the models, as mentioned below.[31]

- Classification.
- Regression.

The classification type of supervised machine learning is designed to figure out or sort out the training items into multiple classes or categories. The most common output-based categories of classification type of supervised ML include:

- Binary or logical outputs.
- Feature detection outputs.

The applications of binary or logical outputs include spam filtering, negative and positive feedback sorting, and other similar applications. On the other hand, the applications of feature detection-based outputs include body movement detection, facial recognition, and others. The most common algorithms used in the classification-based app include:

- Decision tree algorithm.
- Random Forest algorithm.
- Support Vector Machine algorithm.

The regression is the second type of supervised machine learning based on the predictive output result generation. This model is used to predict numerical values in relation to certain variables to establish a predictive relationship between the input data and the output data. The most common examples of numerical predictions based on the input data include:

- The average prices the customers will be willing to pay after one year or so.
- Prediction of prices of the real estate properties in terms of the area or zip code.
- Projection of market sizes of some products or services for many years in the future.

The most common algorithms used in the regression category of the machine learning field are mentioned in the following list.[30,31]

- Logistic regression algorithm.
- Linear regression algorithms.
- Linear discriminant analysis algorithm.
- Bayesian linear regression algorithm.
- Non-linear regression algorithms.
- Polynomial regression algorithms.
- Decision tree algorithms.
- Random forest algorithms.
- Support vector machines (SVM) algorithms.
- Neural networks.

Choosing the most suitable algorithm, either in the category of regression or classification, is based on the suitability of the projection or prediction type and a few other parameters, such as variance and bias within the algorithms, and the complexity of the model. Meanwhile, the accuracy, linearity, heterogeneity, and redundancy of training data should be properly assessed and analyzed so that the most desired results can be achieved easily.

Unsupervised machine learning

Unsupervised machine learning is one of the three fundamental machine learning types that are used for analyzing and grouping the information in the training datasets. The training datasets used in unsupervised learning are not labeled or tagged, as is the case in supervised machine learning. The algorithms used in machine learning find out the features or characteristics of items or other information and group them on the basis of similarities and differences. The most similar items are grouped together or placed in the nearer area of the plane. The diverse items with many disparities are not placed in a group and are placed at a distant location from the similar items. Thus, a cluster of dissimilar items is formed in the clustering area or plane. The main features and characteristics of unsupervised machine learning are summarized here:[32,33]

- As the name implies, it is a type of machine learning that uses algorithms that can learn without any human intervention.
- The identification of the information in the unlabeled datasets is accomplished through different commonalities of features or characteristics.
- It discovers similarities and differences of features to group the items.
- Unsupervised learning is used for accomplishing three main tasks:
  - Clustering.
  - Association.
  - Dimensionality reduction.
- To perform the above-mentioned tasks, unsupervised machine learning uses different algorithms and approaches, which will be covered in this topic later on.
- It uses two major probabilistic methods known as:
  - **Cluster analysis** – This method is used to form groups with common features or characteristics for extrapolating algorithmic relationships.
  - **Principal component analysis (PCA)** – Analysis of huge data, which contains a large number of characteristics/features/dimensions for each observation. It increases the interoperability of data and preserves the maximum information.

The workflow and procedure of unsupervised machine learning are shown in Figure 2.8.

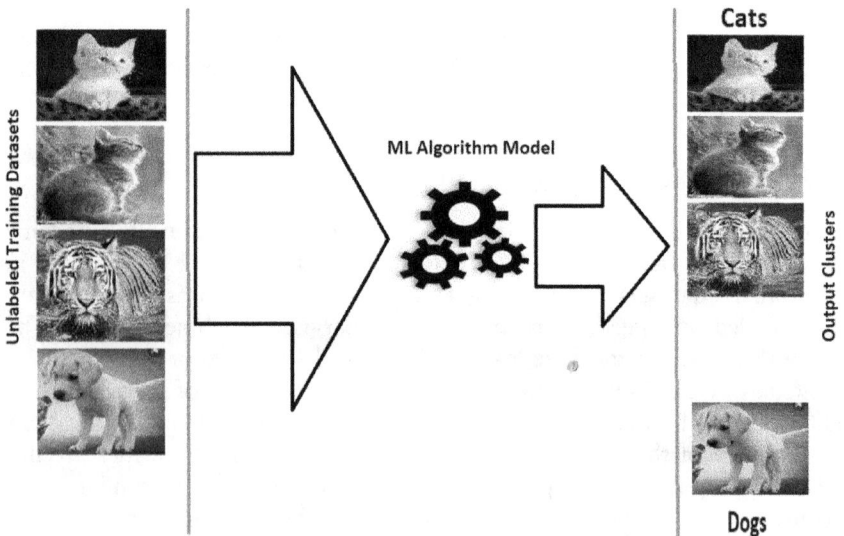

Figure 2.8 Schematic diagram of unsupervised machine learning.

In Figure 2.8, the training datasets consist of four images. Three of those four images are of cats and tigers. The remaining image is a dog. The data is not labeled and is fed to the machine learning algorithm, which performs a clustering process on the input data without any explicit labeling, finds the features of each figure, and compares them with the others. If the features are similar to each other, they are grouped together and placed in a group or cluster. In our example, two images of cats and one image of a tiger are placed into the broader category known as "Cats" because they belong to a similar family with little disparity. The fourth image is of a dog. The features of the dog do not match the features of the other images classified as cats. Therefore, it has been classified into another category or group known as "dogs". Thus, the basic process of clustering in unsupervised machine learning is complete. If more items are fed as data input through training datasets, they are also categorized in terms of their features and categorized with respect to similarities and differences.

There are three basic approaches that are deployed in unsupervised machine learning. They are as follows:[32,33]

- Clustering.
- Association rules.
- Dimensionality reduction.

Clustering

As described earlier, the clustering is an approach that is used to make groups of the information based on the features and patterns of the entities that are similar or dissimilar to each other. Thus, the grouping is done on the basis of commonalities and differences. There are different types of clustering algorithms that are commonly used in unsupervised machine learning. A few very popular groups of algorithms include:

- Exclusive clustering.
- Overlapping clustering.
- Hierarchical clustering.
- Probabilistic clustering.

Initially, the weightage and threshold values are chosen randomly before getting started with the machine learning procedure through neural networks. The results of the first input will be nonsensical or ridiculous. The output of the neural network will be compared with the known and correct value of the output. The data will be compared, and feedback will be given to the system through the neural network feedback mechanism. This process continues repeating till the correct result is achieved. Thus, the neural network continues learning through training datasets fed to the system continuously. For training such networks, you need huge volumes of data to make them more reliable, accurate, and efficient in performance, so that you can deploy them into real-world testing and learning environments easily.

In this entire process, the weightages of the neurons in the artificial neural network are continuously adjusted to make sure that the correct structure of the machine learning model is achieved. The adjustments in the weightage are done through the feedback system that compares the output of the model to the accurate value or known value of the input.

Exclusive clustering

This type of clustering uses the features or characteristics of information that can exist only in one group exclusively. This clustering is also known as hard clustering. The hard clustering, or exclusive clustering, uses the K-means clustering algorithm as the most fundamental tool for grouping the information in an exclusive group. The K is the number of clusters or groups and the K-means is the mean distance between two groups. The details of this algorithm will follow.

Overlapping clustering

As the name indicates, the overlapping clustering is a type of group in which the attributes or features of a single entity or information can co-exist in multiple numbers of groups. This type of clustering is also referred to as soft clustering. The belonging of a data point to multiple groups is governed by the separate degree of membership. The most common algorithm used for performing overlapping clustering is the Fuzzy K-means algorithm, which will be discussed at length in the upcoming topics in this chapter.

Hierarchical clustering

Hierarchical clustering, which is also known as hierarchical clustering analysis (HCA) in the machine learning field, performs the clustering or grouping process in two different ways, as mentioned below.

- Agglomerative clustering.
- Divisive clustering.

The agglomerative clustering is a bottom-up approach. Initially, the data points in this clustering are separated into isolated groups, and later on, they are merged together on the basis of commonalities iteratively until one single group is formed. On the other hand, the divisive clustering uses a top-down approach in which a large group or a cluster is further divided into multiple groups based on the differences of features among the entities.

To measure the commonalities in agglomerative clustering, different methods are used for establishing them, such as:

- Ward's linkage.
- Single or minimum linkage.
- Maximum or complete linkage.
- Average linkage.

The formulas behind establishing the above-mentioned types of linkage include Euclidean distance and Manhattan distance. The schematic description of agglomerative and divisive clustering can be shown in a diagram named a dendrogram.

Probabilistic clustering

The probabilistic clustering is also a soft clustering. It is used to solve the density estimation issues by establishing data points, which are formed based on the likelihood that they are linked to a particular distribution. The most commonly used clustering algorithm in this clustering approach is known as the Gaussian Mixture Model, precisely referred to as the Gaussian Mixture Model (GMM) algorithm, which is based on the Gaussian mathematical equation.

Association rules

The identification and establishment of an association or relationship between different variables in a training dataset is called the association rules. A range of businesses are using powerful association to figure out the valuable information between two or more variables in online marketing or online sales. The most commonly used algorithm for establishing relationships used in modern machine learning is the Apriori algorithm. The other algorithms used in association rules include the Eclat algorithm and the FP-Growth algorithm.

Apriori algorithm

The most commonly used algorithm to find out the relationship between multiple variable parameters in a training dataset is the Apriori algorithm. This is designed for basket market analysis applications in online shopping and sales. Numerous recommendation engines on a range of digital product, entertainment, and e-commerce retail sales companies use this algorithm for product recommendation purposes.

Dimensionality reduction

Dimensionality reduction is a process of unsupervised machine learning in which the dimensions or features are reduced to a level where the integrity of the dataset is not compromised. As we know, the number of dimensions of an item in a dataset produces the most accurate results. But sometimes, the number of dimensions goes beyond a certain limit, where the performance of the computer systems gets affected. To maintain a balance between the performance and accuracy of the results without compromising the integrity of the information in the training dataset, the dimensionality reduction technique is used. As the name implies, it will reduce the number of dimensions of an entity or information in a dataset to such a level that it does not lose its integrity and the performance of the computing system, eventually, it becomes more desirable. The data input size becomes more manageable and easier to handle. The main application of the dimensionality reduction approach is the preprocessing of data storage and other applications. Different types of algorithms for achieving different functionalities in data training sets are used. A few of them are mentioned below.

Principal component analysis (PCA)

By using this algorithm, the number of redundancies in datasets is reduced to compress the datasets in such a way that the features of the datasets are extracted. The representation of data is formed by using the linear transformation to build a set of principal components. The first component sets the direction, such as orthogonal or perpendicular, to reduce the variance of datasets.

Singular value decomposition (SVD)

Singular value decomposition, precisely referred to as SVD, is another algorithm to reduce the dimensions of a dataset. The principal matrix is factored into three low-rank matrices. A range of noises in audio, image, and other data is reduced by using this algorithm. It uses a formula $(A = USVT)$, where U, V are orthogonal matrices, and S is a diagonal matrix that has the singular values of matrix A.

Autoencoders

This technique of reducing the dimensions of the training datasets is commonly used in neural network models of unsupervised machine learning. The autoencoders use neural networks for compressing the data first and then representing the input data in a new form in such a way that the data integrity is not compromised, but the irrelevant dimensions are reduced to improve the system performance significantly.

Major application domains of unsupervised learning

Unsupervised machine learning is extensively used in numerous industrial and business domains in the modern world, powered by artificial intelligence. A few very important areas of unsupervised ML are listed below:

- Computer vision (CV).
- Medical imaging (MI).
- News sections sorting apps.
- Recommendation engines.
- Customer personas.

Like other types of machine learning applications, the use of unsupervised machine learning is expected to grow significantly in the future, too.

Semi-supervised machine learning

As the name implies, it is a partially supervised and partially unsupervised type of machine learning. It uses techniques and algorithms used in both supervised and unsupervised machine learning. This type of machine learning uses a small volume of output labeled training datasets associated with each tuple and a huge volume of data with pseudo-labels used in the unsupervised machine learning. The combination of supervised and unsupervised machine learning is known as semi-supervised machine learning. It is not a fundamental kind of machine learning, but rather it is a derived type that shares the techniques, features, and procedures of both fundamental types of machine learning, such as supervised and unsupervised machine learning.[34]

The main driver of using a combination of both types of machine learning is the high cost of a limited application spectrum and the complexity of unsupervised machine learning. The best tradeoff between cost, accuracy, and performance is semi-supervised machine learning. Supervised learning requires manual labeling of the tuples of training data by data scientists or specialists. The cost of labeling the data is huge for companies to bear. On the other hand, the application spectrum and performance of unsupervised machine learning are very limited.[35] The semi-supervised machine learning uses unsupervised learning to cluster the data into groups of a huge volume of data, and then the labeled data is linked to those groups to create more accurate and faster results. Those groups can be labeled through the existing labeled data.

Step-by-step workflow of semi-supervised machine learning

Semi-supervised learning uses different algorithms used in supervised and unsupervised learning, network models, and neural networks to complete the process of partially supervised and partially unsupervised machine learning. The complete workflow of this procedure is described below in a step-by-step manner.[34,35]

- In the first step, the compute system is trained with the labeled dataset associated with each tuple until the machine generates accurate results.
- In the second step, the algorithm ingests unlabeled data with pseudo-labels to train on. The results achieved in this step may not be accurate.

- In the third step, the labels from the labeled data and pseudo-labels from the unlabeled data are linked together.
- In the fourth step, both the input data from the labeled and unlabeled training datasets are also linked together.
- In the last step, the accuracy and performance are improved by training the model again on the combined input achieved in the fourth step.

Assumptions made in semi-supervised learning

To establish relationships between unlabeled and labeled objects, semi-supervised machine learning uses different assumptions, as mentioned below.

- **Cluster assumptions** – The data is divided into multiple discrete clusters, and the data points in the same cluster use the output labeled data.
- **Continuity assumptions** – It is assumed that objects near each other share the same cluster or group. With the smoothness assumption in low-density boundaries, the decision boundaries are incorporated.
- **Manifold assumptions** – According to this assumption, the density and distance are used, and data lies on a manifold of fewer dimensions than the input space.

Real-world application of semi-supervised learning

The real-world application of supervised machine learning and unsupervised machine learning is limited to certain fields. The combination of both types of machine learning in the form of semi-supervised machine learning increases the spectrum of real-world applications because it owns characteristics and capabilities of both fundamental types of machine learning. Semi-supervised machine learning can be used in numerous real-world applications. Some are mentioned below:

- **Online content classification** – The online content posted on websites and applications can easily be sorted out in terms of their characteristics and response to any related query. It is not possible for professionals to manually label the data on a huge arena of online website content. Semi-supervised machine learning is the best option to rate and classify the content on websites. Google uses semi-supervised learning for this purpose to rate and rank the websites in terms of their content relevancy and accuracy.
- **Text document classification** – The classification of millions of text documents can be done with the help of semi-supervised machine learning. Otherwise, classifying or labeling manually would be a nightmare for professionals as well as for businesses.

- **Speech analysis** – The application of semi-supervised machine learning, or SSL, can provide the capability of analyzing numerous audio files effectively. Otherwise, labeling such huge audio data manually would be an uphill task.
- **Protein sequence classification** – Considerable human intervention is required to analyze and classify the DNA (deoxyribonucleic acid) protein sequences, which are extremely large and complex. The application of semi-supervised machine learning in the identification and classification of protein sequences is extensively feasible in modern medical sciences.
- **Cybersecurity** – The application of semi-supervised machine learning in the cybersecurity field, especially in the banking and finance sectors, is very critical. It can be used to identify the activity patterns of thieves and fraudsters, provide a suitable response, and generate alerts for professionals to take appropriate action.

Other than the above-mentioned uses, this type of machine learning can be custom-applied to numerous other applications where bulk data is involved to be analyzed for making decisions by automatically finding the business value in the raw data.

Reinforcement machine learning

Reinforcement learning, precisely referred to as RL, is one of three funda-mental types of machine learning used in the modern artificial intelligence field. This type of learning is based on the reward and punishment of desirable and undesirable behavior of an action taken by the machine learning algorithm on the unlabeled datasets. The reward may be in the form of a positive parameter or value, and punishment can be in the form of a negative parameter or numeric value. The computer model learns on the basis of those patterns and takes subsequent steps by keeping the results of the past steps that it learned. Thus, slowly and gradually, intelligent machines start learning about the input data or environments and can make suitable predictions for the next steps. This type of learning is also known as learning through *trial and error*. The most common features and character-istics of reinforcement learning are:[36,37]

- It is based on a pattern of actions, based on taking suitable steps to maximize the rewards.
- There is no labeled output for a particular action in training data, as is the case in supervised learning. In this learning, the artificial agent has to learn from its experience without any prior availability of data or labeled data.
- The input of a reinforcement learning model is the initial state from which the learning process starts.

- The output may vary because there can be numerous solutions based on reinforcement learning.
- The most suitable solution is decided on the basis of the maximum reward.
- The model continues to learn as the previous information keeps helping.
- It is a type of sequential decision-making model. The state of the current input decides the output or results.
- The current state of input is dependent on the output of the previous input.

The operational example of reinforcement learning is depicted in Figure 2.9, in which the fire is considered as the negative step, and a punishment or negative value will be awarded, and the diamond is the maximum reward that the robot or learning agent is supposed to achieve.

The learning agent will keep a record of learning in this entire process and will incorporate this learning into the next moves to conduct them in a more knowledgeable way. The analysis of the pattern to reach the maximum value will be calculated every time it achieves the goal. Thus, it will come to know the most rewarding path or pattern after certain learning attempts.

Types of reinforcement learning

There are two types of reinforcement learning commonly adopted in the modern artificial intelligence field. They are:[36]

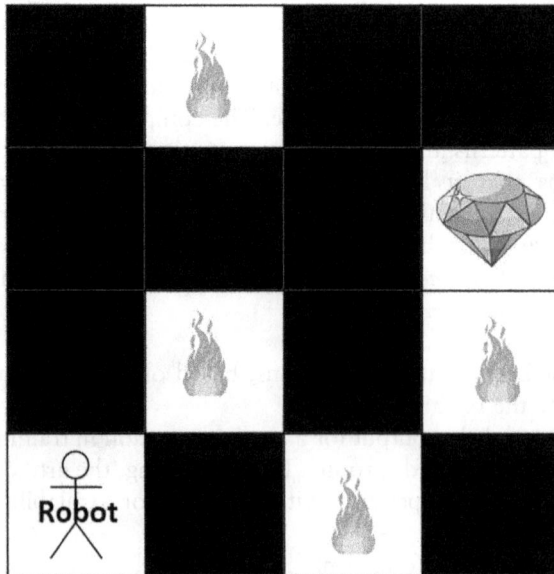

Figure 2.9 Schematic diagram of reinforcement learning example.

- Positive reinforcement learning
- Negative reinforcement learning

Positive reinforcement

The positive reinforcement is an increasing effect of an event that enhances the frequency and strength of a particular behavior in reinforcement machine learning. The major attributes of positive reinforcement include the sustained change for a longer time, maximization of behavior performance, and others.

Negative reinforcement

Negative reinforcement learning is a type of learning in which the negative conditions are minimized or even avoided to strengthen the behavior. It increases the behavior value by defying the minimum standards of performance.

Algorithms used in reinforcement learning

Reinforcement learning is continuously evolving, and new approaches and algorithms are being devised to make machine learning more effective. The most common types of algorithms used in the present-day machine learning field include the following.[36]

Q-learning

The Q-learning algorithm mostly focuses on self-training without any explicit policy provided to the model. The policy is also known as the information provided to the computer system that a particular action will result in a punishment or reward. This type of learning hits and tries without any particular policy to follow.

State-action-reward-state-action

This type of algorithm is used in reinforcement learning, in which a particular policy of actions is provided to the compute system through the algorithm. The algorithm is well aware of certain odds of actions that may result in rewards or punishments.

Deep Q-networks

This algorithm uses both reinforcement techniques and neural networks that provide help on the basis of past learning for taking certain actions that will be helpful. This algorithm uses self-directed exploration of the reinforcement learning environment to decide future actions based on random samples taken from past beneficial actions.

Real-world applications of reinforcement learning

- Industrial automation and robotics.
- Data processing and big data management.
- Gaming and entertainment industry.
- Personalized recommendations.
- Enterprise resource management system.

The newer domains and applications of reinforcement machine learning are emerging in the field because machine learning is gaining stronger roots with over time due to numerous factors, such as the availability of huge data and tools capable of data analytics of gigantic piles of raw and unstructured data. So, it is expected that the real-world applications will keep increasing even in the future as innovative technologies and platforms emerge in the technological sphere.

MODELS OF MACHINE LEARNING

In machine learning, readers should be very aware of the nitty-gritty of the concepts that are very confusing and interlinked, with a vague boundary between them. There are two very important concepts among these concepts, such as machine learning algorithms and machine learning models. Both of them are very confusing terminologies used in modern AI technology. Let us now dive a bit deeper to clarify those two interrelated concepts before moving forward to describe different models of machine learning.

Machine learning model vs. machine learning algorithm

A machine learning model is the output in the form of a formula, a code structure, any other presentation, even a pattern achieved by running a computer program (algorithm) on the data to achieve an output. In other words, a machine learning model is the representation of the question of what has been learned from running the algorithm code or program on the training data. It contains a set of functionalities of an algorithm applied to the data.

On the other hand, the algorithm is a computer program or sequence of instructions to execute on the data to achieve an output. The output of an algorithm instruction or procedure is known as a machine learning model, which specifies what has been learned by running the algorithmic procedure on the data.

The finally achieved model through algorithm execution can also be saved as an equation or short code program by using the previously stored functionalities for projecting or predicting the future estimations when some kind of new test data is encountered by the machine learning systems. The other major differences between a machine learning model and a machine learning algorithm are figured out below:[38]

- A model is an output of an algorithm, which is a procedure based on a computer program to generate an output or a mathematical representation.
- The algorithm runs on data to create an ML model.
- *ML Model == Model Data + Prediction Algorithm* (Sometimes "data-set" again).
- A suitable algorithm is required to be selected for generating a desired model of machine. learning. This means the model defines which algorithm to choose to achieve the best results.
- Models use well-defined formulas based on the computations that are created as the results of running ML algorithms on data.

DIFFERENT MACHINE LEARNING MODEL CATEGORIES

After having clearly understood the difference between the concepts of algorithm and machine learning model in the previous topic, let us explore the categories and different models. Machine learning models can be classi-fied into four major categories based on their functionalities and tasks, as listed below.[39,40,41]

- Regression Models.
- Classification Models.
- Clustering Models.
- Dimensionality Reduction Models.

Both regression and classification models are used in supervised machine learning systems, while clustering and dimensionality reduction models are used in unsupervised machine learning. Each category of the above-men-tioned ML models consists of other subtypes of models based on certain techniques, equations, and outputs.

REGRESSION MODELS

This category consists of those sub-models that deal with the prediction in regression problems to generate a numeric value as an output. That means the results of all models falling in this category produce predicted results or outputs in the form of numeric values. The most common sub-models in this category include:[41]

- Linear regression model.
- Decision tree model.
- Random forest model.
- Neural network model.

Linear regression model

The linear regression model, as the name implies, is a machine learning model to predict the output value based on the input variables through a linear relationship based on the linear mathematical equation of a line. The model may vary a bit based on the types of dependent and independent variables. The relationship between an input (x) and an output (y) is linear, found through a linear line based on the linear equation of the line. The most common features and characteristics of the linear regression machine learning model are:[42]

- It is used for performing linear regression on variables to forecast the relational value.
- This model is used in supervised machine learning, where intelligent compute systems are trained with labeled output data against the input training datasets.
- The regression dependent variables are referred to as endogenous variables, criterion variables, outcome variables, or regressand variables.
- The regression independent variables are also named as exogenous variables, regressor variables, or predictor variables.
- The main objective of linear regression is to find the best-fit line to represent the relationship between dependent and independent variables with the minimum error ratio.
- The examples of uses of linear regression are forecasting sales, prices, demand, supply, and other similar kinds of factors under constrained conditions.

Decision tree model

A decision tree is another very popular model extensively used in both classes of supervised machine learning, such as regression models and classification models. In regression-type modeling, the decision tree model is used to find the predicted value or an output against the input values. The decision is made on the basis of a flowchart that consists of nodes and branches. The nodes are the elements of the decision structure, which is also known as "Test", which is used to decide the output based on certain regression rules of the model. The output of the test is referred to as a branch of the regression model. As mentioned earlier, this model is used in both regression and classification; therefore, the terminologies differ a little in both of those categories of models. The main characteristics and features of the regression decision tree model include:[43]

- Decision trees are used for decision analysis and operations research purposes.
- The larger number of nodes makes it more accurate in its decision-making applications.
- Each internal node represents a test on any attribute in the training dataset to produce logical results based on the internal rules of the node.
- There are three main types of nodes:
  - Decision nodes.
  - Chance nodes.
  - End nodes.
- Each node in the decision tree model is a splitting node (burst node); there is no converging path node (sink node) in the entire structure.
- The definitions of nodes, branches, and decision rules are all built through software applications or a program known as a regression model, if it is designed for regression purposes.

A decision tree is a very simple and intuitive model of machine learning. The results produced by this model are comparatively less accurate (if other advanced rules are taken into consideration).

Random forest model

The random forest model is one of the most commonly used regression models in supervised machine learning, in which multiple decision tree models are combined to make a more reliable decision or output. As the name implies, it consists of multiple units of decision tree models deployed in the form of a forest, where multiple trees are planted. All those decision tree models produce their respective outputs, which are combined and averaged to find a more accurate output. The average output is further processed through the random forest decision rule to find out even more accurate results of the analysis.[44]

As mentioned earlier, the decision tree model is very simple and intuitive. The accuracy level of the model is low; therefore, to increase the output accuracy, multiple decision tree models are combined together to form a random forest model of decision-making in the machine learning field. The output produced by the random forest model is highly accurate, which makes this model one of the most powerful machine learning models. The other main characteristics and features of the random forest machine learning model are mentioned below.

- The random forest model combines multiple models through a machine learning model merger technique known as the ensemble technique.
- All models joined together are allowed to predict separately in parallel with the other models in the random forest structure, without any common rules or sharing of processing or output support at all.
- The final results produced by all those models are collected and averaged by the next step or layer of the model. The averaged results are further processed through the random forest predictive module to produce the final output.
- Forecasts of prices, salaries, or other market parameters are the major use cases of the random forest model of regression because it generates more accurate results than all other popular models used in supervised machine learning.
- The random forest model of machine learning is also used in both regression and classification modeling of machine learning.

Neural network

A neural network is a model of learning in which the decision is made on the basis of a layered structure of processing units that resemble human neurons in the brain. The entire structure of machine learning mimics the structure and functioning of the human brain to imitate the human learning process through artificial intelligent neural networks.

A neural network, also known as an artificial neural network, consists of multiple layers of connected processing units, named artificial neurons. A neural network should consist of at least three layers as listed below.[45]

- Input layer – One.
- Hidden layers – At least one, but may contain more than one layer too.
- Output layer – One.

The number of hidden layers measures the power of the neural network to build a reliable and efficient artificial neural network to create accurate results or output. The larger the number of hidden layers, the more powerful the artificial neural network. Each neuron node has its own weight and threshold value. When the input fed to the node is higher than the threshold value, the node gets activated and passes its value (weight) to the next node connected to it. If the value of the input is less than the threshold value of the node, it will not move forward in the network. The output of one node fed to the other node or neuron is the input for the latter neuron.

Initially, the weightage and threshold values are chosen randomly before getting started with the machine learning procedure through neural networks. The results of the first input will be nonsensical or ridiculous. The output of the neural network will be compared with the known and correct value of the output. The data will be compared, and feedback will be given to the system through the neural network feedback mechanism. This process continues repeating till the correct result is achieved. Thus, the neural network continues learning through training datasets fed to the system continuously. For training such networks, you need huge volumes of data to make them more reliable, accurate, and efficient in performance, so that you can deploy them into real-world testing and learning environments easily.

In this entire process, the weightages of the neurons in the artificial neural network are continuously adjusted to make sure that the correct structure of the machine learning model is achieved. The adjustments in the weightage are done through the feedback system that compares the output of the model to the accurate value or known value of the input.

CLASSIFICATION MODELS

The classification models are designed to produce logical outputs in the form of different labels, categories, or classes learned from the input training datasets with the help of certain algorithms selected for generating the desired outputs. The most important types of classification models used in modern machine learning include:[40]

- Binary classification.
- Multi-class classification.
- Multi-label classification.
- Imbalanced classification.

The details of all these subcategories of classification modeling are described (with associated algorithms used for that purpose) in the following subtopics.

Binary classification

The binary classification model is one of the most fundamental models extensively used in the classification of data points into two categories, as the name implies. The basic principle of this machine learning model is to group the items (data points) into two classes, such as Yes or No, Right or Wrong, Is or Not, and others. Binary classification is used in supervised machine learning, in which the labeled data is ingested into the model to produce the desired results automatically. The major applications of the binary classification model include:

- Categorization of spam and normal emails.
- Projecting a churning or non-churning trend.
- Predicting conversion (purchase or not).

The other characteristics and features of the binary classification model of machine learning are mentioned in the following list:

- It uses the Bernoulli probability distribution for all of the purposed tasks to assess the probability of a falling data point on one class or another.
- The major algorithms used in the binary classification model of machine learning are listed below and will be covered at length in the next topics.
  - K-nearest neighbor.
  - Support vector machine.
  - Logistic regression.
  - Decision tree.
  - Naïve Bayes.
- The core principle of the classification model of machine learning is based on the identification of the features or characteristics of the data to categorize them.

Multi-class classification

Multi-class classification refers to the grouping of the data points on the basis of multiple features of a single data point to differentiate it from many other data points (in comparison). This classification model deals with numerous features that make one data point different from the other data points. Thus, it is contrary to the normal and abnormal (Yes/No) conditions used in the binary classification. Other main features and characteristics of the multi-class classification model of machine learning are mentioned below:

- The unique feature of a data point is identified, which is unique to a particular class as compared to many other data point classes.
- The main examples of applications that deploy multi-class classification include:
  - Optical character recognition (OCR).
  - Facial recognition.
  - Plant species classification.
- This model handles a large number of features or labels that can help the ML model make a reliable decision of correct categorization.
- The multi-class classification model uses the Multinoulli probability distribution for the discrete distribution of probability to generate a large number of classes of features.
- Numerous algorithms used for binary classification can also be customized and used for multi-class classification.
- The most popular algorithms used in multi-class classification are:
  - Decision tree.
  - Naïve Bayes.

- Gradient Boosting.
- K-Nearest Neighbor.
- Random Forest.
- Multiple algorithms used in binary classification can be deployed for a single output based on binary classification for numerous classes. This method can be customized in two ways for use as mentioned below:
  - **One-Vs-One** – In this customized application of binary classification algorithms, the algorithm is used to fit for one pair of features to classify into two groups.
  - **One-Vs-Rest** – One binary classification model is customized to make it fit for the rest of the other classes.

Multi-label classification

Multi-label classification of a data point is the process of classifying different objectives with multiple labels within one data point. An example of this type of classification is to label multiple objects in a single image, such as a bicycle running on a road and a cat sitting by the road. In this image, there are three main items, such as a road, a bicycle, and a cat. This classification performs an activity to classify all those objects into different labels for the grouping of information. In this type of classification, multiple labels are expected from the machine learning model to work out one single data item. The main difference between multi-class and multi-label classification is that in a multi-class model, only one class is expected as an output, while in multi-label classification, multiple labels are expected for each example of the dataset.

Other main features and characteristics of the multi-label classification machine learning model are listed below.

- This model can use multiple binary classification functionalities on one example of data to label them properly.
- Multi-label classification uses customized and specialized versions of algorithms to process the multi-label activities.
- A few very important specialized versions of classification algorithms used in multi-label classification are listed below.
  - Multi-label random forests.
  - Multi-label decision trees.
  - Multi-label gradient boosting.
- Using a separate classification algorithm for every label on objects (in each example) is also commonly used in multi-label classification modeling.

Imbalanced classification

As the name implies, in imbalanced classification modeling of data, the number of examples varies or is distributed unequally among groups. In this type of classification modeling, the majority of the training dataset examples are normal, while a small minority of training dataset examples are not normal or abnormal. The applications of this model in real-world environments include:

- Outlier detection.
- Fraud detection.
- Medical diagnostic tests.
- And others.

The main features and characteristics of an imbalanced classification model of machine learning are:

- The modeling of problems in this classification model is done as binary classification tasks or activities.
- Although the modeling is done like binary classification, specialized versions of algorithms are required to process the training datasets.
- Changing sample composition by oversampling the minority class and undersampling the majority class can be one of the main specialized techniques used in this machine learning classification modeling.
- Two major techniques used at algorithmic levels in imbalanced modeling include:
  - SMOTE oversampling.
  - Random undersampling.
- Although imbalanced classification uses binary classification by adopting the above-mentioned techniques, specialized or customized versions of commonly used algorithms in binary classification are still required.
- The main specialized algorithms used in the imbalanced classification model include:
  - Cost-sensitive decision trees.
  - Cost-sensitive logistic regression.
  - Cost-sensitive support vector machines.
- To track and report the accuracy of the specialized algorithms and the entire imbalanced classification model, alternative performance metrics are needed.
- A few very important alternative performance metrics used in this type of machine learning classification modeling include the following.
  - F-measure metric.
  - Precision metric.
  - Recall metric.

CLUSTERING MODELS

In the clustering model of machine learning, the objects, entities, or data points are grouped together on the basis of their similarities and differences. The similar data points are put into a separate group, and dissimilar information is placed away from that group in another category. This grouping model of machine learning has further subtypes, such as:[42]

- K-Means Clustering.
- Mean-Shift Clustering.
- Density-Based Clustering.
- Hierarchical Clustering.

These different models, classified on the basis of the applied procedure, are used in the grouping of the data points to make clusters of information. The details of each type of clustering model are expressed at length below.

K-means clustering

K-means clustering is a subset of the clustering model of machine learning. It is a type of unsupervised machine learning model in which no labeled training datasets are used, and the machine is not trained explicitly on known results. The K-means clustering uses inference to classify the data points into different clusters through repetitive learning and cluster optimization. To infer the classification of data points into clusters, this model uses the input vector technique.

The most common characteristics and features of K-means clustering are:[46,47]

- The main objective of this machine learning model is to group similar data points together on the basis of their similar features using the K-means vector technique and understand the underlying patterns of the data points.
- The letter K in the K-means clustering model is the number of clusters to be considered in the definition of features of data points into groups or clusters. The number of K is identified either manually or automatically by the model.
- After the definition of the number of clusters, the center of the cluster is located imaginarily, and the input vector is used to optimize the position of the center of the cluster, technically known as the centroid of the cluster.
- All data points in the training dataset are assigned to the clusters through the reduction of the in-cluster sum of squares.
- The centroids are kept as small as possible in this model.
- The centroid optimization to make the most reliable, accurate, and smaller groups or clusters is governed by two factors – a predefined number of repetitive processes (iterations) or the cluster stabilization.
- The stabilization of the cluster is achieved by reducing the associated distance of the data point from the center of the cluster by varying the position of the centroid.

- The step-by-step workflow of this model of clustering machine learning is given below:
  - Choose the number of clusters or K value.
  - The random imaginary centroids are chosen.
  - Each data point in the training data is aligned to the nearest centroid of cluster.
  - Optimize the centroids by changing the square position to achieve the most accurate positions of the centroids of the clusters.
  - Once the centroid stabilizes, add all nearest data points to their respective clusters based on their similarities.
  - The K-means clustering model is ready to go!

Mean-shift clustering

The mean-shift clustering model is one of the most powerful and extensively used machine learning models in the unsupervised machine learning category for computer vision and image analysis applications. The working principle of this model is almost similar to the K-means model, in which the number of clusters is predefined manually by the data scientists, and the K-means vector is used to optimize the centroid of the cluster. Similarly, the mean-shift model for clustering does not support predefined numbers of clusters, but the model automatically builds the centroids on the basis of the mean-shifting principle, which is based on Kernel Density Estimation, precisely referred to as Kernel Density Estimation (KDE). The KDE defines the probability distribution for a set of data points. It is also referred to as a probability density function (PDF) for the set of data used in this unsupervised form of ML training. The schematic diagram of mean-shift clustering is explained in Figures 2.10 and 2.11.

In Figure 2.10, the data points are located and scattered on the entire data point surface. The application of the mean-shift model will set the boundary

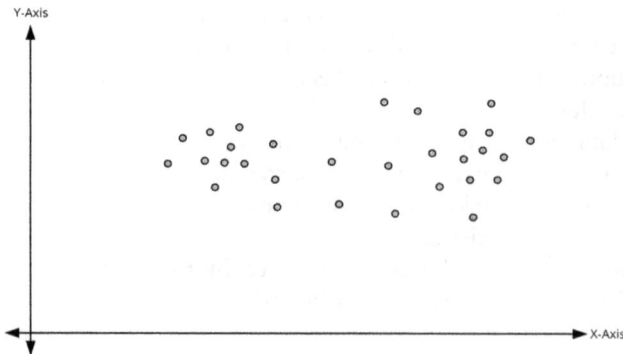

Figure 2.10 Data point surface for mean-shift model.

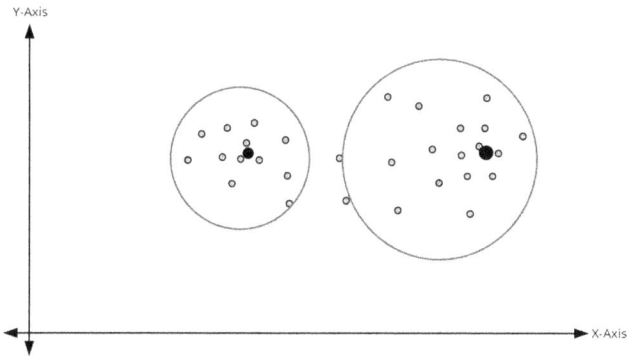

Figure 2.11 Bandwidth-based KDE surface in mean-shift to centroid.

circles based on the bandwidth value, as two boundary circles have been formed. The central point is imaginary, located by applying the mean-density function or the mean weightage of the data points. In Figure 2.11, the solid-filled black point depicts the centroid point. Now, the mean-shift starts optimizing all the data points through a smoothing process to converge into one peak as the centroid point through the mean-shift process. The mean-shift process moves each data point to the centroid by the mean value of all other data points in the cluster. This process is iterative and will continue till the entire landscape of scattered data points is merged into one point to form an uphill peak.

The most important features and characteristics of the mean-shift clustering model are:[48,49]

- This machine learning model is also centroid-based, which uses the density of the weight function of the data point to converge to the center of the cluster.
- The optimization of the cluster takes place through shifting data points to the centroid of a cluster iteratively based on the mean distance of the other data points in the region.
- This model is also known as the mode-seeking algorithm or model in other terminology.
- The KDE (Kernel Density Estimation) finds out the probability density function of a data point, which is also known as the weightage of the data point.
- The data smoothing takes place through the KDE function to infer the population of data points.
- The bandwidth parameter is the main factor that impacts the resultant density function variation in the mean-shift model.
- Each data point in the KDE surface is shifted to the centroid, which is equal to the average distance of other points in that particular cluster. This process is repeated for every data point in the cluster and is shifted toward the centroid, which is a peak in the cluster.

- The number of clusters is defined by the mean-shift model itself on the basis of the data contour scattered with data points.
- This type of machine learning clustering model produces highly reliable results in image processing and computer vision applications, but a huge amount of computation or processing power is required for this model.
- Each data point is assigned the number of clusters, which should be the closest cluster to that data point. The direction for the data point to which the data point will be shifted for data smoothing is also assigned.
- The assignment of the cluster and direction may change as the iteration of shifting data points continues in all cluster centroids. The final convergence of the centroids, or the clusters, will have the cluster numbers for all data points in those particular clusters.
- The kernel is the weightage function for every data point used in the mean-shift machine learning model.
- Different kinds of kernels are normally used in developing mean-shift machine learning models. The most important of them is the Gaussian kernel.
- The kernel bandwidth forces the results to vary as the value of the bandwidth changes in the kernel mathematical equation.
- The Python programming language is used for the development of mean-shift machine learning models or algorithms.

Density-based clustering

As the name implies, the density-based clustering methods, or models, are those techniques in which the clusters are formed on the basis of the density of the data points on a surface. A cluster is a group of data points that are merged into one entity based on the similarities in features and characteristics of data points. This model uses a technique in which the surface of data points is scanned for the availability and density of the data points, and also the sparse and empty areas. The formation of a cluster is decided on the basis of the concentration of the data points in a particular area that also encompasses the surrounding data points at maximum.

The most common characteristics, features, and types of density-based clustering in the machine learning field are:[50,51,52,53]

- Density-based clustering models are used in unsupervised machine learning.
- The density-based clustering can be further divided into three major categories, through which you can find the clusters of the data points based on the density of those data points in a particular cluster space.
- Those three categories are mentioned below:
  - DBSCAN – It is a density-based scanning model in which the clustering is found on the basis of the density of the data points. According to this approach, the dense space of data points on a density-based surface is a cluster, which is separated by the region

that has either very low density or sparse regions. DBSCAN stands for density-based spatial clustering of applications with noise. It uses an "n" dimensional shape to map different data points that appear on the plane. Similar data with equal dimensions that fit in the given "n" dimensional shape are used for mapping the similarities of the data points. Thus, we can say it will separate the data into n-dimensions. This model scans all data points through an n-dimensional object or tester and classifies the objects into three major categories, such as 1) core points, 2) border points, and 3) noises. The core points are assigned a particular cluster number because they are similar to each other. The border points are also assigned the cluster number of the cluster (on which border it is laid). The noise points are not assigned to any cluster and are treated as noise in a particular input training dataset, and will be classified in the other categories with more similarities or common features. To be considered as a core point, there should be certain points within the epsilon distance, which is the radius distance, of the core point. Otherwise, it may not be considered a core point. The number of minimum data points to declare a cluster and the distance between one point and another one should be predefined for this model. The distance between two points to be considered in a cluster is based on the epsilon distance, which is equal to the radius of the circle encompassing the core point and is decided in the first step. It is also known as the defined distance model of unsupervised machine learning.[51]

- **HDBSCAN** – Hierarchical Density-based Spatial Clustering of Application with Noise, precisely referred to as HDBSCAN, is an unsupervised machine learning model for clustering the unlabeled data to develop understanding in the machine models. The selection of an area of similar data points in this model is based on three main steps: 1) estimation of densities, 2) picking up high-density regions, and 3) combining multiple points in selected areas of data points. The last step is done on the basis of hierarchical order to merge data points into one large cluster to create high-density areas, which can be combined together to form a bigger cluster. That's why this model is referred to as the Hierarchical DBSCAN (HDBSCAN) model.[52] The estimation of density is accomplished through the definition of core distance. The core distance is the distance between the core point and its Kth point, which is defined by the data scientist in this model for performing the clustering process. This model requires the least data inputs from the users and is extensively used for producing efficient results.

- **OPTICS** – Ordering Points to Identify the Clustering Structure, precisely known as OPTICS, is another very important model used for unsupervised machine learning's clustering process. It is another important model that is inspired by the DBSCAN model. It uses core distance for estimating the cluster initially, i.e., the distance between the target point, defining as a core point, and the adjacent point to declare the target point as a core point. The minimum points are defined to declare a cluster under the core distance. The area covered under the epsilon distance is the space jurisdiction of the cluster. The other distance that is used in this model is known as the reachability distance. It is the sum of the maximum core distance between point A and point B and the Euclidean distance between those two points.[53]

- This model uses three main factors for defining the cluster, such as 1) Input Point Features, 2) Output Features, and 3) Number of features to constitute a cluster.
- The minimum number of features to form a cluster is a very important factor in this model of machine learning for clustering data in a reliable manner. If the number of features is kept large, the objects with fewer than the features defined in the cluster will fall in the category of noise, and thus, the accuracy of the data point clustering deteriorates. Thus, it is a good idea to keep the number of features to a minimum to create multiple clusters with similar characteristics and features and to minimize the noise in the space.

Hierarchical clustering

Hierarchical clustering is another important model for forming groups or clusters of data points in unsupervised machine learning. The machines are not trained with the labeled data in this model, but the model has to understand the characteristics of the data points and form groups based on differences in those data points. The hierarchical clustering is almost similar to the K-means metrics in which the number of clusters was predefined by the data specialists. In this model, all data points are considered at separate clusters or groups, and then different clusters are merged together through the dissimilarity metrics method.[54]

Other main features and characteristics of the hierarchical clustering model are mentioned in the following list.[54,55]

- Hierarchical clustering is also referred to as hierarchical cluster analysis, or precisely HCA, in the machine learning field.
- The binding of two different clusters is done by finding the dissimilarities in those clusters.
- The metrics to combine two separate groups or clusters can be decided on the basis of either Euclidean distance or the Ward linkage formula.
- The schematic diagram of the hierarchical cluster appears in the form of a tree that is also known as a dendrogram presentation.
- In certain cases, the output of hierarchical and K-means clustering appears to be the same, but the working principles of both methods are different.

- The hierarchical clustering model uses two different approaches to carry out the desired procedure, as listed below:
  - **Agglomerative approach** – This approach is also called the *bottom-up* approach. In this approach, in the first step, all data points are considered as separate groups or clusters. In the second phase, the data points with lesser differences or dissimilarities are merged together to form a bigger cluster. This is done through two methods – distance or linkages.
  - **Divisive approach** – In this approach, the bigger clusters are broken into smaller ones to achieve a hierarchical tree of clusters. This is also referred to as a top-down approach based on finding dissimilar characteristics.
- The most widely used approach in hierarchical clustering is the agglomerative approach, which is based on a bottom-up methodology.

How does agglomerative-based hierarchical clustering work?

The step-by-step working process of agglomerative-based hierarchical clustering is mentioned in the following procedure.

- First of all, the model marks all data points as unique clusters. That means if there are six data points, there will be 6 unique clusters based on their unique characteristics without any analysis of differences or similarities in comparison with other data points in the plane. Once all data points are marked as separate clusters, the process of merging those separate clusters or groups is accomplished through different agglomerative approaches.
- In the second step, the merger of the data points that are slightly different from the main data point under consideration are merged as shown in Figure 2.12.

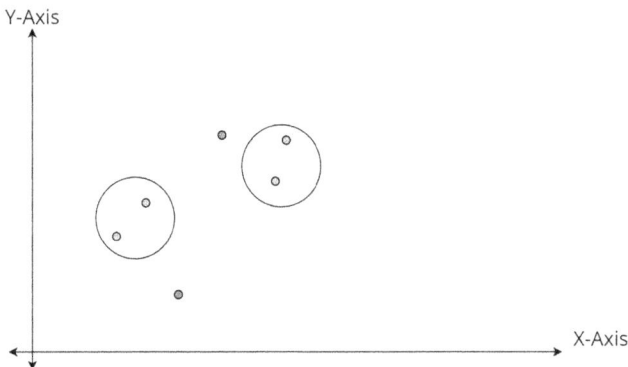

Figure 2.12 Step 1 and step 2 of hierarchical clustering.

- In the next step, the nearest distance data points, which are also separate clusters, are merged into the nearest distance upper-level clusters that were formed by merging two different data points in step 2. Thus, the nearest smaller clusters are merged to form two bigger clusters from the six clusters that were formed at the start of the process. The result of the third step is shown in the graphical diagram in Figure 2.13.
- In the final step, both clusters formed in the previous step are merged to form a single cluster (see Figure 2.14). In this step, too, the dissimilarities of clusters are used to combine the data points in such a way that they appear in a hierarchical position.

The dendrogram of the final merger of the clusters into one cluster through the agglomerative approach in this hierarchical clustering is shown in Figure 2.15.

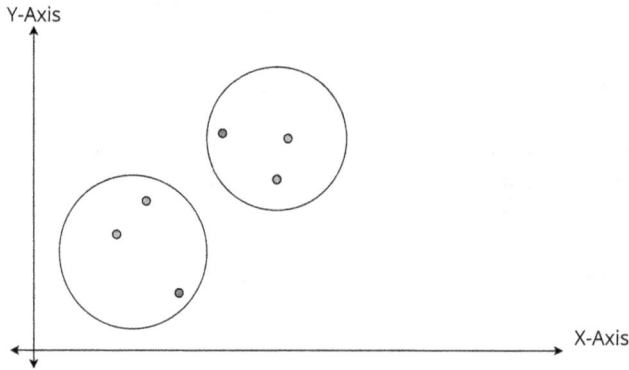

Figure 2.13 Hierarchical clustering merger.

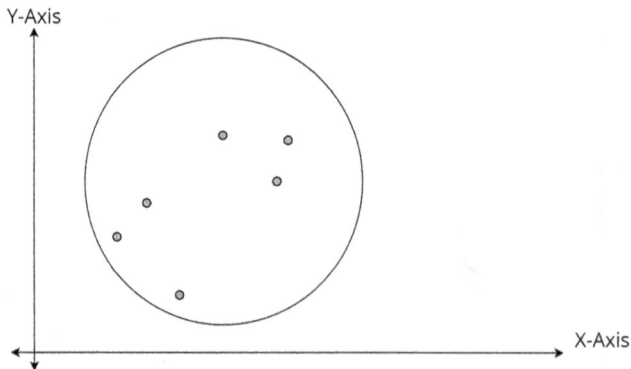

Figure 2.14 Final merger of clusters in hierarchical clustering.

Cluster Hierarchy

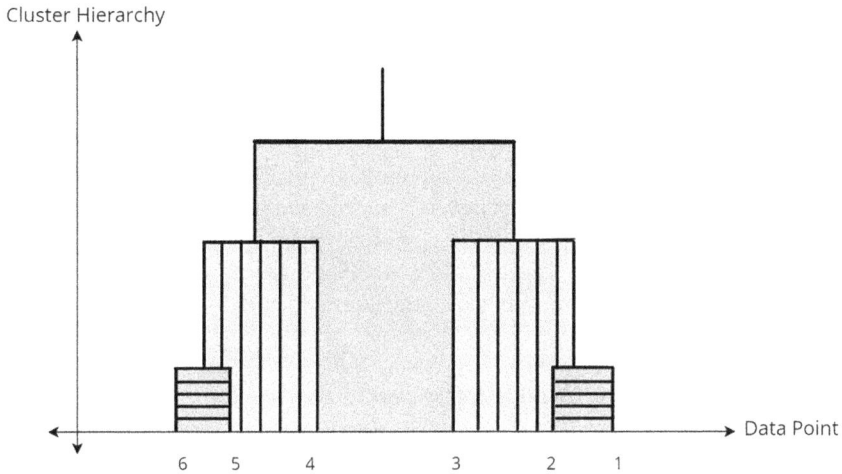

Figure 2.15 Dendrogram of cluster hierarchy.

It is very important to note that each data point is differentiated by the level of the hierarchy in terms of the dissimilarities of features or character-istics. The entire information of the features of each data point is known to the computing machine.

In Figure 2.15, the six data points are placed on the data point axis named 1 through 6 sequentially. The first two similar data points, such as 1 and 2, are merged to form a cluster, and similarly, two other points with minimum distance or difference – points 6 and 5 – are merged to form another cluster, as shown in the horizontally striped boxes. The remaining points, 4 and 3, are merged through distance calculation to add to the matching group or clusters, as shown in the vertically striped boxes. Those two vertically striped boxes (clusters) are merged to form a higher-level cluster, as shown in the solid-filled big box. Thus, the entire merger takes place.

Distance measurement between two unique clusters

The merger of two separate or unique clusters is done on the basis of the distance between them. The measurement of the distance between two clusters is known as linkage. The linkage is a method of measuring the distance between two clusters. There are numerous linkage methods used in the merger of clusters in hierarchical clustering applications. A few very important linkage methods commonly used in agglomerative clustering are mentioned below.

- **Single linkage** – The shortest distance measure between two data points of a cluster in a hierarchical data point plane is known as single linkage.
- **Complete linkage** – The complete linkage is the maximum distance between two data points on the hierarchical clustering plane in which all other data points of both clusters are encompassed or covered completely.

- **Average linkage** – In the average linkage method of measuring distance between two points of two separate clusters, the overall average distance between each point in cluster one with each point in cluster two is added together and then divided by the number of pairs to generate the final average linkage distance.
- **Centroid linkage** – As the name implies, in this method of calculating the distance between two clusters, the distance between the centroids of the clusters is measured. The centroids of each cluster are measured by finding the sum of the distances of all points in a cluster and then averaging it by the number of data points in that particular cluster.

DIMENSIONALITY REDUCTION MODEL

A dimensionality reduction model is a type of machine learning model in which the number of features or attributes is reduced or eliminated. In this model, those features of a data point are discarded or eliminated that have low importance. This is done to categorize the data points with higher precision while maintaining the tolerable reduction in the data point feature. The word "dimensionality" refers to the features or attributes of a data point in machine learning predictive models. The predictive models use a range of dimensions to categorize the objects or information that the machines encounter for learning. The reduction is a process to reduce the dimensions of a data point that have low importance and result in overfitting of the results. Thus, the term "dimensionality reduction" is used for reducing the attributes (random variables) of data points that are not important enough to be considered in a particular predictive analysis. This avoids the chances of overfitting the results of the predictive models used in different forms of machine learning techniques.[56,57]

Dimensionality reduction can be divided into two major categories commonly referred to as dimensionality reduction components. They are listed below:

- Feature selection.
- Feature extraction.

Each of the categories of the above-mentioned processes uses different methods and techniques to accomplish the desired objectives associated with them. Let us discuss the details of those categories of dimensionality reduction models.

Feature selection

The feature selection is a process to obtain the subset of the most relevant features that are very important for creating accurate results and leaving the irrelevant features that do not make much sense and have little importance on the results. In simple words, achieving the optimal set of features of an entity is known as feature selection.

The feature selection method uses numerous techniques for obtaining the most relevant or optimal subset of features. A few of them include the following.

- **Filtering** – This is the most fundamental technique in which the irrelevant features of a data point are filtered through certain criteria, and the most relevant ones are allowed to pass through the filter and form a set of relevant dimensions. The filtering may use different formulas such as ANOVA (analysis of variance), information gain, feature correlation, chi-square test, and others.
- **Wrapping** – As the name implies, in this method of feature selection, a few models are fed to the machine learning model, and the performance of the model is monitored to check whether to use those features or not on the basis of the performance of the model. This process is commonly referred to as the wrapper method. The wrapping technique uses numerous subtypes or processes, such as forward selection, backward selection, bi-directional elimination of features, and a few other models.
- **Embedded techniques** – There are certain other embedded techniques that are designed to deal with the features and their respective performance while ingesting them into the machine learning. If the performance remains under the desired limits, the features are retained automatically; otherwise, they are removed from the system. Some of the most commonly used techniques include elastic net, LASSO, and Ridge regression.

Feature extraction

The second most important process of the dimensionality reduction technique is feature extraction. In this process, the larger number of relevant features of a data point space is merged into similar types of features to achieve a smaller number of resembling features. For example, dew and water are two factors available in a data point space. Using both features, it is a great idea to merge both features them either into water or dew to produce accurate results while maintaining the better performance of the model and avoiding overfitting.

In the dimensionality reduction model of machine learning, numerous techniques are used for feature extraction. A few very important ones are:

- Principal component analysis.
- Linear discriminant analysis.
- Quadratic discriminant analysis.
- Generalized discriminant analysis.
- Kernel principal component analysis.

The above-mentioned techniques are used for either linear feature extraction or non-linear feature extraction based on the type of machine learning model, dimensionality reduction objectives, underlying machine learning algorithms, and many other factors. The linear feature extraction is extensively used in numerous modern dimensionality reduction applications. In linear feature extraction techniques, principal component analysis, or PCA, is mostly used. Let us have a deeper insight into the most commonly used linear dimensionality reduction technique, known as principal component analysis, or precisely as PCA, at length in the upcoming subtopics.

Other main dimensionality reduction techniques

As described earlier, dimensionality reduction is classified into two major categories, such as feature selection and feature extraction. In both of the categories, different formulas are used for reducing the dimensions of the data points. Those techniques are either based on component reduction or projections. The most common techniques based on component or factor reduction include:

- Principal component analysis.
- Independent component analysis.
- Factor analysis.

While the projection-based techniques used for dimensionality reduction include the following:

- Isometric mapping (ISOMAP).
- Uniform Manifold Approximation and Project (UMAP).
- T-Distributed Stochastic Neighbor Embedding (T-SNE).

On the other hand, numerous other techniques are used for feature selection and feature extraction. A few of them include:

- Low variance filter.
- Missing value ratio.
- High correlation filter.
- Forward feature selection.
- Random forest.
- Backward feature extraction.

All of the above-mentioned techniques used for different purposes in the dimensionality reduction procedures are of very high importance. But, a few of them are more critical to be introduced here in this section for a better understanding of dimensionality reduction.

SALIENT TECHNIQUES OF DIMENSIONALITY REDUCTION

A few very critical techniques extensively used in the dimensionality reduction process of unsupervised machine learning that should be described with further details here are mentioned in the following list.

- Principal Component Analysis (PCA).
- Forward Feature Selection (FFS).
- Backward Feature Elimination (BFE).
- Low Variance Filter (LVF).
- Missing Value Ratio (MVR).
- Factor Analysis (FA).
- High Correlation Filter (HCF).
- Autoencoders.

Principal component analysis

This is a linear correlation statistical procedure, which transforms the results of correlated features into a set of linearly uncorrelated features by using an orthogonal transformational mathematical approach. The newly converted features are referred to as principal components. Principal component analysis (PCA) is highly used in different applications related to predictive modeling and exploratory data analytics in machine learning and data science.

The most salient features and characteristics of principal component analysis are summarized in the following list:[58]

- A statistical process to reduce a large number of features or characteristics of a data point into a smaller number that are easy to visualize and analyze while maintaining the accuracy and integrity of the data points simultaneously.
- It uses an orthogonal transformation function to carry out the component analysis for feature reduction.
- Preserving the maximum variability or statistical information while reducing the parameters or features of a data point significantly is the core purpose of the principal component analysis technique in machine learning.
- For dealing with every component, the machine learning model should process to solve an eigenvector or an eigenvalue problem. Thus, finding a new component out of multiple components that are linearly correlated to a new or principal component is called the procedure of finding a principal component. That principal component is processed in the further analysis of the features of the data points.
- Dimensionality reduction can be used in a wide range of unsupervised machine learning models. A few very important ones include:
  - Power allocation in different communication channels.
  - Image processing applications.
  - Recommendation engine applications.

- It uses two main methods for finding out the principal components in the data points, as listed below:
  - Correlation matrix.
  - Covariance matrix.

The PCA is one of the oldest and most effective models extensively used in the dimensionality reduction field of machine learning.

Forward feature selection (FFS)

In the forward feature selection technique, the best or the most relevant features of a data point are chosen so that they can increase the performance and accuracy of the model. This procedure is accomplished through different steps as mentioned below:

- A single feature is chosen, and the computing system is trained on it.
- The assessment of the feature is done for every feature.
- The best feature that enhances the performance of the model is chosen.
- This process is continuously repeated until the desired level of machine performance is achieved.

Backward feature elimination (BFE)

In this model, the bad-performing features of the data points are eliminated after training the machine learning model on all features of a data point. This model is extensively deployed in logistic regression and linear regression models for performing the dimensionality reduction process. The main steps of this technique are listed below:

- All possible features "n" number are chosen, and the machine learning model is trained on them.
- Performance of the model is assessed in terms of features.
- The reduction of one single feature is done, and the machine is trained to assess the performance.
- This process is repeated for "n" times till the number of features reaches zero.
- Any feature that has impacted the performance of the computing system negligibly is dropped one by one till the optimum performance point is reached.

Low variance filter (LVF)

Low variance filter, precisely referred to as LVF, is another important technique extensively used in dimensionality reduction of machine learning models. In this technique, those columns of variable information are deleted that have an average variation in the feature below the threshold value predefined by the data scientists. If the changes in variables are much lower than a predefined threshold value, there would be very little impact on the main prediction output. Thus, that column can be discarded to improve the performance of the model. This model helps filter double-compatible columns that have the variance value below the cut-off level predefined by the data scientist.[59] Those columns are more likely to distract certain machine learning algorithms, especially those that are based on the distance formula; therefore, removing them from the predictive calculation improves the performance of the model.

Missing value ratio (MVR)

Missing value ratio, precisely known as the MVR technique, is a very simple and effective technique mostly used in dimensionality reduction models to improve the performance of the machine learning model. If the number of missing values in a column is very high, the impact of the column data will be very low on the main predictive model. Therefore, that column can be removed to improve the performance of the machine learning model. A threshold value is set for the number of missing parameters. If the number exceeds that predefined threshold value, the entire column is discarded in the predictive machine learning model.

The missing value ratio is calculated in percentage, which is equal to the number of missing values divided by the total number of readings or observations and then multiplied by 100. The threshold value can be defined arbitrarily because it is not a rigid quality in the dimensionality reduction mechanism, but it can improve the performance of the model, at the same time, it may lose a little accuracy if the threshold value is set very high. Thus, an optimal value should be set for calculating the feature reduction value in any column to generate reliable performance and accuracy.[60]

Factor analysis (FA)

Factor analysis is another very useful technique used for reducing the features on the basis of similarity or a high level of correlation. It is extensively used in the dimensionality reduction models for unsupervised machine learning applications. In this technique, different variables with high correlation are identified and merged to form a separate group with a name very relevant to the overall meaning of that particular group's features. Those factors that are highly related to each other can be assumed to be the same, with very little impact on the overall predictive machine learning model. Thus, a substantial improvement in the performance of the dimensionality reduction model can be achieved by using this technique. This technique can be accomplished through the following steps:[61]

- In the very first step, different types of tests are implemented to detect the features of the variables, such as the KMO (Kaiser-Meyer-Olkin) test and Bartlett's Sphericity Test, etc.
- In the second step, the number of factors is identified.
- In the next step, all those factors are assessed for the highest level of correlation among them with minimum differences.
- In the last step, all those factors identified in the third step are merged to form a group, and a relevant name is given to that group.

Now, all features or factors in a group are considered as one single entity to offer greater ease for the computing system for improving the performance.

High correlation filter (HCF)

High correlation filter, precisely referred to as HCF, is a dimensionality reduction technique commonly used in different models in unsupervised machine learning. In this technique, one of the most correlated factors is dropped out of the model calculation to maintain high performance and relevance of results in the ML model. This method is extensively deployed in logistic regression, linear regression, and similar models of machine learning.[62]

The high correlation value of two factors will mean that both factors are bearing almost similar types of data without any additional information. The factor with a higher correlation coefficient in relation to the threshold value is discarded, and the other one is maintained in the predictive model for better performance. The correlation coefficient is calculated in relation to an independent numerical value. The higher coefficient value factor is removed to avoid any kind of degradation in the performance of the model.

Autoencoders

Autoencoder is a very popular dimensionality reduction technique extensively adopted in artificial neural networks (ANN). This technique is based on compressed knowledge learning, in which the features of the input of a machine learning model are compressed into a dataset of independent features or variables to overcome the bottlenecking in the neural network to reconstruct the output based on the compressed representation of the features of the input. This saves time and computing power in a bottlenecking condition of a neural network.[63]

The main features and characteristics of this dimensionality reduction technique are summarized below:

- It is used in unsupervised machine learning that leverages artificial neural networks (ANN) for learning purposes.
- The main task of this technique is representation learning through compressed input to produce or regenerate output.
- Deployed to overcome the bottleneck in artificial neural networks.

- The bottlenecking constrains the data to traverse through the deeper layers of neural networks with all features and forces the network to learn from the compressed data of the input to produce an output.
- This technique has two major parts or functions, such as:
  - **Encoder function** – This function compresses the input data to build a latent-space representation for the neural network to pass through the bottlenecked network.
  - **Decoder function** – The main activity of this function is to reproduce an output from the latent-space presentation ingested into the neural network for learning purposes.

MISCELLANEOUS MACHINE LEARNING MODELS

There are some other techniques extensively used to enhance the performance, accuracy, predictability, and other features of a machine model:

- Ensemble Model.
- Anomaly Detection Model.
- Transfer Learning Model.

The above-mentioned machine learning models are a few more models that can be used in customized applications and in hybrid models of machine learning, where the standard techniques or models fall short of the desired objectives. The details of these miscellaneous machine learning models are mentioned separately.

Ensemble model

Ensemble modeling is most commonly used in data mining and predictive analysis applications of machine learning. The combination of more than two different analytical models (simultaneously) is used to produce more reliable results and then combine them for further synthesis to get highly accurate outputs in numerous data mining and data analytics applications.[64]

It has been observed in real-world environments that the predictive analysis of data based on a single machine learning model leads to poor results with a large number of biases and other anomalies. To reduce those anomalies and biases, two different machine learning models are deployed in parallel to analyze the data in two different paths, and then the outcome is synthesized to produce the most reliable and accurate results. For instance, a decision tree is one of the most popular techniques in the regression predictive models, but the result of this model is less reliable due to numerous biases. Therefore, multiple decision trees are merged with the help of an ensemble process to form a new model known as a random forest. This produces way better results than a simple decision tree model.

Anomaly detection model

An anomaly detection model is a technique to find abnormal conditions, events, observations, or other behaviors in a data analysis. This technique is extensively used in modern data mining, cybersecurity, big data management, and many other fields. The most common features and characteristics of anomaly detection techniques are listed below:[65]

- Anomaly detection technique is also known as outlier analysis or detection.
- With the help of this technique, real-time as well as past abnormal events or conditions can easily be detected and responded to automatically through machine learning-enabled mechanisms in modern applications.
- The most common applications of this model include:
  - Detection of cyberattacks.
  - Fraudulent activities detection in banking systems.
  - Real-time technical faults.
  - And many other similar types of activities.
- This technique can be used in the following technological domains in the form of different algorithms and models.
  - Time series analysis.
  - Machine learning anomaly detection.
  - Neural network anomaly detection.
  - Supervised/Unsupervised ML outlier detection.
- This model can be used in detecting different types of anomalies, in which the most common categories are:
  - **Contextual anomalies** – These abnormalities are bound to certain contexts or backgrounds. For instance, any person purchasing a combo of warm clothes in the winter season is normal, but the same is abnormal in the hot season. Thus, the anomalies that do not satisfy the context or background information are called contextual anomalies.
  - **Point anomalies** – In this category of abnormalities, the abnormal data point lies far away from the normal data points. For instance, a person normally spends US$200 per day. If his credit card is debited with a bigger transaction, say, US$2000, it is a point anomaly that significantly differs from the routine activities.
  - **Collective anomalies** – The collective anomalies pertain to the combined (not individual) abnormal response of different factors in an ecosystem. The example of this category of anomalies includes the rhythm break in an electrocardiogram or ECG.
- The most commonly used techniques in the entire anomaly detection model can be classified into two major categories, such as:

- **Parametric techniques** – In these techniques, the data scientist knows the normal population condition in the data prior to deploying any algorithm. If not known, it can be easily approximated through average or mean values to show the normal conditions of the population.
- **Non-parametric techniques** – In the non-parametric techniques, the fixed parameters of a given population are not required prior to the deployment of the anomaly detection model. Thus, it is independent of population parameters. They are distribution-free techniques and are getting more and more popular nowadays. This is due to their low complexity and the fact that no assumption is required in such techniques.
- This model is equally useful for both supervised and unsupervised machine learning applications.
- It uses numerous algorithms for anomaly detection in the data analysis that are normally used in supervised and unsupervised machine learning. But the most important ones specifically used for the anomaly detection models include:
  - Support Vector Machine (SVM).
  - Local Outlier Function (LOF).

Transfer learning process

The transfer learning process is a procedure or a set of activities in which multiple machine learning models can be used in an existing ML-based solution to solve new challenges in a new environment. In simple words, it is the process of reusing existing machine learning models in solving new problems or challenges. In this process, any model – supervised, unsupervised, or any other – that has already provided a solution to certain challenges is redeployed in a new environment or machine ecosystem to solve another challenge or problem. Thus, we can say it is the transfer of machine learning abilities from one machine or computing system to another one to solve new challenges. The most salient features and characteristics of the transfer learning process are mentioned below for a better understanding of the concept.[66]

- It is a process of reusing an existing machine learning model for solving new problems or challenges in machine learning ecosystems.
- It is not a machine learning model or algorithm; rather, it is a complete process of reusing the existing models.
- The recycling of previously learned knowledge by a machine into another environment to solve new challenges is the core principle of transfer learning.
- This process saves substantial time on developing a new machine learning model from scratch for every new challenge.

- It reduces the cost of data labeling required for building a unique machine learning model every time a new problem is encountered.
- The most common areas of machine learning applications where the reuse of previously learned data is heavily deployed include:
  - Computer vision (CV).
  - Natural language processing (NLP).
  - Artificial neural networks (ANN).
- In the transfer learning process, the large amount of source data and source labels in large volumes are transferred to the new environment along with the source model of machine learning powered by a source algorithm.
- There are numerous models that are used in deploying the transfer learning process in a machine learning environment. A few of them include:
  - Inception Model.
  - Xception Model.
  - ResNet Model.
  - Visual Geometry Group (VGG) model.
- All those models are based on different layers of convolution matrices to generalize, categorize, and classify the subjects in the training datasets.

How does the transfer learning process work?

The entire process of transfer learning consists of numerous steps and models to use for generalization of training data, selection of additional training models, and other activities. In a generalized way, the previously trained machine learning model with previous experience of data points is chosen for similar kinds of problems or challenges. The generalized learning in the previous model is transferred along with the source data and source labels. The remaining or additional data required for learning the new environment of the new challenge is trained through another suitable model decided by the data scientists. For example, an existing model is trained with 24 million images with their labels classified in 50 generalized categories of subjects. If the new model is almost similar in logical architecture to a few additional data points, the learning experience of the previous model can be recycled or reused in the new challenge environment. The additional training for the new challenge is provided through any form of machine learning. Thus, the entire learning experience of millions of images and their respective subjects was transferred to the new model, and any additional customized training required for the new challenge is provided to the machine learning model. It is much easier than developing and designing an ML model from scratch and training the model with millions of labeled images and other objects.

MAJOR ALGORITHMS USED IN DIFFERENT MACHINE LEARNING MODELS

Most commonly used machine learning types, models, and other techniques have already been covered in this chapter separately and categorically. The most important component of all machine learning models is machine learning algorithms, which act like the breath and soul to the entire machine learning ecosystem, irrespective of what type of machine learning class or models are used for training the computing systems. Here, let us discuss the most important algorithms used in different classes and categories of the entire machine learning technology.

Fundamentally, the machine learning algorithms can be classified into three major categories based on three major processing models used in all types of machine learning technologies. Each of those categories supports a wide range of ML algorithms to perform the activities associated with those groups or categories. The most important categories of machine learning algorithms extensively used in modern machine learning include:

- Classification Algorithms.
- Regression Algorithms.
- Clustering Algorithms.

A number of algorithms can be placed under each category of machine learning algorithms. Those are discussed separately under each category in the following topics.

CLASSIFICATION ALGORITHMS

Classification algorithms, or classification machine learning algorithms, are those types of functions that are designed to weigh the features of the input training dataset in such a way that they can be classified into two separate categories, such as either positive value or negative value.[67] There are numerous machine learning algorithms that are trained through classifier training so that they can easily identify the weights of the features to accurately categorize the subjects in any training or testing datasets. The most important machine learning algorithms extensively deployed in the classification training include:

- Random Forest.
- Decision Tree.
- Naïve Bayes.
- K-Nearest Neighbors.
- Support Vector Machines.
- Gradient Boosting.

The details of each of the above-listed machine learning algorithms are expressed in full length in the following subtopics separately.

Random forest

The random forest algorithm is about a forest, or a combination of multiple random trees. This machine learning algorithm has evolved from the combination or ensemble process of multiple decision tree algorithms to produce the most accurate and reliable output in the machine learning training process. The random forest algorithm is extensively used in the supervised machine learning field, in which the labeled data is ingested into the algorithm to produce the mapped output results. It can be used in two major categories – classification and regression problems. This topic mainly focuses on the classification process in ML training. The most important characteristics and features of a random forest ML algorithm are:[68]

- The core factor of this algorithm is the decision tree algorithm combined through the ensemble process.
- It is designed to provide more accurate output in complex problems.
- Different decision tree algorithms are used to classify different subsets of data used in this algorithm for machine training.
- The second stage of this algorithm is to take the average or mean of all decision trees combined for data classification to generate more accurate results.
- In the last step, the prediction function is applied to finally predict the output against the given challenge or problem through a test dataset.
- The number of decision trees combined is directly proportional to the accuracy, performance, and reliability of ML output.
- All decision trees used in this algorithm are not the same; rather, they have unique attributes and features as compared to other trees. This capability is also known as the miscellany of the random forest algorithm.
- The feature space is much smaller due to immunity to dimensionality because features are not processed in this algorithm.
- There is no difference between training and testing data because a decision tree checks less than 30% of the entire data.
- A schematic diagram of the random tree algorithm is shown in Figure 2.16.

In this figure, each decision tree is depicted with a circle, and "n" number of decision trees have been used in this random forest algorithm. Those decision trees will select the random samples from the training datasets ingested into the machine learning model. The algorithm assigns a separate decision tree for each training dataset. The results of all those decision trees – for instance, n numbers of trees – are polled or voted through different functions such as averaging or taking means. The averaged value is fed to

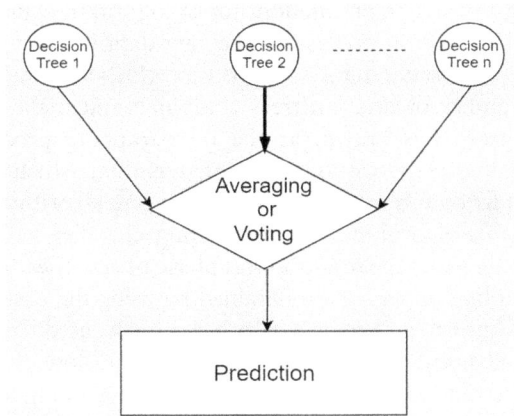

Figure 2.16 Schematic diagram of the random forest algorithm.

the prediction module, which makes the decision and understanding about the problem and the training datasets.

As we know, combining multiple algorithms is referred to as an ensemble process. In our case, multiple decision tree algorithms have been combined to form an ensemble. There are two major methods used in creating the ensemble in machine learning models. Those methods are:

- **Bagging** – In the bagging method, for each dataset, a different training subset is created with replacement. This is a parallel method of machine learning used in the ensemble process. It is also known as bootstrap aggregation in the random forest algorithm. The random data is chosen and arranged into samples that are known as bootstrap samples, and the entire process to choose and rearrange the datasets is called the bootstrapping process. Then each model is trained individually to generate unique results. The individual training and generation of different results by the models is referred to as aggregation. Finally, the unique results are achieved by combining the results through averaging or majority voting, accomplished with the help of the ensemble classifier. The entire process of combining and producing the final result is known as the bagging process in the random forest algorithm.
- **Boosting** – In this method of the random forest algorithm of machine learning, the weak learners are combined with the strong learners to improve the accuracy of the output results. In contrast to the bagging method, the boosting method is known as a sequential process. Multiple sequential models containing strong and weak learners are formed to improve the accuracy of the modules. Those modules produce the boosted results. That is why this method is known as the boosting method. A few examples of boosting techniques include XG Boosting, ADA Boosting, and others.

The functioning process of the random forest algorithm consists of multiple stages governed by certain processes. The raw data in the form of training datasets are fed to the random forest algorithm, which identifies a few datasets based on the number of decision trees combined and makes the bootstrap samples. This process is known as the bootstrapping process. The third process that goes after bootstrapping is aggregation, which deals with the generation of individual results in each decision tree algorithm that has been combined into this algorithm. The aggregating classifier helps the random forest algorithm generate the results in this phase of activities. The final results based on the pooling or voting are obtained by using the ensemble classifier. This process is known as bagging, which is mostly used in random forest algorithms for classification purposes. The entire workflow of the activities or procedures in the random forest algorithm is depicted in Figure 2.17.

The results produced by the random forest in the classification category of machine learning are much more accurate than those created by the decision tree alone. The major applications of random forest for classification include facial recognition, body movement detection, image processing, and many other types of applications in modern businesses.

Decision tree

A decision tree is one of the simplest forms of algorithms used in the machine learning field. It is very intuitive to understand. A decision tree is a non-parametric algorithm. It is extensively used in both regression and classification applications. A decision tree is also referred to as an algorithm designed for supervised machine learning. It is hierarchical in nature, like the formation of a tree with branches and leaves. This is the reason that the name

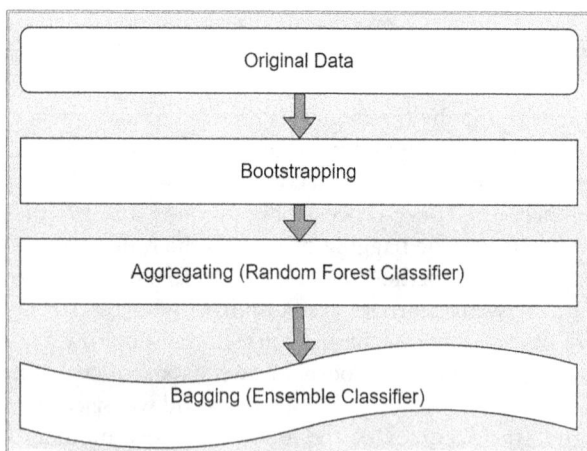

Figure 2.17 Random forest algorithm workflow.

"decision tree" was given to this algorithm. A decision tree algorithm consists of two main components.

- Branches.
- Nodes.

The nodes are further divided into different types based on their capabilities and characteristics, such as:[69]

- Root nodes.
- Internal nodes.
- Leaf nodes.

The branches in a decision tree are divided into two types in terms of their flow of input and output.

- Incoming branch (input branch).
- Outgoing branch (output branch).

All nodes other than the root node have one input or incoming branch and two outgoing or output branches. The root node has only two output branches and no input branches, while the leaf node has no output branches and only one input branch that displays the output value. The schematic diagram consisting of all components, such as nodes and branches, to describe a decision tree algorithm is shown in Figure 2.18.

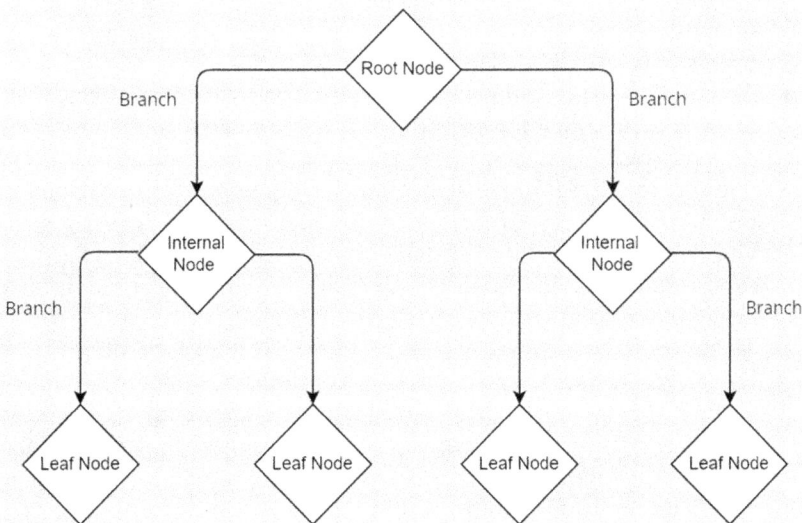

Figure 2.18 Decision tree algorithm block diagram.

In Figure 2.18, the first node of this algorithm is the root node; that means the decision tree starts from the root node. This root node does not have any incoming branch. This node makes an evaluation of the data and builds a homogeneous subset based on the logical classification. The output of the subsets is fed to the internal nodes, which are also referred to as decision nodes in this structure. They also assess the input data on the basis of logical classification or criteria to generate two possible outputs, which may further be fed to another layer of internal nodes to decide on more subsets. This process may continue till multiple layers of decision nodes are formed. The final outputs of the datasets are presented through leaf nodes. The other main features and characteristics of the decision tree algorithm are mentioned below.

- This algorithm is based on a very basic and simple principle of logic known as "*if … then*" to present the decision-making structure in a way that is very easy to digest.
- This algorithm uses the strategy of "divide and conquer" to figure out the most relevant solution for a particular problem through a greedy search for finding the most optimal split points within the decision-making tree.
- It is a top-down algorithm in which each output is further split on the basis of further logic until all records or the maximum number of data records have been classified into different categories.
- If dealing with a complex problem, the decision tree may expand significantly, which may lead to very little data falling under the sub-tree, called data fragmentation.
- It is very difficult to maintain the purity of the decision node if the complexity of the decision trees increases hugely. Such types of decision trees often lead to overfitting due to data fragmentation that occurs at lower levels of decision nodes.
- Attaining the pure leaf nodes is possible through smaller trees, which provide better accuracy and relevancy as compared to the most complex systems.
- Initially, the decision tree algorithm was developed for understanding the human learning process in psychology in 1960. It is known as Hunt's algorithm, which was later adopted for machine learning applications for making decisions, especially in the supervised form of machine learning.
- There are three main types of algorithms that have been derived from Hunt's algorithm. They are mentioned below.
  - **ID3** – Iterative Dichotomiser 3, precisely referred to as ID3, is one of the basic decision tree algorithms developed by Ross Quinlan. This algorithm is based on two very important components for evaluating the candidate splits. Those two factors include 1) entropy and 2) information gain. These terms will be further discussed later.

- **C4.5** – This is an advanced version of the ID3 algorithm with additional capabilities and features. It is known as the Decision Tree Identifier, which is an effective algorithm in data mining applications. The use of gain ratio or information gain is the main principle of finding the candidate split points.
- **CART** – Classification And Regression Tree, precisely known as CART, is another important type of algorithm used in both classification and regression tasks. It uses the Gini impurity method for finding out the most suitable attributes for candidate data splitting. This approach will be further discussed later on.
- The most common applications or areas where the decision tree algorithm is extensively used in the artificial intelligence (AI) field include knowledge discovery and data mining applications.
- A few benefits of the decision tree algorithm include the following:
  - Simple and intuitive.
  - Either very little or no data preparation is required.
  - Highly flexible for customized uses.
- The most important downsides of the decision tree algorithm include:
  - Very prone to overfitting and data fragments.
  - More expensive in terms of training datasets.
  - The Scikit-Learn library does not support it.
  - Little variation in the datasets can lead to very different types of decision trees.
- Decision tree algorithms can further be classified into two major types based on the nature of the targeted variables, such as:
  - **Categorical variable decision tree** – These types of decision trees focus on the variables that classify the data points into categories.
  - **Continuous variable decision tree** – This type of decision tree deals with the numerical values in regression tasks.
- The capability of the decision tree algorithm to deal with different types of variables makes it effective in both regression and classification tasks simultaneously.

Major techniques used for data splitting

The decision tree algorithm is one of the most fundamental and basic types of algorithms used in machine learning applications. It uses two very important techniques for deciding the candidate splits in the decision-making process. Two major techniques include:

- Information Gain.
- Gini Impurity.

The information gain technique uses a very important technical term known as *entropy* for making decisions. Thus, the understanding of entropy is very important for grasping the concept of the above-mentioned two techniques used in the decision tree algorithm.

Entropy (S)

The measurement of impurity in the sample data values is called entropy. This concept is basically used in information theory. It has substantial importance in physics and other domains of study. The value of entropy ranges between 0 and 1. The 0 is a value with minimum impurity or disorder. If all samples or data points fall under one single class, the value of entropy will be zero. Meanwhile, if the sample data points are classified into two different categories with equal volumes or numbers, the entropy value will be maximum, i.e., it will be 1. It is always desirable to choose the split with the minimum entropy value. In other words, the attributes with the smallest amount of entropy should be used or selected.

The formula to calculate entropy in any data point ecosystem is given below:

$$\text{Entropy } (S) = -\sum_{C \in C} p(c) \log 2 \, p(c)$$

In this equation:

S = Dataset whose entropy is to be calculated.
C = Classes in set (S).
P = Proportion of data points associated with class C to the total number of data points, which belong to set (S).

Information gain

Information gain (IG) is a ratio of the values of entropies before attribute split and after attribute split in a node of the decision tree algorithm. The entropy is the core factor that influences the value of information gain; therefore, the entropy was explained in full detail in the above topic. In the information gain method, the greatest value of IG will produce the best split, which leads to the production of the most accurate classification of the data points in decision tree algorithms.

The information gain function is based on entropy (S) and the attribute of a data point (a). It can be calculated through the following mathematical equation.

$$\text{Information Gain } (S, a) = \text{Entropy } (S) \sum_{v \in vcalues(a)} \frac{|Sv|}{|S|} \text{ Entropy } (Sv)$$

In the above equation:

a = Attribute label.
S = Dataset.
Entropy (S) = Entropy of dataset S.
$|Sv|/|S|$ = Proportion values of Sv and S in the dataset.
Entropy (Sv) = Entropy of dataset Sv.

Each attribute of the training or test dataset is measured with the help of the above-given formula to get the value of information gain (IG). Any attribute with the highest value will be considered as the first split point in the decision tree algorithm. After selecting the first split of the data attribute, the other sub-trees are calculated under the first tree that was chosen on the basis of a higher value of information gain. The formula for further splitting is also the same and repetitive for the next split, and so on and so forth till the final outcome is achieved.

Gini impurity

Gini impurity is another very important method used in the classification of data points after the information gain technique. It is very similar to the entropy function. It measures the impurity of an attribute or label that is labeled incorrectly. If the Gini impurity of an attribute is zero, that means the attribute is fully classified and correctly placed. If the value of Gini impurity is greater than zero, the attribute is not fully classified to its designated category. Thus, the repetitive tests are processed to finally place them in the right class.

The Gini impurity function is expressed in the following mathematical equation.

$$\text{Gini Impurity} = 1 - \sum_i (Pi)^2$$

In the above equation:

Pi = Probability of each class
$\sum_i (Pi)^2$ = Sum of squared probabilities of each class

In simple words, the Gini impurity is equal to the sum of all squared probabilities of each class subtracted from 1. This helps the algorithm decide the best class for a data point or find out the best split for an attribute in the decision tree algorithm.

Naïve Bayes

The Naïve Bayes machine learning algorithm is very simple, fast, and effective for use in numerous classification tasks in supervised machine learning models. It is very simple (naïve), based on the probability theorem enunciated by the famous scientist Thomas Bayes. The Naïve Bayes algorithm has numerous unique features and characteristics that make it one of the most efficient algorithms for supervised machine learning models, especially in determining the classification tasks in those models. A few of those characteristics are listed below:[70,71]

- The combination of two words, Naïve and Bayes, forms this algorithm, powered by the simplicity and Bayes probability theorem.
- According to the definition of the word "naïve", the algorithm assumes that the occurrence of a certain attribute is not dependent on the occurrence of other attributes or features. There is no relationship between two features of a data point and the other features.
- Naïve Bayes theorem is extensively used in text classification, which requires a high-dimensional training dataset for supervised machine learning.
- It is considered the fastest and simplest algorithm for faster machine learning and making faster predictions.
- It uses the power of probability of being a class or category; therefore, it is also known as a probabilistic classifier or algorithm.
- The most common domains of applications of the Naïve Bayes algorithm include sentiment analysis, spam filtration, article categorization, and others.
- This algorithm is equally useful for both multi-class classification and binary classification.
- It is considered the most effective multi-class classification algorithm in the field of machine learning models.
- It has a downside in that it assumes that all features of a data point are independent or not related to each other. This bar machine establishes relationships between multiple features of an object.
- Naïve Bayes ML algorithm is considered an eager learner algorithm that makes it highly suitable for real-time applications of classification tasks.
- There are three major types of Naïve Bayes ML algorithms, such as:
  - **Gaussian Naïve Bayes** – In this algorithm, the predictor takes continuous values rather than discrete ones, and it is assumed that the attributes or features follow a normal distribution. The sampling of the values is assumed to have been done through the Gaussian distribution principle.
  - **Bernoulli Naïve Bayes** – When the independent Boolean variables are consumed in a multinomial distribution, the classifier is known as the Bernoulli Naïve Bayes model. It is extensively used for document classification tasks.
  - **Multinomial Naïve Bayes** – In this type of algorithm, the multinomial data is used. It detects the class of the object based on the frequency of the words used in particular data for the predictors.

Working of Naïve Bayes' algorithm

The fundamental principle of Naïve Bayes' algorithm is Bayes' theorem and its axioms in terms of other mathematical relationships, such as the Bernoulli theorem and other types of distributions. The addition of Naïve is to notify that this algorithm takes into account the assumption that all features are independent. To have a better understanding of this algorithm, a deeper insight into Bayes' theorem is necessary.

Bayes' theorem

This is a mathematical expression that is used to determine the probability of a hypothesis with prior knowledge to verify. This theorem is based on the conditional probability principle. Bayes' theorem is also known as Bayes' law or Bayes' rule in certain fields. The mathematical expression or equation to find out the probabilities is given below:

$$P(A|B) = \frac{P(B|A)P(A)}{P(B)}$$

In the above equation:

$P(A|B)$ = Posterior probability of hypothesis A on observed event B.
$P(B|A)$ = Likelihood probability of evidence that the probability of the hypothesis is correct.
$P(A)$ = Prior probability of hypothesis before observing the evidence.
$P(B)$ = Marginal probability of evidence.

To understand the Naïve Bayes working principle, let us explore the major steps used in making a certain decision on the given conditions or raw data, as mentioned below:

- Construct a frequency table out of the given dataset that describes the situations for a particular action in the probability paradigm.
- In the second step, form the likelihood table by finding the probabilities of certain attributes given in the problem description.
- Apply the Naïve Bayes theorem mathematically to calculate the posterior probability.

K-nearest neighbors

K-Nearest Neighbor, precisely known as KNN, is a very simple and effective machine learning algorithm used for both regression and classification tasks. The deployment of this algorithm in machine learning problems is very easy. It is used for supervised machine learning applications or models. According to the assumption of the K-nearest neighbor algorithm, similar items would be available in close proximity. On the basis of this principle or assumption, the further process of understanding the dataset is accomplished.[72]

There are several features and characteristics of the K-nearest neighbor algorithm. A few of them are listed below:[72,73]

- The distance, closeness, or proximity are the fundamental terms used in the K-nearest neighbor algorithm, which would decide the features of objects in a given dataset.
- The letter "K" in the name of this algorithm indicates the number of groups or neighbors that the data can be classified into.
- There are certain methods implemented to determine the distance between two features or objects in a dataset. Those methods include:
  - Euclidean distance.
  - Minkowski distance.
  - Hamming distance.
  - Manhattan distance.
  - And others.
- The most commonly and extensively used method for calculating the distance in the K-nearest neighbor algorithm is the Euclidean distance between two points.
- Euclidean distance between two points is calculated through the following mathematical formula:

$$d(x, y) = \sqrt{\sum_{i=1}^{n} (yi - xi)^2}$$

- It is a non-parametric algorithm, which means no additional hypothesis is required to be assumed in algorithmic calculations.
- The assignment of labels to the object in classification problems is done through majority voting or plurality voting, in which the majority number is used to assign the label of that particular class. For instance, in a two-category problem, the ratio of the voting or number of votes should be more than 50%, while in the case of multiple categories, the ratio may be much less than this one. In certain cases, it may be well below 25% of the votes, too.
- On the other hand, for the regression problem, continuous values are taken for labeling the datasets. It is contrary to the classification problems in which the discrete values are taken for classifying the subjects into categories.
- The KNN algorithm is also referred to as the "lazy learning" algorithm family or models.
- This algorithm is also known as a memory-based and instance-based algorithm because it requires substantial memory to store its learning about the environments, and the calculation takes place when prediction or classification is being accomplished.

- The idea of the KNN model was proposed by Evelyn Fix and Joseph Hodges, and further expansion of this model was done by Thomas Cover.
- The most common types of applications in industry that use this algorithm in machine learning models include:
  - Financial market predictions.
  - Recommendation engines.
  - Intrusion detection system.
  - Data mining processes.
  - Pattern recognition.
- The definition of the value of K is arbitrary and should be set in such a way that the output gives you the most accurate results in terms of both classification and regression predictions of the training datasets.
- A small number of K results in low bias but high variance. Again, a large value of K will lead to low variance and high bias. Thus, the definition of the K value is a powerful balancing tool in the KNN algorithm to avert overfitting and underfitting of the outputs.
- It is always recommended to use an odd value of K to avoid a tie in the majority voting of neighbors for a query point for classification or prediction.

How does KNN work?

The working principle of the KNN algorithm is based on finding the distance value between the selected categories or groups and the new data points. If the distance of a new data point is closer to group A than group B, the data point will be categorized as a data point in category A. This entire process takes place through multiple steps. The working steps of the KNN algorithm to categorize a new data point are mentioned below:

- The first step of the KNN algorithm is to determine the number of groups, which is denoted by the "K" value in the metrics. This selection is arbitrary, starting from just "1" and increasing to see the accuracy of the results. The number is chosen by analysis of the outputs to produce the most correct or optimal accuracy.
- The next step is to calculate the Euclidean distances of all neighbors "K" chosen in the K-nearest neighbor algorithm.
- Choose all data points to assign the category with the help of the K-nearest neighbor formula to calculate the distance.
- The data point is assigned to the category in which the maximum number of neighbors are found or the nearest data points are found.
- The K-nearest neighbor algorithm is ready to be deployed on the desired machine learning model to further train and test.
- The schematic diagram of classification through K-nearest neighbor is shown in Figure 2.19.

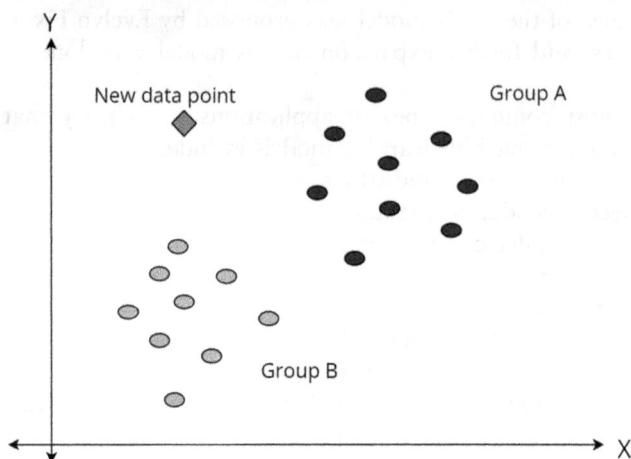

Figure 2.19 Schematic diagram of the KNN algorithm.

In Figure 2.19, there are two main groups or categories shown with gray and black (solid). There is one new data point that is to be classified by the K-nearest neighbor algorithm. For example, we choose a K value equal to 7, which produces the best or most accurate results. First of all, the algorithm will calculate the Euclidean distance of all data points with respect to the new data point. Thus, the values of distances of all data points to the new data points would be found. Now, the nearest points to the new points from both categories will be considered. In our case, where we chose the value of K as 7, there are four points from group B near the new data point as compared to the three data points in group A. Thus, the new data point will be classified as a member of group B.

For any application powered by the K-nearest neighbor algorithm, it is recommended to use at least 75% of the datasets for training purposes to make the machine learning model capable of predicting reliable outcomes and about 25% of the datasets for testing purposes to make sure the machine learning model is producing the desirable results without any overfitting or underfitting or any other confusing outcomes of the model.

The normal range of choosing the value of K in the K-nearest neighbor algorithm is 3 to 10. The most accurate value is that one that produces the optimal value of accuracy in the output or predictions. The output is always checked after assigning different K values in the algorithm. This process is repeated till the desired level of accuracy is achieved.

The selection of the K value is not only to achieve the most accurate results but also to maintain a certain level of performance of the model. If the value of K is increased to a larger number in a complex problem, the time to infer will be longer and will pose certain problems in large datasets. There are certain methods used to choose the optimum value of K in the algorithm. Two notable methods are:

- Square root method.
- Cross-validation method.

Support vector machines

Support Vector Machine, precisely referred to as SVM, is a machine learning algorithm based on deep learning in the domain of supervised machine learning. This algorithm is used for both classification and regression tasks in supervised machine learning models. The main principle of the support vector machine algorithm is to develop hyperplanes with the help of parallel lines to separate the groups or categories in a larger space of data points. The classification is performed on the basis of similarities in the features or attributes.[74]

The most important characteristics and features of the SVM algorithm are summarized below:[74,75]

- It requires labeled training datasets to learn through supervised machine learning models based on the deep learning concept.
- This algorithm is known as a non-probabilistic and binary linear classifier.
- This algorithm was initially invented by Vladimir Vapnik and Alexey Chervonenkis in 1963.
- This algorithm is extensively used for image, text, and hypertext classification in modern business applications.
- The major commercial applications include chatbots, robots, facial recognition apps, driverless vehicles, expert systems, and others.
- This algorithm draws lines or decision boundaries that are the most optimally accurate to divide the multi-dimensional (n) space into the most suitable categories in such a way that any new data point can easily be placed in a particular/relevant group.
- The best decision boundary drawn through this algorithm is referred to as a hyperplane.
- The parallel lines in two-dimensional space that help develop an optimal hyperplane are known as support vectors. In n-dimensional space, the support vectors are equal to the number of dimensions (n).
- The name of this algorithm is drawn from the functionality of support vectors that help achieve the most optimal separation or decision boundary between n-dimensions based on the features or attributes of data points in an n-dimensional space.
- Each feature of a data point is referred to as one dimension in the support vector machine algorithm's terminology.

- The maximum distance between two data points is called the hyper-plane or decision boundary in this algorithm.
- There are two types of SVM algorithms that are mentioned below with some details.
  - **Linear SVM** – The type of algorithm that can classify data points in a two-dimensional space through straight lines is called a linear support vector algorithm. This type of algorithm is applied for a two-dimensional space or the data points with two categories or classes. This type of algorithm is also referred to as a linear support vector machine classifier.
  - **Non-linear SVM** – This type of SVM algorithm is used in an n-dimensional space of attributes when a straight line cannot separate the categories clearly. This type of SVM uses non-straight lines to separate the categories in a multi-dimensional space of attributes or features. It is also known as a non-linear SVM classifier.

How does the support vector machine algorithm work?

The basic working principle of the SVM algorithm is based on finding the best decision boundary in a multi-dimensional space of data points. The most basic type of algorithm that deals with only two attributes or features is known as the linear SVM algorithm. A more complex version of this algorithm deals with multi-dimensional space through non-linear lines to separate the categories or groups of features through the best boundaries. The basic terms used in the description as well as in the diagrams are already explained in the above-summarized list. Let us have a deeper dive into the basic workflow of the linear SVM learning algorithm here by examining the two diagrams presented in Figures 2.20 and 2.21 (which show a two-dimensional space).

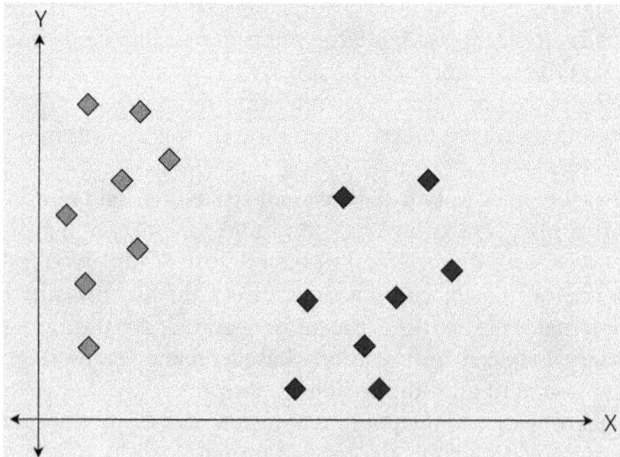

Figure 2.20 Schematic diagram of two-dimensional data point space.

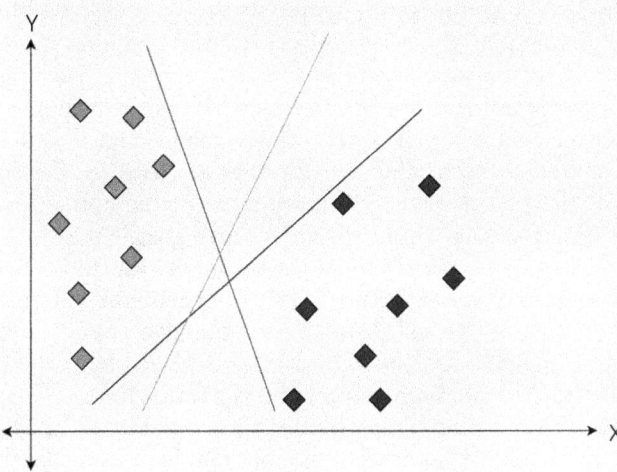

Figure 2.21 Multiple decision boundaries possibility.

In these figures, the two-dimensional space of data points is depicted in black (solid) and gray colors. Any new data point appearing in this space should be classified into a certain category. Before that, those two separate features should be separated by the best line. There can be multiple lines to divide those groups, as shown in Figure 2.21. But the linear support vector determines the best line, which represents the best decision boundary between those two groups or classes.

The application of the linear SVM algorithm is depicted in Figure 2.22. Here, two support vectors are drawn that are the closest lines for each

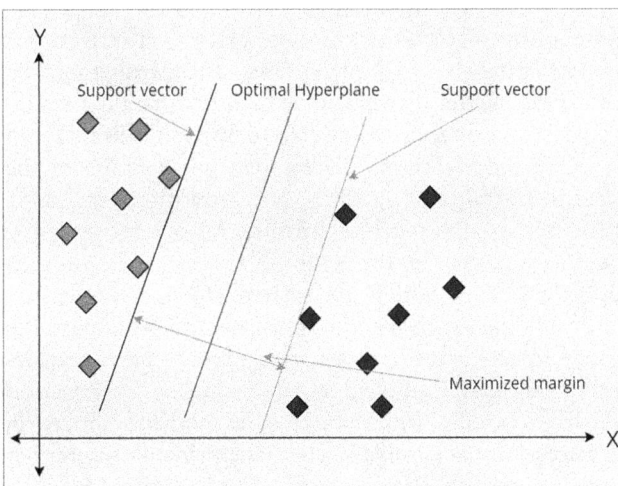

Figure 2.22 Linear SVM best decision boundary.

category or class of attributes of data points shown in this two-dimensional space. One vector is the nearest straight line to the attributes shown in black (solid) color on the right side of the optimum hyperplane. The other straight line is drawn on the left side of the figure, which is the nearest to the data point shown in gray color. It is very important to note that these vectors should be parallel to each other because they are used for determining the final path of the best decision boundary through the optimal hyperplane. Once the support vectors are finalized by moving their positions in such a way that they produce the maximum margin between those two support vectors, the optimal hyperplane line is drawn. The maximum margin is the maximum achievable vertical distance between two support vectors. The hyperplane, or the best decision boundary, is achieved by drawing a line at the midpoint of the maximum margin and is parallel to the support vectors on both sides of the data point classes, as shown in Figure 2.22.

The line in the middle is known as the optimal hyperplane (see the figure) that separates the two categories of data points in a two-dimensional space. The multi-dimensional space uses a nonlinear SVM type to determine the boundaries between multiple classes of data points.

Gradient boosting

The Gradient Boosting Algorithm, or Gradient Boosting Machine, is a type of algorithm based on the boosting of the performance, accuracy, and speed of the prediction model in machine learning, as well as in a few other applications. Gradient boosting machine is precisely referred to as GBM, too. As mentioned, this is an algorithm that boosts the predictive outputs in terms of their accuracy and performance of the entire process of prediction. GBM is used in supervised machine learning for both classification and regression tasks simultaneously.[76]

To understand this algorithm with more clarity, let us have a look at the boosting function extensively adopted in machine learning models. All those algorithms used in machine learning have their own weaknesses that result in inaccurate output. The inaccurate or erroneous results are the most important factors in machine learning. To remove those errors or inaccuracies, different types of techniques, methods, and algorithms are used. The most common technique used in machine learning for enhancing the accuracy of the ML model output includes the ensemble technique. In this technique, the weak learner algorithms, which are referred to as "stumps" in boosting processes, are combined with the strong learners to produce the most accurate results and improve the performance of the entire machine learning model. In the same way, boosting is a technique in which multiple weak learners are used in parallel with the strong learners to improve the accuracy and performance of the ML models. The basic principle of gradient boosting is the loss function, which is very effective in enhancing the accuracy of the models with complex datasets used for the training of the machines.

Basically, the boosting technique involves two steps, phases, or even models as listed below:

- The training dataset model is built.
- An error function correction model is built.

In the first step of building a training dataset model, all data points in a space are assigned equal weights and processed through the machine learning or training model for classification of the objects. Now, the weights of all data points – both rightly classified and incorrectly classified – are updated accordingly. The weights of all objects or data points that are incorrectly classified are increased to increase the probability of right classification of those data points in the second phase, and the weights of the correctly classified are reduced to decrease the chances of reclassification in the second phase of classification. If there are still some data points that are wrongly classified, they would be processed through the same activity to reach the final position where all data points are accurately classified. This entire process is known as the boosting process in machine learning terminology.

Gradient boosting is an algorithm based on the boosting process that has been discussed here. The main features and characteristics of the gradient boosting algorithm extensively adopted in the classification task of supervised machine learning are:[76,77]

- The gradient boosting algorithm is based on the mechanism of boosting output accuracy by exploiting error functions.
- There are two very important types of errors in machine learning, which play a pivotal role in enhancing the accuracy of the prediction and classification methods. Those errors are expressed below:
  - **Bias error** – The errors that occur in the system due to wrong hypotheses in machine learning models. They are errors in which the results of an algorithm are skewed either in favor of an assumption/idea or against the same.
  - **Variance error** – A type of error that measures the variability of a machine learning model to adjust in terms of given datasets. This error occurs in very complex problems or models. The relationship between bias and variance error is inversely proportional; that means the higher the bias error, the less the variance error, and vice versa.
- The gradient boosting algorithm is used to reduce the bias errors in a machine learning model.
- Adaptive Boosting Algorithm, precisely known as AdaBoost, is an example of a gradient boosting technique commonly used in classification and regression ML tasks.
- Multiple models are built in a sequential order to improve the bias errors developed by the preceding model until the entire problem of data point classification is accomplished correctly. This is known as gradient boosting.

- There are two sub-algorithms of gradient boosting used for classification and regression tasks, as mentioned below:
  - **Gradient boosting classifier** – Used for classification models or problems where the target data column is based on continuous values.
  - **Gradient boosting regressor** – It is used for regression problems or models when the target data column is a binary value.
- Both versions of the gradient boosting algorithm are based on the loss function. The different functions are used in regression and classification problems. One example of loss functions used in both versions includes:
  - **Classification loss function example** – Different log-likelihood functions.
  - **Regression loss function example** – Mean Square Error (MSE).
- The loss function for the classification problem based on the log-likelihood is presented through the following function.

$$L = -\sum_{i=1}^{n} Y_i \log(p) + (1-p) \log(1-p)$$

- The entire workflow of the gradient boosting algorithm can be defined in three important and sequential steps as mentioned below:
  - The loss function is optimized in the first step.
  - At the second step, a weak machine learner is asked to make predictions with losses or inaccuracies.
  - The additional weak learners are included in the next model to reduce the loss function created in the previous step. This process continues till the accurate classification of the data points is accomplished.
- One single weak learner is added in every repetitive model creation in a sequential order, while maintaining the old decision trees or weak learners in this model to reduce the loss functions gradually.
- The gradient boosting algorithm has a drawback of overfitting fast due to its nature of greediness in functionality. To overcome this downside of the algorithm, different techniques such as regularization and penalization are deployed to keep it under tolerable limits. Other common techniques used include:
  - Random sampling method.
  - Tree constraints technique.
  - Shrinkage method.
  - Penalized learning method.
- The most important and desirable benefits of the gradient boosting algorithm include the fast speed of processing, greater accuracy of outputs through stepwise improvements, and being very effective for very large and complex problems or models of machine learning designed for both classification and regression tasks.

- Another example of the most popular gradient boosting-based algorithm developed by Google Inc. is XGboost. This algorithm is playing a pivotal role in the Google search engine and is based on the R platform.
- The most common difference between ensemble and boosting is that in the former, multiple weak learners are combined to form a new combo to process the data at a single time. While in the case of the latter one, one weak learner's output is fed into another weak learner to make it more accurate.

REGRESSION ALGORITHMS

Regression is another very important task deployed in machine learning applications. A function or activity that is used to predict and forecast the relationship between two different variables, such as independent variables and dependent variables, is called regression in the machine learning field. The independent variables are also known as features of data points. Dependent variables are referred to as the output or outcome of an ML-based predictive model.[78]

Regression activity is performed by using a wide range of regression algorithms. A few very important algorithms to investigate the relationship between dependent and independent variables are listed below:

- Linear Regression.
- Multiple Linear Regression.
- Lasso Regression.
- Logistic Regression.
- Multivariate Regression.

Let us explore the above-mentioned list of algorithms used for the regression activity in modern machine learning applications.

Linear regression

It is a form of machine learning algorithm designed for solving regression-related problems. It is the simplest type of regression ML algorithm that predicts the target values based on a linear projection through a straight line – it is also referred to as a regression line defined in a mathematical formula. Linear regression is a supervised machine learning algorithm for performing regression tasks to solve for the continuous values of independent variables to find out the target value (dependent variable) by establishing a linear relationship between those two types of variables through a linear line that has the minimum value of errors.[79]

There are numerous characteristics, assumptions, and techniques that are used to establish a continuous relationship between two variables and to reduce the errors in deviation from assumptions. A few such features and characteristics of the linear regression algorithm are mentioned below:[79,80]

- The linear regression algorithm is used in supervised machine learning for regression tasks.
- There are two major types of linear regression algorithms: simple linear regression algorithms and multiple linear regression algorithms. The simple linear algorithm deals with a single independent variable to establish a relationship with an output or dependent variable through a linear regression line. On the other hand, the multiple linear regression deals with multiple independent variables to find out the relationship with a dependent variable through a straight linear regression line. The simple linear regression algorithm, generally referred to as the linear regression algorithm, is covered in this topic, and the multiple linear regression algorithms will be covered in the next topic.
- The linear regression algorithm is used for predicting real/continuous or numeric values. Those predicted values may include price, salary, age, sales, demand, supply, profit margins, market values, and much more.
- The relationship between independent and dependent variables in the linear regression algorithm is accomplished by using the following straight-line formula.

$$y = b_0 + b_1 x_1 + \in$$

In this equation:
y = Target value or output (dependent variable).
x = Predictor factor (independent variable).
b_0 = Intercept constant (for additional freedom in drawing a straight-line relationship).
b_1 = Coefficient of linear regression.
ε = Random error.

- A linear line, or straight line, that defines the relationship between independent and dependent variables is known as a regression line.
- There are two main types of relationships established by the linear line in the linear regression algorithm, such as:
  - **Positive linear relationship** – A type of relationship in which the value of the dependent variable increases on the y-axis with the increase in the dependent value on the x-axis is called the positive linear relationship. The line that depicts the positive linear relationship is known as the positive line of regression.
  - **Negative linear relationship** – A type of linear relationship in which the value of the dependent variable decreases on the y-axis with the increase in the independent variable on the x-axis is called a negative linear relationship. The line that describes the relationship is called the positive line of regression.

- Residual is the distance between a data point and the linear regression line. A longer distance will result in a higher residual value, which is directly proportional to the cost function of simple linear regression.
- The cost function is the value of the coefficient that generates the best-fit regression line on a coordinate plane. The cost function is also used to determine the performance of the linear regression algorithm.
- The mapping accuracy of independent variables (input variables) and dependent variables (output variables) is also accomplished by using the cost function. The mapping function activity is also referred to as the hypothesis function in linear regression terminology.
- The most commonly used cost function in simple linear regression is Mean Square Error, precisely known as MSE. The MSE is the average of the squared error between actual and predicted values.
- The MSE is calculated through the following formula.

$$MSE = 1\frac{1}{N}\sum_{i=0}^{n}(y_i - (a_1x_i + a_0))^2$$

Here in this equation:
$(a_1x_i + a_0)$ = Predicted values.
N = Total number of observations.
Y_i = Actual value.

- Updating the coefficients of a line is done through a process known as gradient descent. This process decreases the MSE value by finding the gradient of the cost function. Initially, the selection of the coefficient value is done randomly, and then the value is changed iteratively to reach the minimum value of the cost function in the linear regression algorithm.
- Optimization is the process by which the best model is identified out of numerous regression models. The best match or fitness of the line of regression with a set of observations determines the performance of the regression algorithm. This is done through the R-squared method. The value of the R-squared method (a ratio of variations) is calculated using the following equation:

$$R\text{-squared} = \frac{\text{Explained variation}}{\text{Total variation}}$$

- R-squared ratio measures the goodness of fit of a statistical model for simple linear regression, which is referred to as the coefficient of determination, and the same for multiple regression is known as the coefficient of multiple determination.

- The other features of the R-squared ratio include the following:
  - Measures the relationship between independent and dependent variables on a scale ranging from 0% to 100%.
  - Measures the minimum difference between predicted and actual values to figure out the best model.
- Linear regression supposes some hypotheses in statistical prediction in different versions of regression algorithms. The most important assumptions made by the linear regression model are mentioned below:
  - A linear relationship exists between the target variable and predictor variables.
  - Either there is no multicollinearity (which is a statistical phenomenon that occurs when two or more independent variables in a regression model are highly correlated) or very little between the predictors that can help determine the real effect of appearing on the target value.
  - The error term is assumed to be the same for all values of the predictor variables. This situation is also known as homoscedasticity.
  - It is assumed that the error term follows a normal distribution pattern.
  - In the linear regression algorithm, it is assumed that no autocorrelation in the error terms exists. That means the accuracy of the model is not affected due to the non-existence of correlation in error terms.

How does the linear regression algorithm work?

The working procedure of the linear regression algorithm in machine learning is very simple compared to many other ML algorithms used in complex problem solutions. The basic objective of a simple linear algorithm is to find the best-fit line that can predict the target values via predictors with minimum error by adjusting different factors, such as line intercepts and coefficients, in such a way that the error or difference between the predicted and actual value is at a very minimum level. Let us understand the workflow by considering Figure 2.23.

In Figure 2.23, the square boxes represent the data points in the linear regression algorithm. The projection of the most accurate value of the predictors that should have the minimum errors should lie on the optimal or the best-fit line of regression. Initially, the value of the coefficient and intercepts (b_0) are chosen arbitrarily and then adjusted interactively to achieve the best-fit line that can predict the most accurate results or target values from the relationship of independent variables or predictors, as shown in the form of data points. The intercept is the value on the y-axis when the value on the x-axis is zero, or the distance at which the line cuts the y-axis. Here in this figure, the value of the intercept is shown by b_0. The vertical distance between the data point center and the linear line of

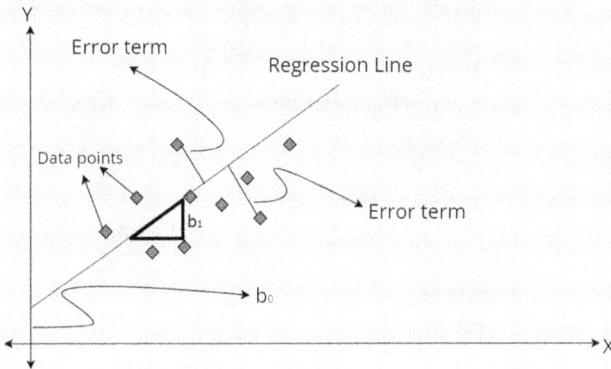

Figure 2.23 Regression line in linear regression algorithm.

regression is called the error term. The main objective of this model is to reduce this value to the minimum level. The data points are also the original values of the variables. The linear algorithm is designed to predict the values on the regression line in such a way that the error term, or the residual, is at the minimum level. The vertical distance between data points and the line of linear regression is called a residual. The residual value is the difference between actual values and predicted values and can be calculated with the following equation.

Residual or Error Term = Actual values − Predicted values

The collective sum of all errors or residual values of individual data points is called the sum of residuals or errors. The square mean of the entire sum of residuals is calculated for the cost function and gradient descent purposes in the linear regression algorithm.

Multiple linear regressions

Multiple linear regression is a very effective and more feature-encompassing type of regression algorithm. It can predict the relationship between a dependent variable in terms of more than one independent variable or predictor. This algorithm is used in supervised machine learning for regression tasks. It is a more advanced and featured algorithm than the simple linear regression algorithm discussed before.[81]

To develop a strong grip on the idea of the multiple linear regression algorithm, let us take an example in comparison with the simple linear algorithm. In the simple linear algorithm, there was only one independent variable or predictor that was used for establishing a regression-based relationship with a continuous value or dependent variable or an output value. For instance, in the simple linear algorithm, the education level as a single factor is considered as the base factor for getting a certain level of salary. But in a multiple linear algorithm, we can use education, experience, skills, expertise, and many other factors to predict or project the matching salary (continuous value).

The multiple linear algorithm has numerous advanced features and characteristics as compared to the simple linear algorithm. A few of them are mentioned below:[81,82]

- The multiple linear regression algorithm deals with complex problems in the forecast and prediction of the continuous value of a dependent variable with multiple independent variables or predictors to establish a complex relationship.
- There are three most important domains of applications of the multiple linear regression algorithm in modern fields:
  - **Relationship quantification** – With the help of correlation analysis, multiple linear algorithms can not only establish the quality of the values, such as negative/positive, upward/downward, good/bad, and others, but also can quantify the relationship in terms of the volume or value of the output based on multiple input independent variables or predictors.
  - **Value Prediction** – The capability of quantification of multiple linear algorithms helps establish a predicted output based on multiple input variables. This is one of the most common application categories of multiple linear algorithms.
  - **Forecasting** – The multiple linear regression algorithm is the forecasting of values, volumes, and projections of other factors based on the input values with time series analysis. It can incorporate two important techniques for forecasting, such as panel data regression and vector auto-regression.
- An example of a real-world relationship is the prediction of a house price in terms of different factors such as location, color, number of bedrooms, number of baths, type of people living in the surroundings, date of construction, and many other factors.
- The mathematical formula for calculating the relationship between multiple independent variables and a single continuous (dependent) variable is given below:

$$y = b_0 + b_1 x_1 + b_2 x_2 \cdots\cdots b_n x_n + \in$$

- The above equation is almost similar to the equation of a simple linear algorithm, except for additional independent variables such as $X_1, X_2 \cdots\cdots X_n$.
- The symbol $(\in)$ denotes the error term or residual of the independent variables.

- The symbols such as $b_0, b_1, b_2 \cdots\cdots b_n$ represent the regression coefficients, which are the slopes between independent and dependent variables with a certain change in the value of the independent or predictor value.
- A certain number of assumptions are incorporated into the formation of machine learning models based on multiple linear regression algorithms. The assumptions are mentioned in the following list.
  - A constant variance is assumed for all residuals.
  - The relationship between dependent and independent variables is linear.
  - All observations are not dependent on other observations in the model.
  - No strong relationship between variables exists.
  - Multivariate normality is followed by all variables.
- The multiple linear regression algorithm is extensively used in complex problems related to forecasting, predictions, control, and planning. It is also able to deal with non-linear problems by exploiting the multidimensional features and capabilities it possesses as compared to a simple linear regression algorithm.

Lasso regression

Least Absolute Shrinkage and Selection Operator, precisely referred to as LASSO, is a form of regression technique used in the modern machine learning field for solving the problems of overfitting in the results of different regression-based machine learning algorithms. This is a type of regression method that uses the "shrinkage" technique to reduce the overfitting of any regression-based ML algorithms. This method determines or shrinks the coefficients toward the center point of the regression lines in such a way that the overfitting problem can be averted. It is also called a regularization technique used in ML algorithms.[84]

The most common features and characteristics of lasso regression are:[83,84]

- It is one of the most effective regularization techniques used to reduce the increased polynomials in a regression equation to minimize the chances of overfitting in different types of regression algorithms.
- This technique determines those variables or predictors that are strongly related to the target variables or dependent variables.
- The number of variables in that makes the equation more confusing and complex. That also creates substantial overfitting in the results, which are discarded through this technique to make the regression equation less complex.
- There are two very important regularization techniques used in regression tasks in the machine learning field; one of them is LASSO, and the other is known as Ridge Regression.

- The LASSO method of equation regularization is also known as the penalized regression technique, in other words, to build a subset of variables that are important ones in the calculation of the regression output values.
- The LASSO regression generates higher prediction accuracy and increased interpretation of regression-based machine learning models.
- This regularization technique is highly suitable for those models that use a huge number of dimensions or features.
- The formula to describe the LASSO technique (D) is given below:

D = Residual sum of squares
+ λ × Aggregate of absolute values of coefficients

Here in this equation:
D = LASSO regularization
λ = Value of shrinkage (Range value 0 to ∞)

- R-Square and RMSE (Root Mean Square Error) metrics are commonly used in the LASSO regression shrinkage technique.
- The regularization used in the LASSO regression technique is known as L1 regularization, and that used in the Ridge regression is called L2 regularization.
- In L1 regularization, the value of the penalty added to the regression equation is equal to the absolute value of the magnitude of the coefficients; thus, the number of coefficients is reduced to build a sparse model.
- Those models that become equal to zero are discarded from the model. The larger values of the adopted penalty will make the coefficient values zero (which are closer to zero already).

The regularization technique based on LASSO regression shrinkage is very useful for those regression-based models that have a high level of multicollinearity. It is also very well-suited for the models in which certain parts of the model selection need to be automated, such as the auto-selection of the variables and the auto-elimination of the parameters.

Logistic regression

Logistic regression is a supervised machine learning algorithm used for both prediction and classification tasks. This statistical model is also referred to as a logit model in the field of data science. It is extensively used for categorical prediction with discrete values in most of the machine learning applications. It resembles linear regression hugely, with a major difference that it is used for both regression and classification tasks, especially the categorical classification of parameters. The most important uses of logistic regression are in classification tasks based on multiple independent variables to predict a dependent variable or target variable more accurately.[85,86]

There are numerous prediction applications in modern businesses that adopt the logistic regression algorithm, such as:

- Expense reduction algorithms in business organizations.
- Improvement in the ROI (Return on Investment) and profit margin projection.
- Optimization of inventory and demand forecasting in the market in terms of a wide range of factors that influence those objectives.
- Enhancement of marketing propensity and other models used for the improvement of effectiveness in marketing campaigns and strategies.
- Weather forecasting for all seasons.
- Risk assessment through multiple impact factors.
- Healthcare preventive action plans and healthcare risk assessment.
- Fraud detection applications and cyberattack predictions.

The use of logistic regression is very extensive in different applications across all businesses. The way it is used in different models generates results suitable for achieving customized objectives. To achieve different objectives, logistic regression is used in different ways, which are known as the types of logistic regression. There are three main types of logistic regression as listed below:

- Binary logistic regression.
- Multinomial logistic regression.
- Ordinal logistic regression.

All types of logistic regression use certain assumptions in their predictive as well as classification models, such as:

- There is no multicollinearity in the independent variables or predictors.
- The dependent variables are categorical or can be classified into discrete categories.

Multivariate regression algorithm

The multivariate regression algorithm is a supervised machine learning algorithm used for both prediction and classification tasks. As the name implies, this algorithm is designed to establish or predict the relationship between multiple independent variables and a dependent variable or output variable. The input variables are more than one, and the output variable is generated based on the impact of multiple input variables simultaneously in this type of machine learning algorithm. The main applications of this model include real estate cost predictions, sales projects, and many others. The calculation of cost factor in real estate, for instance, depends on numerous factors such as the conditions of the building, location, number of rooms, baths, covered areas, available amenities, and many other factors that directly impact the cost of a house.

The most important characteristics, capabilities, and features of the multivariate regression algorithm are listed below:[87]

- The workflow to use a multivariate model or algorithm is based on simple step-by-step activities, like:
  - Feature selection to be considered as independent variables.
  - Normalization of those features to be used in the model.
  - The selection of the loss function is crucial because this model uses a loss function for predictions.
  - Choosing the hypothesis to simplify the projections.
  - Fixing or varying the hypothesis and loss function reduction to achieve the optimal value to produce greater accuracy in predictions.
  - Finally, analysis of the hypothesis function by applying test data to check the results.
- There are two major categories of multivariate regression:
  - Multivariate linear regression.
  - Multivariate logistic regression.
- The multivariate linear regression is commonly used for predictive analysis or predictive results based on multiple input factors, while the multivariate logistic regression is used for classification purposes based on two conditions.
- There are certain assumptions made in multivariate linear regression:
  - A linear relationship exists between independent and dependent variables.
  - There is no strong correlation among the independent variables.
  - The selection of observation (Yi) is random among the population.
- Similarly, there are certain hypotheses assumed in the multivariate logistic regression models to produce classification, such as:
  - The independent variables can be either single or multiple in the form of continuous, ordinal, or nominal values simultaneously.
  - The dependent variable, or target output variable, can be in either ordinal or nominal form.
  - There is no strong correlation among the independent variables.
  - The dependent variables are assumed to remain mutually exhaustive and exclusive in nature.
- Multivariate regression algorithms are the most popular and simple in nature for establishing a relationship among multiple independent variables.
- They are prone to overfitting and complexity issues when the problem under consideration is complex with multiple parameters and features.
- These algorithms are not a good fit for smaller datasets. They are mostly used for huge datasets to generate accurate results in supervised machine learning.
- The most common examples of multivariate regression algorithms include principal component analysis (PCA) and common factor analysis (CFA).

Others

Regression is one of the most commonly used predictive analysis mechanisms in data science as well as modern machine learning fields, especially in supervised machine learning applications and models. The most common algorithms used in regression tasks have been discussed in the above-mentioned sub-sections. Other than these, there are a few other machine learning algorithms that are also used in regression tasks. Like, for instance:

- Ridge regression.
- Neural network regression.
- Decision tree regression.
- Gaussian regression.
- Polynomial regression.
- And others.

CLUSTERING ALGORITHMS

Clustering algorithms are those machine learning algorithms that are used for categorization of unlabeled datasets. These algorithms are designed for unsupervised machine learning that ingests unlabeled training datasets as well as testing datasets to generate automated outputs based on those algorithms to categorize the data points in clusters.[88]

There are many types of machine learning algorithms that are used for clustering tasks in unsupervised machine learning. A few very important ones are:

- Expectation Maximization Algorithm.
- Agglomerative Hierarchical Algorithm.
- K-Means Clustering Algorithm.
- Fuzzy C-Mean Algorithm.

The details of the above-mentioned machine learning algorithms for performing the clustering task are provided in the following subtopics:

Expectation maximization algorithm

The Expectation Maximization (EM) algorithm is a combination of algorithms that is used for the maximization of the likelihood of estimates of unobservable or latent variables in any unsupervised model of machine learning used for clustering tasks. In other words, it is a statistical algorithm that finds the local maximum likelihood parameters of a machine learning model. It can be used for both the observable and unobservable parameters in a model, especially the unobservable or latent parameters in a statistical model of unsupervised machine learning.

Let us explain it further: there are a huge number of parameters in a normal machine learning model, in which all those parameters (variables) are not observed, but a few of them are observed, and the others are predicted by using instances. The unobservable variables, those which are not observed in the standard clustering tasks, are not observed by using the instances, but they are observed by using the estimation maximization algorithm. This algorithm predicts the values of those parameters under the condition of determining the forms of probability distribution governing the latent or unobserved variables.

The most common and salient features and characteristics of an expectation maximization algorithm are:[89,90]

- Expectation maximization is a combination of multiple algorithms used for clustering tasks in unsupervised machine learning.
- This algorithm determines two major things for unobservable, variables as listed below:
  - Local maximum likelihood estimates (MLE).
  - Maximum A Posteriori probability (MAP) Estimates.
- It is also known as the latent variable model because it is used to find out the maximum likelihood estimation in a model where the presence of latent or unobservable variables is noticed for clustering tasks.
- This is a repetitive type of model that consists of sequential steps and continues till convergence is achieved.
- This model normally works with other unsupervised clustering algorithms such as K-means clustering, Gaussian Mixture Model (GMM), DBSCAN, and others based on density, distribution, centroid, and hierarchical models.
- The most common technical steps performed through this algorithm are identified as modes or steps, as listed below:
  - Expectation mode or step.
  - Maximization mode or step.
- In the expectation mode, the missing variables or latent variables are estimated.
- In the maximization mode, the maximization or optimization of the parameter values is accomplished so that the data can be explained more accurately and clearly.
- The entire workflow of the expectation maximization algorithm consists of four major phases as listed below:
  - Assigning the initial values to the parameters, and this process is referred to as initialization of parameters.
  - The second step is known as the estimation step, which is used to estimate the missing variables such that all parameters are known.
  - The third step is known as the maximization step, in which the local maximization of likelihood is accomplished by updating the whole data achieved in the second step to rationalize the hypothesis.

- The fourth step is known as the convergence verification step. If the values have converged, then the workflow ends, and if not, then the control of the flow returns to the second step, referred to as the estimation step.
- The matching of the values of two different given variables is known as convergence in this algorithm.
- The areas of machine learning fields in which the expectation maximization algorithm is extensively used include the following:
  - Natural language processing (NLP).
  - Structural engineering.
  - Data clustering tasks.
  - Image reconstruction.
  - Computer Vision (CV).
  - And others.
- The expectation maximization algorithm supports both forward probability and backward probability simultaneously, in contrast to numerical optimization functions that consider only forward probabilities.
- The typical real-world applications of the expectation maximization algorithm include healthcare engineering applications, mixture clustering models, quantitative genetics, virtual reality and augmented reality applications, and others.
- The complete working lifecycle of the expectation maximization algorithm is depicted in Figure 2.24.

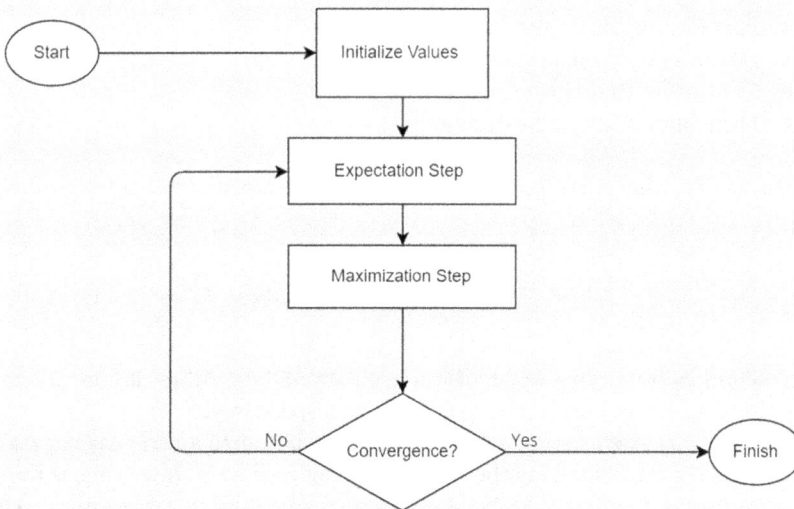

Figure 2.24 Workflow of expectation maximization algorithm.

As shown in Figure 2.24, the process of expectation maximization starts from the assignment of the initial values of the parameters in the kick-start step. In the second phase, the values of the unobserved or latent parameters whose values have been missed are guessed. This process is accomplished by updating the values of the variables. In the third step, the hypothesis is updated locally to find the maximized likelihood of parameters. The final step is designated to check and verify if the convergence in the values of the variables is being achieved or not. If it is achieved, the process ends here. The repetition of step 2 and step 3 is performed until convergence is achieved.

K-means clustering algorithm

The K-means clustering algorithm is one of the most powerful and extensively used machine learning algorithms for the unsupervised version of ML. It is used for clustering tasks for unsupervised training datasets. Before we deep-dive into the nitty-gritty of the K-means clustering algorithm, let us have a look at the technical background of this clustering algorithm.

Basically, there are different categories of clustering that are extensively deployed in clustering tasks for unsupervised machine learning. A few of them include the following:

- Hierarchical clustering.
- Non-hierarchical clustering.

The non-hierarchical clustering is further divided into different categories:

- Partitioning clustering.
- Density-based clustering.
- Centroid-based clustering.
- Distribution-based clustering.

Furthermore, the partitioning clustering is further divided into different formats or types, which are:

- K-means clustering algorithm.
- Fuzzy C-means clustering algorithm.

The details of both types of partitioning clustering algorithms are mentioned here in this section and in the next section, respectively.

In the K-means clustering algorithm, all data points in a problem space are divided into a predefined number of clusters, denoted by K. If we choose K=4, it means that there would be 4 clusters formed in this algorithm. The formation of clusters in this algorithm is based on the similarities in the characteristics of the data points.[94]

The other main characteristics, capabilities, and features of the K-means clustering algorithm are:[94,95]

- The working principle of the K-means clustering algorithm is the comparison of the features or characteristics of data points. Those data points that have similar features or characteristics are grouped together into one group. Thus, predetermined numbers of groups can be formed based on the comparative similarities in features of the data points.
- All data points have their unique identity of group. In other words, one data point can be a part of only one group, not part of two or more groups with some similarities in characteristics that match multiple groups.
- The letter "K" in the name of this algorithm denotes the number of clusters to be created initially. This number is provided by the data scientist to the system.
- After deciding the number of groups or K value, the algorithm randomly chooses two centroid points in the space of data points. These random points are not the real centers but are taken arbitrarily or randomly at any point in the space.
- The data points are individually grouped by measuring the distance between the nearest centroid points. The distance between a data point and both the centroids is measured. The smaller distance will be considered as the nearest point to add a data point to it. Thus, all data points are aligned to their respective centroid points.
- The second activity of this algorithm is the convergence of every cluster by finding the real centroids of each group. This can be done by calculating the distance of all points and the central point iteratively. Once the centroid moves in some direction, the reallocation of the data points is to be calculated to make sure that no point has changed its position in such a way that it also changs the characteristics of that particular group. If the distance of a particular point has changed in such a way that it should be added to another group, that point is added to the new group.
- This process continues changing through repositioning and relocation of the data points till the groups converge or saturate, and no changes in the centroid are observed anymore, and no relocation of points occurs.
- The most common applications of the K-means algorithm in the field of machine learning include the following:
  - Healthcare diagnostic systems.
  - Web search engines.
  - Academic performance evaluation.
  - Wireless-based sensor networks.
- The most common mathematical formulas used for calculating the distance between two data points and centroids include:

- Squared Euclidean distance matrix.
- Euclidean distance matrix.
- Cosine distance matrix.
- Manhattan distance matrix.

How does the K-means clustering algorithm work?

To have a deeper perspective on this algorithm, let us have a look at Figure 2.25, which shows the lifecycle of a single iteration of algorithm processing.

The K-means matrix uses a predefined number of clusters identified by the data scientists and fed to the algorithm to consider. The K values are also known as randomized centroid data points. Initially, it is selected randomly by the algorithm, and then the entire group or cluster is converged to the real centroid point of the cluster. This is done by using the expectation maximization technique discussed before.

In Figure 2.25, there are various data points that are to be clustered in two groups because the value of K is set as 2. The first step of the K-means clustering algorithm is to assign two centroids randomly. The random allocation of centroids for both clusters is shown as colored squares in Figure 2.26.

After the definition of the centroids of both of the centroids, the distances between the two centroids and every data point are measured through different formulas, as mentioned earlier. Any data point that is nearest to any of the two centroids is added to that group or cluster. Thus, two non-overlapping and unique groups are formed as shown in the figure.

The next step in the K-means algorithm is the convergence of clusters, or groups of data points. This is done by using expectation maximization rules, in which the average mean value of the data points in the existing group is calculated, and the centroid is shifted according to that value. Once the

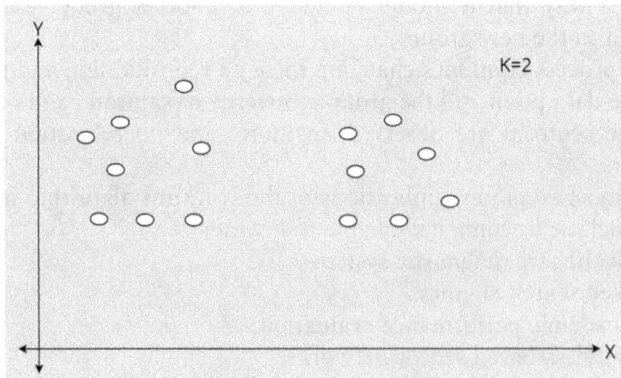

Figure 2.25 Data points to be clustered in two main groups.

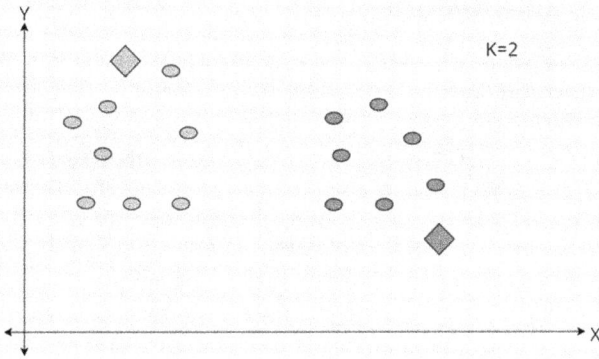

Figure 2.26 Random identification of centroids.

position of the centroid is relocated, the distances of different data points to the centroid also change. This may change the formation of the clusters. Another iteration of re-measuring the distances with respect to both centroids is accomplished, and any data point having dissimilar characteristics is shifted to the other cluster. Again, the relocation of the centroid is calculated. If the centroid again shifts to some other location, the re-measurement of data point distances is done, and this process continues till no difference in distances is achieved and there is no need for any relocation of the centroid or central points, as shown in Figure 2.27.

This situation, in which both clusters settle with no additional changes, is called the convergence of the clustering. This is the final classification of the data points done through the K-means clustering algorithm in unsupervised machine learning.

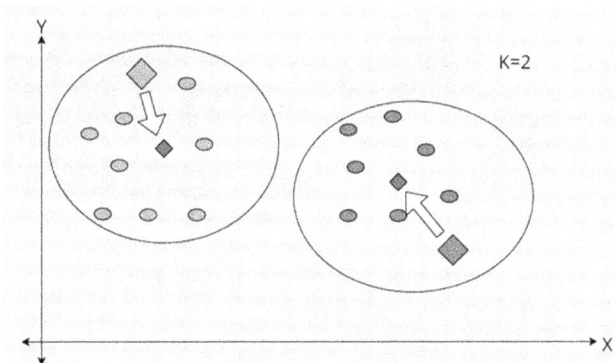

Figure 2.27 Final converged clusters after relocation of centroids.

Fuzzy C-means algorithm

Fuzzy C-Means, precisely referred to as the FCM algorithm, is a type of clustering technique used in the unsupervised machine learning field. This algorithm is also known as soft clustering and the soft-means algorithm. This algorithm is based on the principle of fuzzy logic. As the name implies, the association of the data points is very vague or uncertain in different clusters at the initial level. The fuzzy logic assigns the membership level to every data point for every cluster under consideration in the subject problem.[96]

In contrast to the hard threshold clustering techniques like K-means and others, the Fuzzy C-means algorithm uses loose or soft rules to assign the membership to every data point available in the data point space in terms of percentage for all clusters under consideration in the problem. In other words, each data point of the space is associated with each cluster in the problem solution. The association of a data point with a particular cluster is described in terms of percentage. The data point that is closer to the center of a cluster has a larger value of association or membership for that cluster as compared to those clusters whose centroids are farther.

This is a very important type of machine learning algorithm with numerous features and characteristics that make it more useful than other competitor algorithms. A few of those features and capabilities of the Fuzzy C-means algorithm are listed below:[96,97,98]

- In the Fuzzy C-means algorithm, all data points are added as members of all clusters used for unsupervised machine learning applications.
- The value of each data point determining its association with a particular cluster ranges from 0 to 1 or from 0% to 100%. The greater the percentage of association, the closer the data point is to that particular cluster, and vice versa.
- The number of clusters is determined by data scientists based on the nature and complexity of the raw data under consideration. The number of clusters should always be greater than 1 to initialize the iterations for optimization.
- The types of settings that are implemented manually by the data scientists include the number of iterations for optimization, fuzzy overlapping, the improvement value between two successive iterations, and a few others.
- The Fuzzy C-mean clustering analysis was proposed by J.C. Dunn in 1973, and later on, another data scientist, J.C. Bezdek, improved it significantly in 1981.
- The workflow of the Fuzzy C-means algorithm is based on the following simple sequential steps:
  - Selection of a suitable value for N, which denotes the number of clusters to consider for solving the problem (it should be greater than 1).

- Randomized assignment of coefficient values to each data point for each cluster under consideration. The assignment of a value is known as an objective function, which determines the weighted membership value in correspondence with the distance between a data point and the centroid of a cluster.
- The algorithm calculates the centroids for each cluster in the present conditions to relocate the centroid to the real position.
- The Fuzzy C-means algorithm calculates the values that determine the grade of association of that particular data point to a particular cluster. This calculation will change the landscape and data point values of all factors in the ML space. The new values of the association grade will appear for every data point, and also the chances of changes in the centroid position.
- The calculation of the centroid and values of the grade of association with clusters on each data point is repeated again and again to achieve the convergence of clusters at the most optimal level, from where further optimization is not possible under the predefined threshold value of changes between two iterations.
- The schematic presentation of the above-mentioned step-by-step sequential workflow of the Fuzzy C-Means algorithm is shown in Figure 2.28.
- The most important applications of the Fuzzy C-means algorithm in modern industries include the following fields:

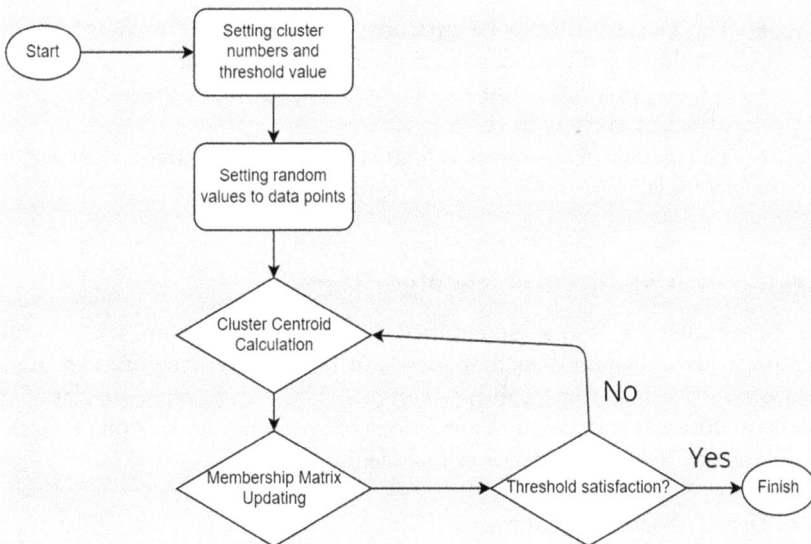

Figure 2.28 Workflow of the Fuzzy C-means algorithm.

- Image and video analysis applications.
- Biometrics and facial recognition apps.
- Digital marketing and retail services.
- Cybersecurity, defense, and national security.
- The number of N, which denotes the number of clusters, also determines the degree of fuzziness of the algorithm. Normally, the value of N is chosen between 2 and 10. The greater the value of N, the greater will be the degree of fuzziness of the solution because a large number of clusters would make all data points much closer to all centroids as compared to a smaller number of "N".
- Fuzzy C-Means runs comparatively slower than competitors like K-means because of the fact that a huge amount of processing work is involved in calculating both the centroid value and the grade of membership of data points with other clusters.
- This algorithm is also sometimes nicknamed "less stupid" than hard association algorithms used in the unsupervised machine learning field.
- This algorithm uses different measures and algorithms, like many other unsupervised machine learning algorithms, as mentioned below:
  - The measurement of the variance analysis coefficient for every cluster.
  - Different entropy-based measuring methods can be used.
  - Two major methods for statistical measurement include Silhouette and Elbow methods, which are most commonly used in it.
  - A homogeneity analysis is assumed for all clusters formed under this algorithm.
  - The clusters should be properly separated from each other and should be homogeneous in their nature of content.
  - F-score, precision, and recall can be considered if the ground truth values of clusters have been achieved.
  - The quality of clusters is validated by using the Pearson Correlation formula.

Agglomerative hierarchical algorithm

Before we dive into the agglomerative hierarchical algorithm, let us recall our previous understanding that there are four major categories of algorithms used in clustering problem solutions. Those categories are classified based on different statuses, and conditions of groupings of data points in the dataset space. The four categories include:

- Density-based algorithms.
- Centroid-based algorithms.
- Distribution-based algorithms.
- Hierarchical-based algorithms.

The agglomerative algorithm falls under the category of hierarchical-based algorithms. There are two main types of hierarchical-based algorithms that are mentioned below:

- Agglomerative algorithm.
- Divisive algorithm.

The agglomerative algorithm is very important and most commonly used in modern unsupervised machine learning models for clustering tasks. Now, it is very clear to dig into the details of the agglomerative algorithm after an overview of the background. Agglomerative hierarchical algorithms are used in clustering analysis applications that use a hierarchy like a tree and its branches. It builds a hierarchical structure that looks like a tree and acts on the principle of *bottom-up*. That is why it is also known as hierarchical agglomerative clustering, precisely HAC.

In this algorithm, each single data point is considered as a separate cluster at the start of clustering analysis, and then starts merging similar types of data points to form bigger clusters, and thus moes on to form even bigger clusters. This process continues until a single unified cluster is achieved. This is the reason that it is known as an agglomerative clustering algorithm. This combining process of clusters occurs in the format of two pairs of clusters or branches in a sequential order of increasing hierarchy.

The main features and characteristics of the hierarchical agglomerative clustering algorithm are summarized in the following list:[91,92]

- This algorithm of clustering analysis is based on a bottom-up approach in which all single data points are considered as separate clusters, and then two similar clusters are agglomerated to form a higher-order cluster. This process continues till a single comprehensive or agglomerative cluster is achieved.
- The matrix used to assess the similarities between two points or clusters is called the distance matrix. The minimum distance between two data points is considered the most similar to each other in this analysis.
- The other matrices used in calculating distances are listed below:
  - Min distance matrix.
  - Max distance matrix.
  - Ward's matrix.
  - Group average distance matrix.
- This algorithm may become very slow as the volume of data increases; subsequently, the number of clusters at the initial stage increases tremendously, which leads to a very complex system that slows down the process.
- The working process involves a few sequential steps as mentioned below:
  - Each data point is defined as a separate cluster.
  - Two of the closest ones are merged to make a combined cluster.
  - This step to merge nearby data points continues until one single unified cluster of all data points is achieved.

- The determination of the optimal number of clusters can be accomplished through a procedure applied to a dendrogram representing the merger of clusters in an agglomerative hierarchical algorithm.
- The procedure to determine the optimal number of clusters involves a few simple steps, as mentioned below:
  - On a dendrogram of the agglomerative hierarchical algorithm representation, find out the maximum vertical distance that does not intersect any additional number of lines at any point of distance. There should be the same number of clusters as the maximum vertical distance cuts.
  - To achieve this, draw two horizontal lines that pass through the extreme points of the maximum vertical line that cuts the same number of cluster lines.
  - The number of optimal clusters is the lines that pass vertically through those horizontal lines during the maximum vertical distance, as shown in Figure 2.29.
- In Figure 2.29, the maximum vertical distance where the number of cluster lines remains the same is the vertical distance between two horizontal lines, line A and line B (see the connecting line between them). You can see, this is the maximum distance that can be achieved in this dendrogram at any point between two horizontal lines. Now, count the number of lines (similar to the line shown between line A and line B) that are cut by the horizontal lines. That number of lines is the optimal number of clusters in this agglomerative hierarchical clustering.

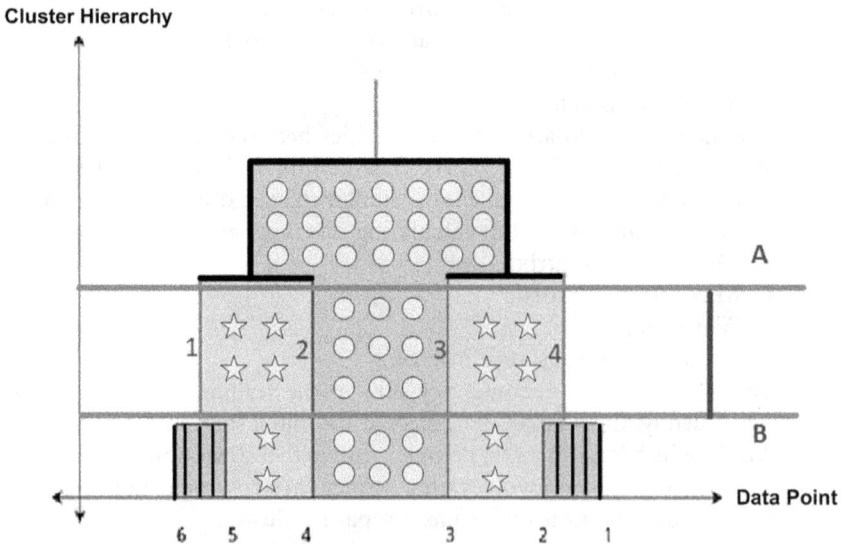

Figure 2.29 Dendrogram to find the optimal number of clusters.

In our case, the number of optimal clusters is 4, as marked with the digits from 1 to 4.

- This algorithm is also referred to as the AGNES (Agglomerative Nesting) algorithm, which is short for the agglomerative nesting algorithm, because it nests different clusters within a larger cluster and continues this method for more and more clusters.
- There are four different criteria used for linking the two adjacent clusters with respect to the distance between them, as listed below:
  - **Single linkage** – In this type of linkage criterion, two points within a cluster are the closest to the other single point distance of other clusters. In other words, the clusters in which the distance between two nearest points is minimum are merged together to form a new cluster.
  - **Complete linkage** – In this criterion, the longest distance between two points in two clusters is considered for complete linkage or merger.
  - **Average linkage** – In this criterion, the average distance between each point of one cluster to every data point in the other cluster is considered, as the core component or criterion for average linkage.
  - **Ward linkage** – The squared distances of each cluster are calculated and then subtracted from the same between two cluster values. The result is the criteria value for the ward linkage process.
- The most important matrices, or mathematical formulas, used for calculating the distance between two data points are:
  - Euclidean distance formula.
  - Manhattan distance formula.

Divisive hierarchical algorithm

The divisive hierarchical algorithm is another type of hierarchical algorithm group. It is the opposite of the agglomerative algorithm described in the above section. In this algorithm, all the data points in a single problem space are considered as one unified cluster. Then those are divided into smaller groups on the basis of their dissimilarities or disparities.

Divisive hierarchical algorithm is also referred to as DIANA, which is a combined word of the short forms of two words: divisive (DI) and analysis (ANA). The combination of the short forms of "divisive" and "analysis" becomes DIANA. It is also known as the inverse agglomerative hierarchical algorithm for clustering purposes in unsupervised machine learning. The working principle of this algorithm is based on a top-down approach. The principle to find out the optimal number of clusters in this algorithm is also the same as in the agglomerative hierarchical algorithm, in which the maximum distance is found between a range of clusters in such a way that the dendrogram explains it clearly, as was done in the agglomerative algorithm (previously presented).[93]

The simple procedure to carry out the splitting of a cluster is to calculate the sum of the squared errors (SSE) of each data point in a cluster. The data points with the maximum value of the sum of the squared errors are grouped together into a separate cluster or group. Now, this process is repeated for every cluster that comes into existence after the splitting of the previous node or cluster. The initial cluster is known as the root cluster, and the other clusters are known as nodes. The last clusters that are not further divided (because the optimal number of clusters is achieved) are known as branch nodes. Those branch nodes are the final outputs of a problem in this algorithm. Ward's criterion is extensively used in the splitting of clusters in divisive hierarchical algorithms.

Chapter 3

Understanding data, datasets, and training for ML

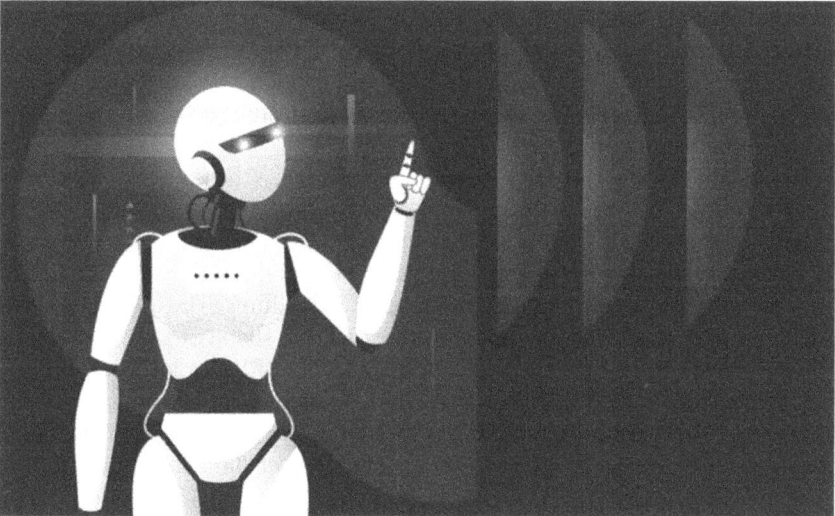

DOI: 10.1201/9781003688327-3

CONCEPT OF MACHINE TRAINING

The concept of machine training is based on the broader concept of machine learning, as discussed in the previous chapter at length. Machine learning is a process to make computers or machines learn and act like human brains do. Training a machine is a part of the machine learning process in which multiple stages are involved, such as building a training model, developing machine learning algorithms to handle input data and processing it, testing the capabilities of the machine that has taken and processed the data to produce human-like output or intelligence, and feeding back to enhance and improve the learning process. The most important part of the machine learning field is the training provided to the machines through real-world data, learning algorithms, and models. The training part of machine learning is called machine training. In technical terms, machine training in the field of artificial intelligence is about infusing real-world data in the form of different types of content into the intelligent machines in such a way that the desired objectives of the machine learning process are produced by the computers under some training processes.[99]

Let us understand the concept with an example. When a kid is born, it is almost unaware of the environments, procedures, languages, behaviors, or other aspects of our lives, as well as our social activities. It is then trained by parents, teachers, environments, and other factors through its experience of dealing with real-world data, activities, and procedures. The data that is fed through parents, such as making it understand the shape of a mango, apple, or different toys, is a part of the training process. When a kid gets training and makes informed decisions based on their experience and training in the real world, they become an intelligent human. In the same way, machines are also trained to make decisions based on the input data through different training datasets fed to different machine learning models governed by machine learning algorithms to learn and make decisions. When machines get sufficient training from the data ingested in different forms of content, it is tested with test data to assess the level of learning or training of the machines. A trained computing machine or computer system that can make correct decisions based on the training it got through different models is known as an artificial intelligence system.

The main features and characteristics of machine training used in the modern artificial intelligence (AI) field are summarized below:[99,100]

- A training dataset, commonly referred to as a training model, is used for training the computers to learn and make intelligent decisions.
- The training dataset ingested into the machine learning algorithm is in the form of text, images, videos, voices, sensors, and others.
- The training data is processed through machine learning algorithms to achieve sufficient sense so that the unknown test data can be recognized and a suitable response or decision can be made by the machines automatically.

- Training the machines is an iterative process that continues for huge volumes of data so that machines can understand the real-world environments. This repetitive process is also known as model fitting in the machine learning (ML) training ecosystem.
- In other words, machine training can also be described as the process of feeding machine learning algorithms real-world data in different forms of content to help machines learn about the features and values of the data to make decisions.
- The training of computer machines can be done through four major machine learning models, as mentioned below:
  - Supervised machine learning.
  - Unsupervised machine learning.
  - Semi-supervised machine learning.
  - Reinforcement machine learning.
- Two types of data formats are fed into the machine learning models to train them – labeled data and unlabeled data.

WHAT ARE DATASETS?

The concept of training machines or intelligent processing systems described in the above topic is fully dependent on huge volumes of data to be fed to those machines for learning about the problem under consideration. The huge volumes of data that are used for the entire training process of artificial machines are called the dataset. The datasets are formed in different classes based on the types of models and the algorithms that govern those models. The most common form of dataset is the basic unit of data that can be used for the training purpose of a machine. The training process of a machine learning model consists of three major stages, as listed below:[102]

- Training or fitting the ML model.
- Testing the model for performance and accuracy.
- Validating the model to render it ready-to-use.

All of the above-mentioned three phases or stages are accomplished through different types of datasets, which are listed below, respectively:

- Training datasets.
- Testing datasets.
- Validating datasets.

All of those datasets are subsets of the original dataset used for machine learning purposes. In other words, the dataset consists of all three formats of datasets used for training, testing, and validating purposes, and is a subset of the original datasets. The testing datasets and validating datasets are sometimes used interchangeably because both of them are the tools used to check

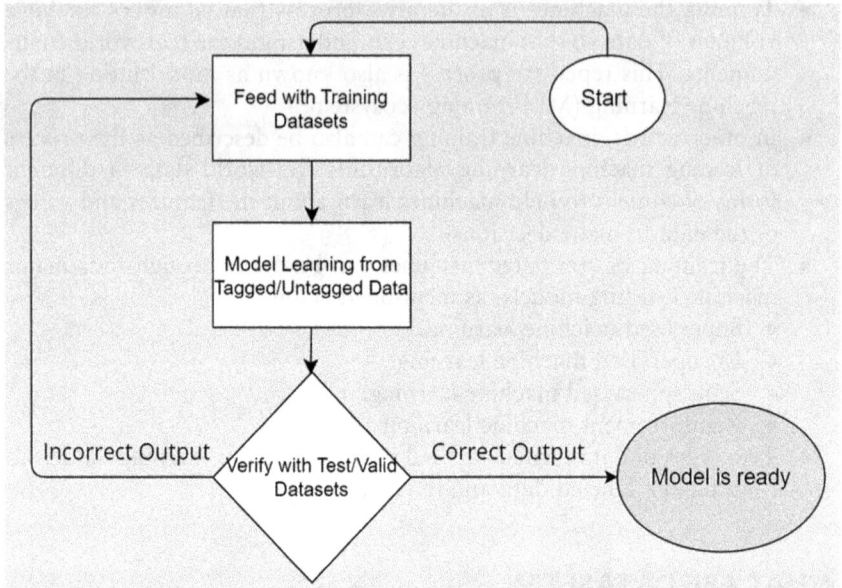

Figure 3.1 Workflow of ML training with datasets.

and verify the performance and accuracy of the model after going through the first phase of machine training by feeding training datasets in bulk volumes. The workflow of the entire machine training process, in terms of different types of datasets used in the training, is shown in Figure 3.1.[101]

The training process in machine learning starts with the creation of a machine learning model with the desired output and the right selection of the type of machine learning. The next step is the feeding of the datasets in the form of training datasets to the ML model. The training datasets may be either tagged datasets or unlabeled ones, depending on the type of ML model used. If the supervised machine learning type is chosen, the labeled training datasets are required to be fed into the machine learning model; otherwise, the untagged training datasets are used in the second phase. The next phase is testing the performance and accuracy of the model it learned through experience and observations made from the training datasets. If the results are satisfactory or accurate, the model will be further verified through validation training datasets, which are the primary versions of the testing datasets and are commonly used to fine-tune and tweak the model to verify if the model is free from any kind of major errors, overfitting, or any other problems.

The last stage of this entire process is the final testing of the machine learning model. In this stage, the entire model is checked and verified in terms of the desired results and tolerance levels in terms of result accuracy and performance. If all parameters of the model are as per the required criteria, the model is rendered as ready-to-use. In such conditions, when the model is performing accurately as it was desired to perform, the machine is rendered as ready to be deployed for the solutions of real-world problems. The testing datasets are frequently used to test the performance of the model during the process of training, too. The final confirmation of the model to render valid is done through final testing on testing datasets. Thus, it can be said that the testing datasets can be used for both testing and validating purposes with a little variation or modification.

The training dataset is more than 80% of the original data, while the testing data is about 20% or even less in certain cases. Normally, the ratio between training and testing datasets is used in three different denominations, such as 70/30, 80/20, and 90/10. The details of all types of datasets described in this section are mentioned below at length:

Training datasets

The training dataset is the subset of the original dataset used for feeding the model in different formats to train the machine learning model. The training data can be either labeled or unlabeled, depending on the types of machine learning adopted in the ML models. The training dataset is the biggest part of the original dataset. It is always more than 60% of the total or original data required for the entire training, testing, and validating process of the model.[103]

Other important features and characteristics of training datasets are mentioned in the following list:[102,103]

- It is the largest set of data. The AI field has grown significantly because of the availability of huge volumes of data generated through different sources in modern information and communication systems.
- The higher the training dataset volume that is fed into the ML models, the better and more reliable the results will be.
- The training data normally comprises two parameters: Either a vector or a scalar as an input parameter and its corresponding output parameter, which may be either a vector or a scalar value commonly known as the target value.
- The observations and experience developed in the machine learning model are based on the training datasets, not the other ones. If the level of accuracy is not achieved by fitting the model with a certain volume of training datasets, more training datasets are fed to develop more understanding through further experience and observations.
- If a model fitted with training datasets develops issues such as overfitting, errors, and other uneven problems, more training and regularization techniques are used to tweak the model to produce the desired results through feeding more training datasets.

- The quality of training datasets plays a very important role in developing a reliable and satisfactorily performing model. It works on the principle of garbage in – garbage out.
- The main features of a good training dataset include the following:[101]
  - **Relevance** – The training data must be highly relevant to the problem that is being solved through the ML model.
  - **Consistency** – The similar attributes of data points should always be linked to the similar labels of the data.
  - **Uniformity** – The data should be taken with uniform attributes from the same or similar types of sources to maintain uniformity.
  - **Comprehensiveness** – This quality deals with the hugeness or volume of the data that can cover all aspects of data points to be used in the solution of the problem through accurate and reliable prediction.
- A few examples of different sources of datasets used in modern business applications include the following:
  - Public government datasets.
  - Open datasets.
  - Natural language processing datasets.
  - Audio datasets.
  - Video datasets.
  - Image datasets.
  - Healthcare datasets.
- Training datasets are always the largest portion of the ML project as compared to other types of datasets, such as test and validation datasets.
- Different formats, such as labeled and unlabeled training datasets, are used for ingesting into the machine learning models for supervised and unsupervised machine learning models, respectively.

Validating datasets

Validating datasets is another major part of a machine learning model used for training artificial systems or machines. This is about 20% of the total volume of the dataset used in the entire training process of an ML model. The validating datasets are used to check or assess the systems during the training process to know about the performance and accuracy of the system. It is also used to check if the system is not suffering from any kind of errors related to overfitting or underfitting that may lead to inaccurate results of the training. With the help of validating datasets, different ad hoc measures or rules can be implemented to overcome the shortcomings of the model during training. It is very important to note that many kinds of fluctuations and glitches happen during the course of machine training, which need to be addressed to streamline the machine training process. This course correction is done after validating the system's learning accuracy and then deploying corrective measures in the training process. The most important corrective measures deployed in the modern training models are:[103]

- Regularization.
- Cross-validation technique.
- Early stopping of the training process.

Testing datasets

Testing datasets are one of the three most important datasets used in the training or fitting of machine learning models. This dataset is used to verify the final performance and accuracy of the model before deploying it in the real-world environment for practical applications. The testing datasets would account for about 20% of the volume of the datasets used in the entire project of the machine fitting process. This is also known as the final testing of the model to verify that all functions and features of the model are as per the requirements of the project. As mentioned earlier, the training datasets are fed to the machines for fitting purposes, and validating datasets are used to check the performance and accuracy of the model during the training process. Certain corrections are also made to set the right course for the training model. The testing datasets are used to finally test and verify the accuracy and performance in light of the set goals of the project and functionalities.

CONTENT USED IN DATASETS

All three types of datasets mentioned in the previous topic are very crucial for the modern machine learning field for fitting the artificial systems to learn from the experience and observations. The datasets are created from numerous types of data available in the real-world environment. The most important domains of data types that are commonly used in modern machine learning can be classified into two major categories:

- Structured datasets.
- Unstructured datasets.

The structured data can easily be used by any computer program or human brain for direct processing purposes because it is in a well-defined and formatted structure. There is no need for any additional processing to make it understandable to the machines. The unstructured data is in the shape of unstructured and undefined rules and formulas; thus, it would require certain preprocessing steps before being ingested into the machines for training purposes. The details of both types of data are mentioned in the following topics at length.

STRUCTURED DATA

The structured data is the type of data that is well-standardized in terms of formats, consistency, structure, flow, compliance with data models, easy accessibility, intuitive understandability, and efficient processing by both machines and humans. The most common features of structured data include the following:[104,105]

- The structured data is highly organized and useful through different programs and human interactions with it.
- It is normally stored in relational databases or other formats that are easy to pull and use instantly.
- The structured data is about 20% of the entire data in the world. It is also a basic foundation of modern technology referred to as big data.
- Structured data is either generated by machines or modern systems or by sifting through the process of structuring the data by humans in different formats.
- Finding the results by using structured data is more accurate and more beneficial for all types of businesses across the globe. This is the reason that the structured data generated by the modern systems and online activities is considered the most precious and valuable not only for the merchant businesses but also for other domains such as governments, defense, security, and many others.
- Structured data can directly and effectively be ingested into the machines through simple computer programs to operate and respond to the queries without any further training or fitting process at all.
- It is compatible with different data models due to its nature as an identifiable structure.
- All attributes and characteristics of the data are properly understood and well defined in their respective tables or formats.
- Different characteristics, features, and attributes are classified and stored in proper groups without any confusion to understand, access, or utilize.
- Allows faster accessing and processing for any kind of problem analysis and finding the respective solutions.
- This data is mostly stored in relational databases for easy access through SQL queries at any time in predefined structures.
- The main sources of structured data in modern businesses include the following:
  - Communication transactions online.
  - Telephone and system logs.
  - Web logs and online shopping.
  - Point of sale details.
  - Banking and financial transactions.
  - Governmental information.
  - Sensor data in different fields.

- Social security personal information.
- Surveys and click-stream activities.
- The ratio of structured data as compared to the unstructured data is continuously dropping due to exponential growth in the unstructured data. It is also very important to note that at present, as much as about 0.5% of the unstructured data is used for analysis to skim business value (from it) nowadays.

CATEGORIES OF STRUCTURED DATA

Structured data is fully organized and properly defined, requiring no further explanation or any other automated process to make machines or software programs understand the meaning of that data or information. The structured information can be directly accessed and used by any simple software application, rather than a huge machine, as is done in the case of unstructured data, where the machines are made to understand and learn the meaning of the data available in unorganized formats. The most important categories, their respective types, and formats of structured data used in modern machine learning and artificial intelligence applications include:

- Quantitative or numeric data.
- Qualitative or categorical data.
- Multivariate or tabular data.

All of the above-listed categories of structured data have even more types of structured data as described in the following sections:

QUANTITATIVE OR NUMERIC DATA

This category of structured data relates to the values in numbers. The numbers can represent a wide range of units commonly used in our day-to-day business and social lives. The examples of such representations include age, price, temperature, length, distance, height, time, weight, and many other similar kinds of units to show the quantities. This category is further divided into two other types:

- Continuous data.
- Discrete data.

Continuous data

The continuous data is in the form of numbers that have value in decimals and fractions. These numbers with decimal values are normally used to express or present the value of a house, profit, sales price, inflation rate, and other similar kinds of quantities. The continuous data provides accuracy of the data at a higher level. The most important forms of continuous data in digital and mathematical fields are known as analog or sinusoidal presentations, respectively.

Discrete data

The discrete data refers to the whole numbers without any fractions or decimals. The discrete values are also used in modern digital systems and logical presentations. Continuous data is used to represent different types of quantities, such as the population of a city, households in a country, the number of Facebook friends, and other similar types of representations.

QUALITATIVE OR CATEGORICAL DATA

The qualitative data is also referred to as categorical data. As the name suggests, this category of data relates to the expression of the values in subjective formats or in the forms of groups, categories, or classes. For instance, the review of a website is either average, bad, or good, and the birthplace of a person will be the name of a country, and other similar types of presentations – these are known as qualitative or categorical data. The qualitative data can further be classified into different types as mentioned below:

- Ordinal data.
- Nominal data.
- Unique data.

Ordinal data

The ordinal data is associated with a number of presentations or data points with a sequential order to describe the quality of that category. This is a definite number, which means that the data points or categories are of fixed numbers, and they cannot be unlimited or indefinite. The examples of ordinal data categories include the performance of an application rating, which can be either bad, good, or average, but it cannot be indefinite. As we look at the order of the rating, we will find that "bad" is the lowest category, "average" is the middle level, and "good" is the upper level of rating of the performance of an application. The other examples of finite and ordinal data include the grading of students in a class, ratings of an Internet service company, performance of employees, quality of air, taste of a food, and so on.

Nominal data

The nominal data pertains to the information of any category of an entity. This data does not have any comparative order or a particular sequential order. The nominal data is also definite in the number of classes or presentations. The most common examples of presentation of classes or categories of nominal data include the country of birth, names of schools a person has studied, the degrees of education a person has achieved, and so on.

Unique data

As the name of this data type indicates, the category presented in it is unique or exclusive in such a way that any other entity cannot be attributed with the same data or information. This data type is also defined in categories, but the number of categories can be extremely large, too. The examples of this data type include the unique ID of products in a store, the area codes of a country, the unique postal or PIN codes of different localities, and many others. The unique data can be expressed or coded in numbers as well as letters, either individually or collectively.

MULTIVARIATE OR TABULAR DATA

The tabular form of data consists of multivariate data that may include multiple types of data forms and categories in tabular form to present different attributes of an entity. Multivariate or tabular data can be in different classes and categories, such as ordinal values, nominal values, unique IDs, and even other formats. The tabular format of data establishes the relationship between different attributes, corresponding data values, and the main entity under consideration for a data analysis. The example includes a unique ID of a product whose attributes are in a tabular format, such as the number of items sold per month, average profit per month, the user reviews analysis, and other similar kinds of attributes associated with a particular unique product in a store. This consists of all types of data in a single table describing the analysis of a unique product.

UNSTRUCTURED DATA

Unstructured data is not in an organized format that can easily be understood through a software program or application by a machine that uses the power of a software application or machine learning model. The unstructured data can be in all formats, shapes, and manifestations that are not organized under relational databases to easily access, understand, and build a required response against any kind of query made through structured or unstructured requests to the machines through software applications.

Unstructured data can be in a wide range of formats, such as numbers, alphabet letters, images, videos, unstructured signals, sensory inputs, voices, noises, light, heat, and others. The most important categories of unstructured data that are used to form training and testing datasets for ingestion into the machine learning models are listed below:

- Text datasets.
- Audio datasets.
- Video datasets.
- Image datasets.
- Sensory datasets.

The most common features and characteristics of unstructured data that are used to form different types of training and testing datasets in machine learning and artificial intelligence applications are listed below:[106]

- It is not properly defined to identify the structure and attributes of the data without any human intervention.
- It does not conform to any model of data presentation, so that a definite analysis of the entire data can be made.
- There is no organized pattern of storage of this data, and it can be stored in any logical way the owner deems right.
- This type of data is not feasible to fit into any database structure.
- The software programs cannot access, understand, and use it easily without any support of either human intervention or machine learning models.
- It is not very fit for the mainstream relational databases used in modern software and computer applications.
- There is no regular or predefined semantic, rule, format, sequence, or organization to be known with.
- The most common sources of unstructured data include memos, MS PPTs (Microsoft PowerPoint files), MS Word documents, survey reports, research reports, raw images and videos, voice files in different formats, webpages, and many others of similar kinds.
- The most important benefits offered by the unstructured data include huge volumes of data useful for machine learning purposes, flexible data to be stored and processed in any format, a high level of scalability, the capability to deal with the heterogeneity of data sources, huge hidden business intelligence, and much more.
- It is comparatively difficult to manage through automated computerized processes due to difficulties in indexing, being prone to errors, and security risks.
- The most common types of unstructured database storage include content-addressable storage systems (CAS), XML formats, and binary large objects (BLOBs) supporting relational database management systems (RDBMS).

All of the above-mentioned datasets are formed from unstructured data available in our real world in the forms of videos, images, voices, texts, and sensory data through different modern equipment powered by computer vision, augmented reality, virtual reality, and other fields of technology extensively used in today's world.

Text datasets

Text data is a very important type of unstructured data available in the real-world environment in different forms and formats. The text data can be processed and analyzed to skim business intelligence from it automatically through computers if they are properly fitted with the unstructured text through certain machine learning models, both supervised and unsupervised types. The text can be in different formats, such as pen-written, typed, scanned images, transcriptions, books, articles, blogs, website content, social media text, and many others. Text is considered the key for all modern business processes, extensively used in digital information systems such as digital marketing, search engine optimization, sales, promotions, training, blogs, and many other activities. The useful content is regarded as the most fundamental component to produce a high level of return on interest (ROI) in modern digital business ecosystems.

The processing of text for achieving automated business intelligence (BI) and other useful outcomes in machine learning (ML) or artificial intelligence (AI) fields is dealt with under the sub-domain known as natural language processing, also referred to as NLP. The NLP field is also capable of handling not only text but also the voices in speech or music forms. The most important applications of NLP in machine learning include:[107]

- Information extraction.
- Sentiment analysis.
- Machine translation.
- Speech transcription.
- Automated response generation.

There are huge sources of text data available for use in machine learning applications. Some of those sources are commercial, while the others are open-source projects. The most common platforms from which the data in the form of text can be obtained for machine learning projects are mentioned in the following list:[108]

- University of California, Irvine (UCI) machine learning repository.
- Kaggle datasets for machine learning projects.
- Governmental datasets shared by many countries, such as India, New Zealand, Australia, European Union countries, and others.
- Amazon's datasets, which are registries of open data on AWS (Amazon Web Services).

- Google's Dataset Search Engine.
- And many others.

The formation of a text dataset for machine learning can vary from model to model, especially from supervised machine learning models to unsupervised machine learning models. The formation of text datasets for supervised machine learning in the natural language processing domain includes different steps, like:[107]

- Language identification.
- Tokenization of words.
- Sentence breaking.
- Lemmatization or stemming of words.
- Parts of speech labeling.
- Chunking or light parsing.
- Syntax parsing function.
- Sentence chaining.

The details of these processes will be covered in the next chapter while diving deeper into the machine learning dataset formation and related activities. The collection of data from different social media platforms, such as Facebook, Twitter, Instagram, and many other platforms, provides enterprises with a great opportunity to have great value through behavioral analysis of the users to tap their interests and habits into the business outcome.

Audio datasets

The audio datasets are formed from a wide range of audio data collected from different sources and different formats in the modern real-world digital ecosystem, as well as through traditional sources and formats. The processing of audio data is done through different activities such as cleaning noises, time stamping, feature extraction, establishing relationships between two different data points in audio data, and other actions. The audio datasets are formed from voice data, which is available from a wide range of sources, such as:[109]

- Google speech command datasets.
- Speech Accent Archives.
- Mozilla Common Voice datasets.
- Own proprietary speech data.
- Telephone conversation data from cloud source customers.
- Field collected in-person voice data.
- And many others.

There are many other open-source and commercial sources from which the data in the voice forms can be collected, with certain conditions of use. A huge amount of voice data is required for training and testing a machine learning model. The formation of voice datasets is another very complex and time-consuming process that costs a substantial amount of money for the organizations.

The voice data can be achieved in different formats and forms from a wide range of open-source, commercial, proprietary, and crowd-sourced data. Overall, voice data can be categorized into three major generalized categories as mentioned below:[110]

- **Controlled voice data** – In this category, the voice data that is scripted and produced for machine learning purposes is considered.
- **Semi-controlled voice data** – This is a type of voice data that is based on the scenario and created under certain scenarios of speeches or conversations. This is neither fully scripted data nor fully natural data.
- **Natural voice data** – As the name implies, this category of voice data deals with the naturally recorded speeches or conversations in our day-to-day social and business activities without any scripted types of voices or scenario-based content.

There are numerous real-world applications of voice data in the fields of machine learning and artificial intelligence. The most important ones of those applications extensively used in modern businesses are:

- Web chatbots.
- Virtual assistants.
- Voice recognition applications.
- Speech-to-text converters.
- Text-to-speech converters.
- Language translators.
- Voice dialing and searching systems.
- Appliance control systems.
- Integrated voice response (IVR).

Huge volumes of voice data will be required for both supervised and unsupervised machine learning projects. In supervised machine learning, the voice annotation services are used to create useful datasets for training machine learning models more effectively.

Video datasets

Video datasets are the processed videos or the combination of image frames used for training the machine learning models or algorithms. The video datasets are formed from different types of videos that show the real-world environments of roads, buildings, objects, human beings, animals, natural landscapes, sky environments, and many others that are used in our day-to-day lives and businesses. The creation of video datasets from raw videos is a proper procedure that involves multiple steps and activities, which will be covered in the next chapter. The most fundamental component for building either training or testing video datasets for machine learning models is the video data of huge volume. A good machine learning model needs thousands of hours of video data for training the model to produce reliable output. The collection of such huge data in the form of videos is a very complex and lengthy task. As we know, video is unstructured data and can be very difficult to manage automatically. The video format of content has become the most powerful and effective data for all major types of business processes in all domains of industry. Video is extensively used for a range of processes, such as:

- Training and education.
- Marketing, sales, and promotional content.
- Entertainment and gaming industries.
- Social media and journalism.
- Digital media and sports.
- Tourism and culture.
- And many more.

The most important fields in which the video training datasets are used in their respective machine learning applications are:[111]

- Video recognition application.
- Facial recognition and surveillance systems.
- Augmented reality (AR) and virtual reality (VR) applications.
- Computer vision (CV) applications in different fields such as retail, e-commerce, entertainment, and digital marketing.
- Gaming applications.
- Autonomous vehicles.
- Manufacturing and robotic applications.
- Done and aviation technologies.
- Agriculture and telemetry systems.
- Defense and internal security.

The video datasets are used for both deep learning models and simple machine learning models based on video learning. The main sources of getting video data for building a large number of training and testing datasets for both types of projects are mentioned below:[112]

- **Open-source databases** – There are many open-source databases that store videos to support the machine learning and deep learning projects for open-source applications and platforms across the industries.
- **Web scraping** – Using AI systems or robots to collect data from different websites, such as social media, entertainment, gaming, sports, and other websites. This process is known as web scraping and is governed by certain copyright rules and regulations.

- **Synthetic video data** – This involves the natural videos that are used for training the machine learning models in autonomous cars and similar kinds of projects. The video gaming platforms can also be a very good example of synthetic video dataset creation.
- **Manual creation of video data** – This is the traditional way in which huge volumes of video data are created through manual recording or crowd-sourcing through different incentivized projects and tasks for the general public to earn extra money for sharing videos in different forms and formats for a particular activity.

Image datasets

Image data or photos are very important forms of unstructured data that would be extensively used in all modern machine learning applications powered by image recognition and image analysis. A huge volume of data of images of real-world entities, places, people, animals, things, and many other items is required to train the machines to automatically recognize and classify. The machine learning training is done through image processing and feeding the systems for image analysis and extraction of useful information from them to make effective future decisions.[113]

For any machine learning application, extremely large volumes of image data are required to form different types of datasets, such as training datasets, testing datasets, and validating datasets, in such a way that the machine starts making correct and reliable decisions when it encounters any image that is not explicitly labeled.[114] The larger the piles of image training datasets that are fed to the ML models, the better the results will be produced by the systems. The most common applications in which images are extensively used include the following:

- Image recognition applications.
- Computer vision applications.
- Augmented reality/virtual reality apps.
- Gaming and entertainment applications.
- E-commerce, retail, and digital marketing apps.
- Cybersecurity, defense, and homeland security systems.

The most common sources of collecting image data for building training and testing image datasets are:[115]

- Kaggle databases of image datasets.
- AWS databases.
- University of California, Irvine (UCI) Repository for machine learning.
- Google Dataset Search engine.
- Government databases of different countries.
- Microsoft Datasets.
- Computer vision datasets.

The proprietary images created by an organization for exclusive usage are also one of the main options to collect high-quality image data for machine learning project training purposes, but it may be a bit costly to create exclusive data for a particular ML project. The processing of images for making the usable datasets consists of a few detailed steps, which will be covered in the next chapter.

Sensory datasets

Sensory datasets are formed through a wide range of sensory data. The field of sensory data is also huge and consists of numerous types of data collected through different sensors, gadgets, sources of energy, chemical and physical properties, cosmological and astronomical data, and many others. The most common sources of collecting sensory data that can be used for building sensory datasets to fit the machine learning models are mentioned below:[116,117]

- Ultrasound signal sensors.
- Radar signal sensors.
- Magnetic field sensors.
- Electrical signal sources.
- Physical energy sources.
- Chemical property sensors.
- Human wearables and gadgets.
- Light signal sources.
- Temperature sensors.
- Moisture and damp sensors.
- And many others

All of the above-mentioned sources of sensory data can generate their respective forms of data in different formats that can be used either directly by the machine learning models or processed through certain processes to make them usable for machine learning models. The processing of raw sensory data to build an annotated dataset for a machine learning model is extensively used in supervised machine learning, while the raw data fed to the ML model for classification and regularization of the data points is the most common way in the unsupervised machine learning process. The combination of the two models makes a good comprehensive model of machine learning in numerous fields such as telemetry applications, agricultural fields, smart city systems, cybersecurity and defense systems, and many other similar kinds of applications.

The most common forms of sensory data collected from the above-mentioned sources are mentioned below:

- Electrical voltage signals.
- Electrical current signals.
- Physical pressure or weight.

- Body movement or gestures.
- Rhythmic beats.
- Electromagnetic waves.
- Light and heat signals.
- Digital and logical signals.
- Magnetic images.
- Frequency signals.
- Sound signals.
- Collision or thrust.
- Chemical properties.

The formation of datasets from those formats may vary with every type of data structure. The raw data in the form of the above formats or versions is also a part of unstructured data that is collected through different sources and is expanding significantly. To utilize the data for training the machine learning models, different types of techniques are required to make them usable for feeding the ML models. In most cases, those sensory datasets are used as unlabeled formats directly into the ML models through sensors to access and analyze them properly. Many formats can be directly accessed and analyzed by the software programs, such as digital, analog, electric, and electromagnetic waves, without any intermediary ML models, too.

Chapter 4

Building training and testing datasets

DOI: 10.1201/9781003688327-4

HOW DOES A MACHINE CONSUME DATASETS?

A dataset is the relational information of different features of a body or entity in the structured format of data, and in the unstructured format of data, a dataset is the labeled data made understandable for the machine learning models through predefined machine learning (ML) algorithms. The unlabeled datasets can also be used in machine learning for classification purposes, with machine learning models falling in the category of unsupervised machine learning.[118]

The datasets used in both types of machine learning categories are consumed by the ML models as an input or a feed to learn through experience and observations. The ways the machine consumes the datasets can be classified into two major ways:

- Annotated dataset consumption.
- Raw dataset consumption.

In the first way of dataset consumption in ML models, the raw and unstructured data is collected from different sources in different formats, such as text, audio, video, images, and senses, and labeled through different techniques to make the unstructured data understandable (or legible data for machine learning models). This process of data annotation is a comprehensive data treatment method that consists of numerous steps. Those steps will be covered in full detail in this chapter later on. These datasets are used in supervised machine learning.

The other way of data consumption in ML models is known as an unlabeled dataset feeding into the models. The raw data without any data annotation is fed into the machine learning models powered by unsupervised ML algorithms. The algorithms ingest the data and analyze it in light of the similarities and dissimilarities of the data points available in the datasets. This form of data consumption is much easier than the former one, in which a huge procedure is required to make the data understandable to the supervised machine learning models.

It is very important to note that the structured data stored in any type of relational database can directly be taken by a simple software program installed on any machine without any further understanding of that data, but the unstructured data is required to be fed into the machine learning model to scan and analyze that data in huge volumes from different angles and perspectives so that the data fed into the machine learning model can easily make decisions for any new testing data environment it encounters in the real-world environment in the form of image, voice, video, movement, gestures, senses, and other formats. To form a reliable one, a machine learning model needs huge heaps of unstructured data, either through annotated datasets or unlabeled datasets. The more input data is fed, the better results can be achieved through the machine learning models.

Creating legible datasets for a supervised machine learning model is a time-consuming and costly process based on certain steps and the exploitation of resources.

HOW ARE DATASETS BUILT?

Dataset building is a comprehensive process that involves numerous steps to achieve a reliable and high-quality dataset. There are numerous readymade open-source resources that provide larger volumes of datasets in different forms, such as video, images, sensory data, audio, and text. Any open-source project can use those datasets directly. To build a reliable dataset of any format, the first step is the collection of high-quality data in the required format – text, image, video, or audio, etc. The next step is to clean the data files of any kind of noise or irrelevant data. This process is called the data cleaning process. After cleaning the data, the three most important aspects of data marking or labeling in the form of categorization, classification, and data annotation are covered through different professional-grade dataset formation tools.[119]

For the formation of reliable datasets for a robust machine learning model to produce the desirable results, they should qualify for four important aspects as listed below:

- High-quality.
- Huge-volume.
- Efficient usability.
- Faster scalability.

Maintaining high-quality datasets is very crucial because they are the very foundation of reliable model development and for testing the accuracy of the model (through training and testing datasets, respectively). Therefore, dataset building should comply with all the major criteria mentioned in the above list to produce the best results of the model.

DATASET BUILDING PROCESSES

Building useful datasets is a lengthy activity that involves numerous processes. The dataset creation process starts from the identification of the problem and its solution through machine learning models. This helps you choose the right data to collect. The data collection is the second step or process in this entire activity. The sequential processes commonly used in the creation of effective and high-quality datasets after identifying the problem and the suitable solution to that problem through an ML model are mentioned below:[120,121]

- Data collection.
- Data cleaning.
- Data categorization.
- Data classification.
- Data labeling or annotation.

In certain models, another important process known as data exploration is also used before data cleaning and after the data sourcing or data collection step. That step is designed to make sure that the data that is collected is understandable in terms of its variables and their inter-relationship with other variables in the data to produce the desired objectives. This step allows the data scientist to remain focused on the problem formulation and its associated machine learning model to solve the problem effectively and accurately. The details of each process mentioned in the list above are provided with process characteristics and examples in the following subtopics.

Data collection

The data collection or data acquisition process is one of the most important parts of this entire activity of creating useful datasets. In this process, data is gathered through different sources and platforms in huge quantities so that the machine learning model can be trained to produce the most reliable results. This data collection process can further be divided into two major approaches, as mentioned below:[120]

- Data generation.
- Data augmentation.

In the data generation category or approach, different sources and methods are used to collect data in bulk quantities for further processing of the dataset creation. This technique is very useful when there is no data available for making datasets, and the data scientists need to generate data from scratch. A few common methods applied to generate data include the following:

- **Crowdsourcing** – In crowdsourcing, numerous platforms for data generation are available that host numerous groups of people providing services for creating the desired data required for building datasets. Those people charge for the services they provide in generating data. Two examples of crowdsourcing platforms are:
  - Amazon Mechanical Turk (MTurk)
  - Citizen Science
- **Synthetic data generation** – This is another important method of generating data. This method is applied when you have a small- or medium-sized dataset generated through other methods and want to

increase the size of the training database for your machine learning model. This method uses computer software programs to generate synthetic data. One of the most popular such programs to generate synthetic data is the Generative Adversarial Network (GAN). This software uses two different contesting networks, named the Generator and Discriminator networks. The former learns to map latent space to data distribution, and the latter compares examples taken from the generated distribution and the true distribution to increase the error rate of the discriminator network. The increased error ratio would prompt the generator network to generate more accurate examples. Thus, the database also expands, and the model starts getting more accurate. The generator network uses the existing data in the form of text, video, audio, and images, and creates new data out of them to look like the original data.

In the second way of collecting data, named data augmentation, the existing data is augmented by performing certain steps such as flipping, increasing or decreasing brightness, cropping images, rotating images, reducing or increasing the contrast, and similar types of other activities to generate new copies of the data that can expand the existing database for training the machine learning models more extensively to produce the best results.

Data cleaning

Data cleaning deals with different types of simple tasks that help improve the effectiveness and understanding of the data for machine learning models. Data cleaning removes different types of anomalies and discrepancies in the data acquired from different sources. The most important tasks performed in this stage include the following:[121]

- Identification of discrepancies and inconsistencies in the data.
- Figuring out the outliers, missing data, repetitions, and other issues.
- Rectification of all types of issues and inconsistencies.
- Removal of blank fields or irrelevant parameters.
- Adding the missing parameters to make the data meaningful.
- A few data cleaning tools extensively used for gathering valuable data include MLClean, ActiveClean, BoostClean, HoloClean, and others.
- If the missing values are not filled, they should be marked as neutral to avoid ML models from getting more confused and misguided.
- Using different techniques and software tools such as Pandera, Great Expectations, PyTest, and others for validating the data after cleaning.

The cleaning process is very important for improving the quality of data that leads to building highly reliable and effective datasets for the ML models.

Data categorization

The data categorization is another very important process that helps machine learning models learn from the datasets accurately, avoiding overfitting, underfitting, and other issues. Most of the machine learning models generate incorrect results or predictions when they are fed with raw and unstructured data for learning. If the data is more structured or categorized into different categories or classes, it will become more useful for ML models to learn from. The categorization of data means that the data is categorized into different groups, such as a range of values, a group of items, and similar types of other categories. Two very important tricks or techniques are applied to categorize the data into suitable groups, which are mentioned below:[121]

- **Binning data** – In this technique, the bins of equal number, size, or any other attributes of data are created. This allows ML to reduce the bias errors. Binning is characterized by two main tricks – equidistant and equi-statistical tricks.
- **Smoothing features** – This technique is used to reduce the variance in the machine learning model by preventing the model from any kinds of misinterpretations due to statistical fluctuation in the datasets.

Data classification

The organization of the data into different classes in such a way that it makes more sense for the readers as well as for the machine learning algorithms during the ML model training. The classes or categories of data make it easier to find, manage, store, and analyze. The main features and characteristics that are the core components for the classification of data include:[122]

- Available types of data.
- Sensitivity of data.
- Location of data.

The criteria for classification of structured and unstructured data are different depending on the nature of the data, problem formulation, and ML model. The classification of data is not only helpful in building machine learning training datasets but also useful for organizations and businesses to optimize the storage space, access instantly, maintain high-level security, perform faster data analysis, comply with regulations, and many other tasks. The classification of data can be accomplished in three different groups, as mentioned below:

- Content-based classification of data.
- User-based classification of data.
- Context-based classification of data.

Properly classified data is very convenient to build desired datasets to feed to the machine learning models for more accuracy and reliability (in any kind of machine learning).

Data labeling

Data labeling is one of the most important processes in the machine learning field, especially in the supervised form of machine learning. The data labeling process starts with the identification of the raw data collected for building ML training datasets, and it puts a few additional labels on the raw data in such a way that ML models can easily understand and learn from the data ingested into the model. The labeling provides a smoother learning experience to ML algorithms by adding tags, metadata, and other information about the raw data file fed into the machine learning model. The example of data labels attached to the raw data may include the name of an entity on an image – man, dog, building, or others; file type – audio, video, text, or any other; what action is required to be performed; what information is enclosed in the file; and similar types of other information. In simple words, this is about adding meaningful tags that are helpful for ML models to understand and learn from the datasets easily and accurately. Labeling helps the advanced ML algorithms learn from the detailed information about the elements of the data fed into the ML model.[123]

Data labeling is a manual process in which the role of humans is important. This is the reason that the labeling process requires a human-in-the-loop (HITL) intervention. The main approaches that a human is involved in or a data scientist works on in the process of labeling the data to build effective and high-quality datasets include the following:

- **Internal labeling** – This is done through a dedicated in-house team of labelers to build high-quality and reliable datasets.
- **Outsourcing labeling** – It is one of the most popular approaches to get the raw data labeled through different models within the outsourcing used nowadays in the world, such as offshoring, onshore outsourcing, freelancing, and others.
- **Synthetic labeling** – The expansion of the existing databases through the creation of duplicate copies of the data, with some cropping and other changes, with the help of powerful computers, is known as synthetic labeling.
- **Crowdsourcing** – There are numerous crowdsourcing platforms that offer different groups for different services, like data labeling and many others. A suitable group is chosen for data labeling tasks for certain charges of the service.
- **Programmatic labeling** – Computer programs or scripts are used for labeling the datasets. This may not be able to provide the desired quality of labeling due to the involvement of a computer program to identify the tags and labels.

The quality of the labeling is very critical for producing the best and most accurate results out of the supervised machine learning model.

Data annotation

Data annotation is the most fundamental technique to label the data and relevant components within the training dataset. With the help of data annotation, the machine learning or artificial intelligence (AI) models are provided with the most relevant information about the data, which is fed to them in such a way that the model can understand and learn from that data more effectively and easily. We can also define data annotation like this:

> The process or technique through which the training data fed to the ML or AI models is labeled with the most relevant and most important data about that particular dataset so that the AI and ML models can learn accurately from that annotated data.[124]

Data annotation is a very important process that is also very lengthy and time-consuming in terms of labor needed to accomplish the data annotation or labeling tasks. This is the most fundamental requirement of any ML or AI project, and without data annotation, no supervised machine learning project can be completed. Through data annotation, the input data formats and forms are marked, and proper identification of the items or entities in the data is also marked with a category or class of the entities. For instance, the training datasets are built from different types of raw or unstructured data, such as videos, audios, text, images, sensors, and others; data annotation provides the information about the types of data and file formats, along with the identification of the objects available in those files. In an image, the data annotation can identify an animal, human, tree, vehicle, or other similar kind of item or entity so that the machine learning can understand that the labeled entity is either a tree, human, vehicle, or any other thing that is explicitly mentioned by the data annotation.

Data annotation and data labeling are very closely related to each other, with a very vague differentiating line between them, so that many times those terms are often used interchangeably. In reality, the labeling is a comprehensive process of marking or tagging the datasets with the relevant and meaningful information for the machine learning or artificial intelligence models to understand and learn easily for correct projects in the future. The annotation of data is a technique or method in which the labeling of the datasets is done.

Data annotation is normally done manually by the data labelers or annotators, who use different types of software tools to annotate different types of data in the form of texts, images, videos, audios, and other sensory formats. The data annotation tools are available in commercial applications as well as in the open-source license that you can deploy in both on-premises and in-cloud environments to use in a shared manner. The data annotation process is supported by both natural language processing (NLP) and computer vision (CV) applications. Professional-grade remote data annotation services are also available to use for a small fee, as compared to the huge cost incurred due to on-premises or an in-house team for annotation purposes.

CATEGORIES OF DATA ANNOTATION

Data annotation is categorized according to the type of data that can be annotated through this process of data labeling or tagging. The most important categories or types of data annotation supported are mentioned below:

- Text annotation.
- Image annotation.
- Video annotation.
- Audio annotation.

Each of the above-mentioned types of data annotation uses different techniques and tools for labeling or tagging the content of the datasets developed for the training of ML/AI models. The details of each category with the relevant techniques and tools have been expressed in full length in the following subtopics.

DATA ANNOTATION TECHNIQUES USED IN DIFFERENT DATA CATEGORIES

There are four major categories or types of data annotation extensively used for building the training datasets for machine learning or artificial intelligence models, as listed in the above topic. Each type of data annotation uses different methods, techniques, and approaches to label the content of the associated data. The details of each type of data annotation, such as text, image, video, and audio data annotation, are described in the following topics separately.

TEXT ANNOTATION

The text annotation is a process of labeling datasets in the form of digital text to provide the relevant information in the datasets for the machine learning model to learn and produce the desired output or predictions when it encounters a similar type of problem in the future. The text annotation is the most fundamental component of the natural language processing (NLP) field of machine learning (ML) or artificial intelligence (AI).

It is very important to note that text is one of the most basic sources for businesses to scan for useful business intelligence. It is very useful for businesses in the form of social media posts, comments, internet surfing patterns, written communication through different sources, and many others. Understanding text with a complete sense of sentiments, intentions, and other abstracts such as happiness, sadness, anxiousness, anger, and many others is very complex, and machines cannot understand it without explicit training to do so. That explicit training of understanding all aspects of text data is done through effective text annotation. The most important domains of the NLP field that use the power of text annotation include:[125]

- Neural machine translation (NMT).
- Sentiment analysis.
- Auto speech recognition.
- Text-to-speech synthesis.
- Auto Q&A platforms.
- Smart chatbots.
- Virtual assistants.
- And others.

The main purpose of the text annotation is to make the text more legible and understandable to the ML/AI models. As mentioned earlier, the text is a very complex and difficult form of content to understand, not only for AI/ML programs but also for human beings who are very well trained and knowledgeable about a range of abstract things described in the text.

Entity annotation

Entity annotation is the widest area of text annotation because it covers numerous aspects of labeling the entities present in the text file and its content. Entity annotation is a process in which the address or location is found, and the identity extraction of a range of entities is done, and then labeled accordingly so that the ML/deep learning (DL) models can easily understand and learn from the text annotation. The most important type of entity annotation process is known as:

- **Named Entity Recognition (NER)** – This is the most important method used for entity annotation in modern data annotation. Through this type of annotation, proper names of the entities are labeled, such as locations, names of organizations, times, days, persons, values, and others.

The other main named entity recognition sub-processes for text annotation are:

- Text classification.
- Parts of speech tagging.
- Key-phrase labeling.
- Product categorization.
- Document classification.

Text classification

Text classification is a process in which either the entire body of an article, a paragraph, or a line of text is tagged as a single identity. This type of annotation provides general information about the text portion for effective learning.

Parts of speech tagging

The functional elements in a document, paragraph, or sentence in the shape of all parts of speech are annotated through a tagging technique referred to as parts of speech tagging. The example of Parts of Speech (POS) tagging includes verbs, nouns, pronouns, adverbs, adjectives, conjunctions, interjections, and prepositions.

Key-phrase labeling

Key-phrase labeling is alternatively referred to as keyword extraction, too. In this type of named entity procedure, the keywords used in the text are marked or annotated. The use of this tagging is very common in search functions in e-commerce platforms, knowledge bases, and other online self-help support platforms.

Product categorization

The use of product categorization is very useful in modern e-commerce, recommendation engines, and other similar kinds of services powered by ML/AI applications. In this process, the products, items, and entities are sorted out into groups or categories.

Document classification

The classification of text-based documents such as books, research papers, theses, journals, articles, dissertations, letters, and many others into different classes is referred to as text classification. In ML/AI document named entity annotation, those documents are classified into different groups so that they can be automatically sorted out by ML models.

Text sentiment annotation

Different abstracts, such as humor, sarcasm, emotional feelings, and similar kinds of expressions, are very difficult to understand in plain text, not only for AI-enabled machines but also for human beings. Text sentiment annotation helps the AI, ML, DL, and NLP models understand and learn the sentiments in the sentimental analysis processes in different applications such as chatbots, virtual assistants, and others.

Entity linking

Entity linking is a very useful text data labeling used to link the details of a word or group of words in a text document, paragraph, or sentence in such a way that machine learning models can easily understand the definition of those terms or words. This process is done through the linking of an entity to the detailed online resource through a uniform resource locator, or URL.

IMAGE ANNOTATION

Image annotation is the process of marking or labeling images with different attributes, such as class, category, name, and others, to build datasets used for training the machine learning models. The image annotation is mostly done through a manual process on different tools used for the purpose by data annotators through different image annotation techniques or types. The image annotated dataset is fed into the machine learning or artificial intelligence models for further processing to learn from the given labels of the functional entities in the images. This process is extensively applied in numerous machine learning models under the supervised category of machine learning.[127]

Once the deep learning (DL) or Machine Learning (ML) models learn through manual annotation sufficiently, they can process the image annotation activity automatically as the new image data is encountered. The automated process of image annotation is also referred to as model-assisted labeling. The most important domains where image annotation is used extensively include neural networks and computer vision (or CV)-based machine learning applications. The most important tasks that are performed in the form of image annotation while building datasets for deep learning or machine learning models include the following:[126,127]

- **Image classification** – Tagging the images with the predefined categories or classes with different names, such as unique IDs, text tags, one-hot encoding, or class numbers, is known as an image classification task.
- **Object recognition or object detection** – Object recognition and object detection are two terms used interchangeably for an image annotation activity in which the objects in an image are detected or recognized through different techniques of image annotation.
- **Image segmentation** – Image segmentation is a task of annotation in which the image boundaries are more precisely detected and separated from the other images for clearer data labeling in the datasets.
- **Semantic segmentation** – It is a form of image segmentation in which the regions of the images are separated with the help of pixel density to divide each region of the image into its respective categories and classes.
- **Instance segmentation** – The separation of an object from the rest of the image is known as the instance segmentation task. It is very useful or helpful in sorting out similar types of images from a group of images, too.
- **Panoptic segmentation** – This segmentation task deals with a combination type of segmentation that includes both instance and semantic segmentation activities. The separation tasks of objects in terms of categories and instance-level segmentation are performed simultaneously in this type of activity.

All of the above-mentioned activities are performed through different techniques of image annotation. Those techniques are deployed as per the requirements for the precision and quality of the machine learning applications. Some of the different techniques or methods, commonly referred to as types of image annotation, are listed below:

- Bounding box annotation.
- Polygon annotation.
- Cuboid annotation.
- Key-point or landmark annotation.
- Polyline annotation.
- Semantic segmentation.

To accomplish the most important image annotation tasks or activities listed earlier in this topic, the above-mentioned types of image annotations are used in modern dataset building for ML/DL/AI applications. Let us discuss the types of image annotation in full length in the following section of this chapter.

IMAGE ANNOTATION TYPES

The most important types of image annotation used for building datasets for different types of supervised machine learning models are described below:[126]

Bounding box annotation

In the bounding box type of image annotation, a box that bounds an object in an image is used to identify or detect it. It is the most fundamental type of image annotation for detecting objects in an image. Bounding box offers lesser precision as compared to other major types of image annotation used for object detection activities. The image annotated through bounding boxes is shown in Figure 4.1.

Each box in Figure 4.1 bounding an object provides information about an entity. The accuracy of the entity body is much lower in this type of image annotation. The bounding box type of annotation deals with two dimensions of an object.

Polygon annotation

The polygon annotation provides more details compared to bounding boxes. It masks every corner, angle, and side of an object with a polygon masking technique in two dimensions to provide more accuracy and precision of masking an entity in an image. The bounding boxes technique is limited to four angles that form a square, but a polygon can cover multiple angles. This type is extensively used for object detection purposes, like the bounding box type, but to achieve greater precision. Medical imaging is one of the well-known fields that uses this technique in different solutions.

Figure 4.1 Bounding box annotation. (Pixabay).

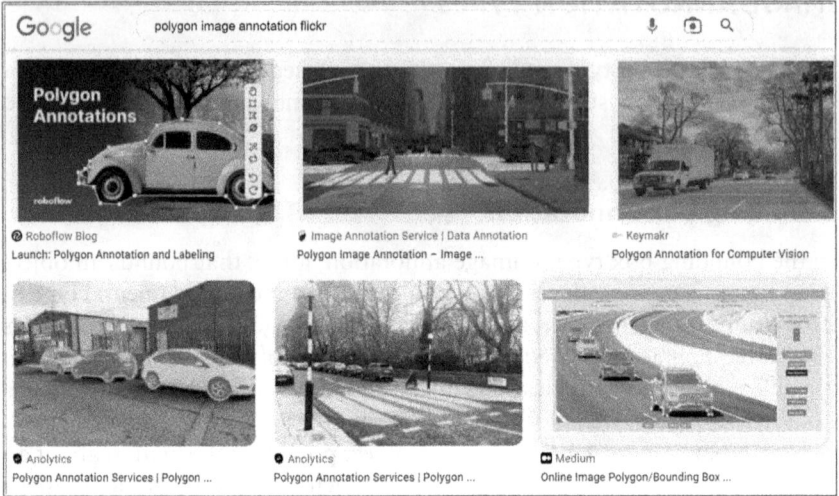

Figure 4.2 Polygon annotation Google image search.

It is used to identify or detect an object in its right size and original shape in two-dimensional space, which provides more details of the features and curves of that object in an image. Thus, polygon annotation is used for all those applications that require a high level of precision in locating the features of any entity in an image. A few major domains of the usage of polygon image annotation are:

- Facial recognition.
- Medical imaging.
- Street signs.

The Google image search for polygon annotation is shown in Figure 4.2, which contains numerous results marked with some polygons.

3D cuboid annotation

Three-dimensional (3D) cuboid annotation is used to mark an object on an image in three dimensions so that the depth, width, and height of an object are clearly found. This is another type of high-quality and high-precision image annotation. Both bounding box and polygon annotations deal with two dimensions of an image, while the 3D cuboid annotation marks an entity in three dimensions to provide more precise object identification in mission-critical applications of machine learning or artificial intelligence.

This type of image annotation is used in numerous domains powered by machine learning (ML) and artificial intelligence (AI) projects, such as:

- Driverless cars.
- Engineering designs.
- Warehousing and logistics.
- And many others.

The pictorial examples of the 3D image annotation are shown in Figure 4.3, pointed to through arrows. This figure is a screenshot of a Google search for 3D image annotation.

Semantic segmentation

Semantic segmentation is another important type of image annotation in which all parts of a frame are marked at the pixel level to separate each entity or object in that particular image. This provides complete details of all objects, points, surfaces, and other information available in that particular photo or image under consideration for semantic segmentation annotation. The semantic segmentation is used for marking the images at sub-parts, object contour, and hue levels.

This form of image annotation is considered the most detail-oriented, precise, and accurate for marking any kind of ML project that requires the highest level of precision. Semantic segmentation annotation is available in both two- and three-dimensional labeling. The most common examples of use cases for this type of image annotation include:

- Driverless vehicles.
- Medical imaging.
- And other computer vision applications.

The pictorial presentation of the semantic segmentation type of image annotation is shown in Figure 4.4's screenshot based on the Google image search for the semantic segmentation keyword. The arrow in this image shows how all parts of an image in a frame are marked and highlighted at the pixel level to separate from one another.

Lines and splines

The lines and spline image annotation is used to mark the continuous lines and grooved or curvy lines that help identify the boundary of an object in an image or frame. This type of image annotation is extensively used for mapping road lines, pedestrian lines, road-crossing lines, zebra crossings, different types of turns on the road, and similar types of lines.

The main pointers used for image annotation in line and spline types of annotation are straight and curvy lines. No other symbols are used in this form of image annotation. The most important real-world machine learning applications that use the line and spline image annotation extensively are mentioned in the following list:[128]

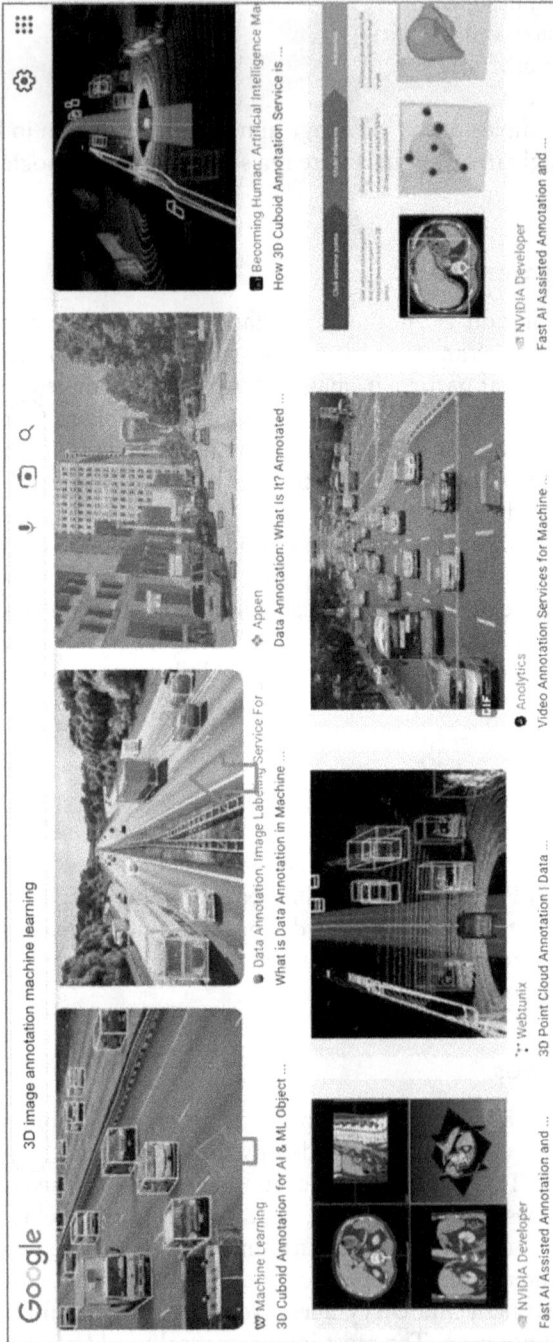

Figure 4.3 Google image search for 3D image annotation screenshot.

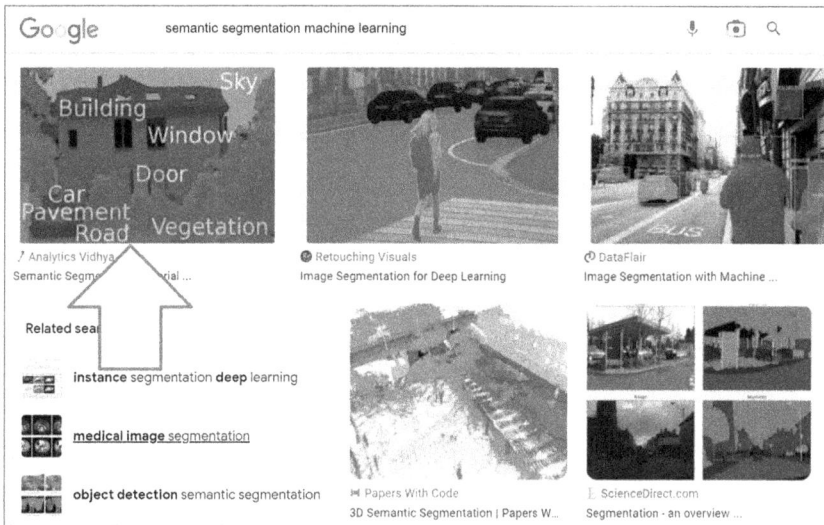

Figure 4.4 Screenshot of Google image search (semantic segmentation).

- Self-driving vehicles.
- Warehouses and store robotics.
- Manufacturing assembly lines.
- Street and lane detection apps.
- Path detection in different applications.

The pictorial explanation of lines and splines image annotation is shown in Figure 4.5, which is a screenshot of a Google image search for line and spline image annotation.

Key-points or landmark annotation

Key-point image annotation is used to detect the features and landmarks in an object or an image. This type of image annotation is also referred to as landmark annotation. The most minor parts of an object are distinguished through dotted points known as key-points, which are joined together to detect or draw the boundaries of an object or a part of an object. This annotation is also helpful in providing enough data for the machine learning algorithms to learn the distance between two parts or landmarks of an object and the pattern of the landmark.

The most common applications of key-points or landmark annotation in modern real-world machine applications include:[129]

- Facial recognition application.
- Fashion designing or fashion landmark detection.
- E-commerce applications.
- Emotion detection.
- Pose estimation or body gesture detection.

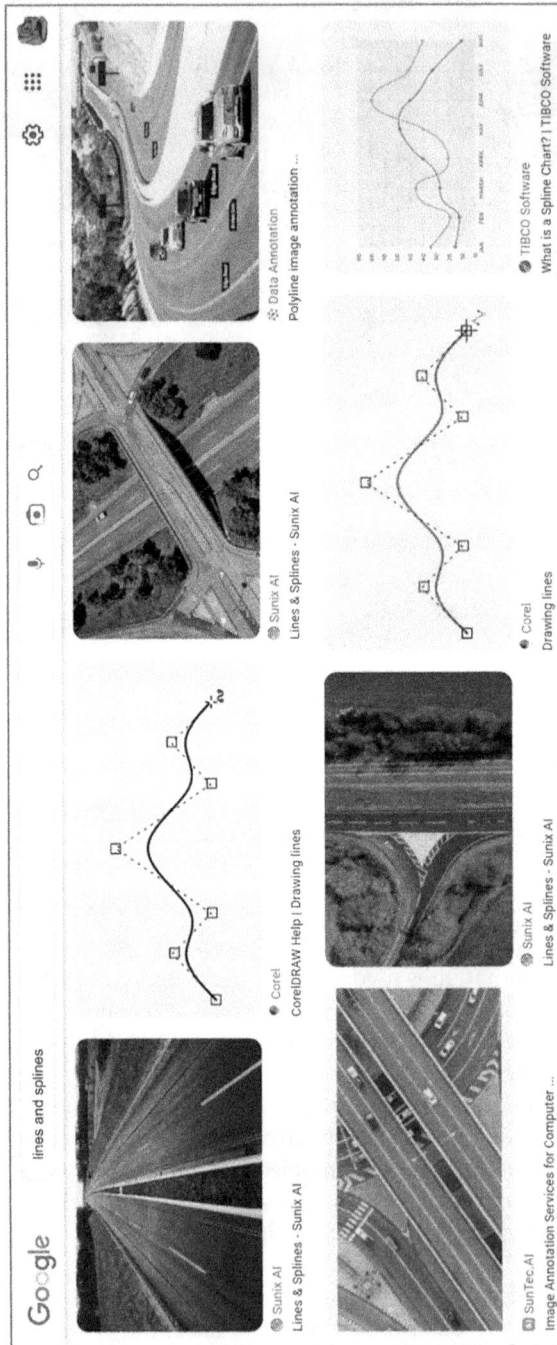

Figure 4.5 Screenshot of Google image search for lines and splines.

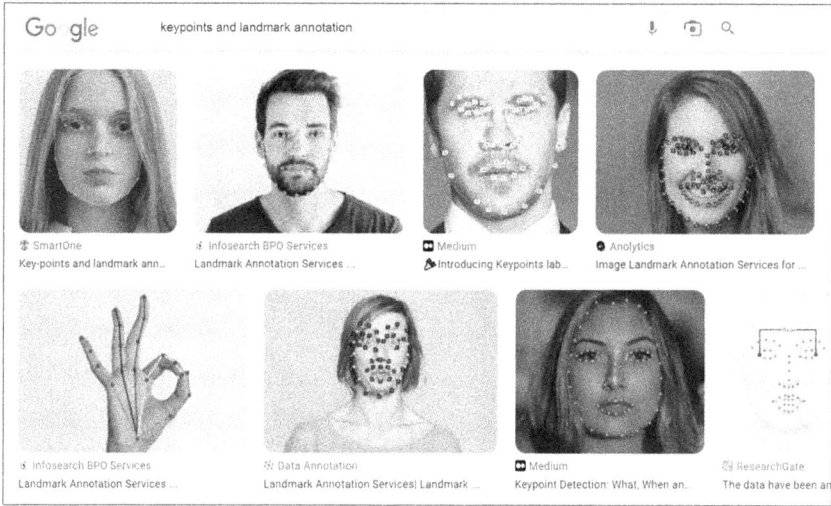

Figure 4.6 Screenshot of Google search for key-points and landmark annotation.

The way key-points or landmark image annotations work is shown in Figure 4.6, which is a screenshot of a Google image search for key-points and landmark annotations.

Polyline annotation

Polyline image annotation is almost similar to the lines and splines image annotation technique, mainly focused on self-driving cars for detecting lanes, edges of roads, broken lines, one-way lines, and roads, streets, intersections, and others. In this type of annotation, multiple lines are used to mark different identifications of lanes, boundaries, edges, centers, or any other markings while developing image training datasets for ML models. The most important features of the polyline image are further summarized below:[130]

- Uses multiple lines for different labels.
- Offers a greater level of accuracy.
- Best for automated driving applications.
- Identification of different types of roads and streets.

The pictorial presentation of polyline image annotation can be understood through different images available in the snapshot of a Google search for the polyline image annotation keyword (see Figure 4.7).

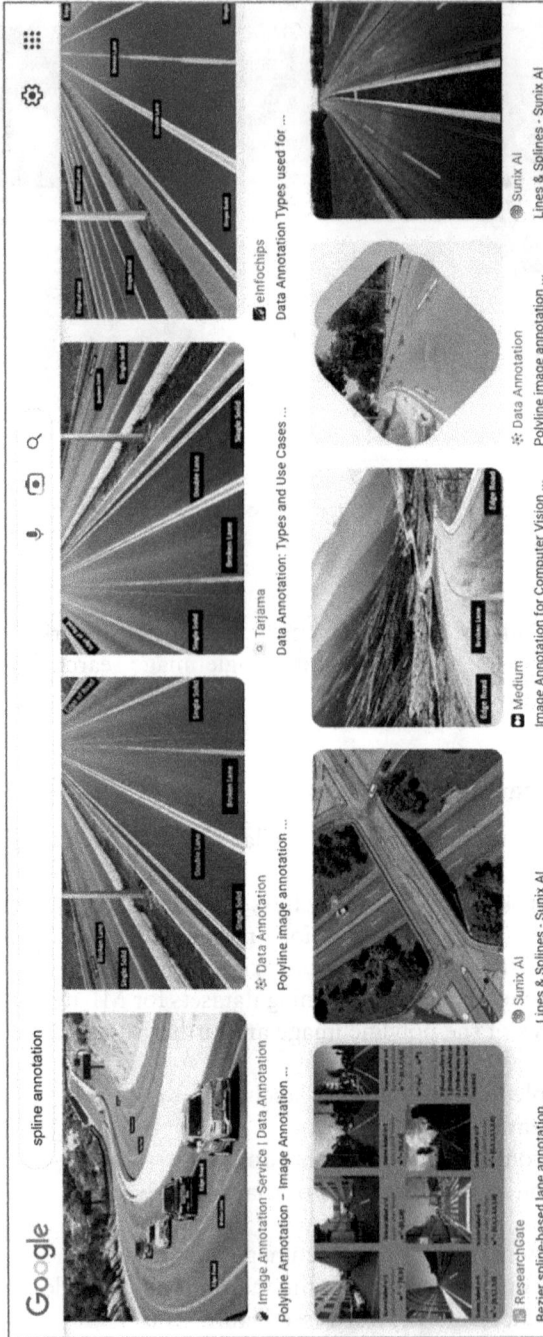

Figure 4.7 Screenshot of Google image search for polyline annotation.

VIDEO DATA ANNOTATION

Video data annotation is almost similar to image annotation with the extension of frames. In video annotation, multiple frames are labeled with different techniques and types of annotations for making the computer algorithms or ML models understand and learn from those labels in a real-time video when the model encounters a challenging situation or problem scenario.[131]

Video annotation is accomplished using different techniques commonly known as types of video annotations, and the tasks performed through those techniques in machine learning or artificial intelligence projects. The details of tasks, activities, objectives, and types of video data annotation are explained in separate sections below.

MAIN TASKS OF VIDEO ANNOTATION

Video annotation is used to perform certain activities to achieve the desired objectives for making the machine learning models learn from the training datasets. The most important objective-oriented activities performed through video annotation include the following:[132]

- Object localization.
- Object detection.
- Object tracking.
- Activity tracking.

Object localization

Locating the position of an object in such a way that the machines can understand easily by providing data about how far the object is, which side it is located on, and what its position is in comparison with other objects is known as object localization.

Object detection

As the name implies, this activity is used for making the machine understand how to find out the objects in the frames as soon as they appear and decide what the object is. Object detection is very crucial in all computer vision applications.

Object tracking

Object tracking is another major objective of video annotation, in which the movement of an object, the arrival of any landmark object, and the difference between the motions of multiple objects are tracked and traced continuously.

Activity tracking

The activity tracking is almost similar to the object tracking, with a small difference that in activity tracking, the functions of an object are tracked continuously, such as walking in different ways, body movements, gestures, and other activities related to body movements. This function helps detect normal and abnormal activities or behaviors of an object. The object may be a human, an animal, or similar.

METHODS OF VIDEO ANNOTATION

Like image annotation, video annotation also uses numerous techniques that are common in both image and video annotation, with a little difference of moving frames in videos and a fixed frame in image annotation. The details of those methods are mentioned below.

Bounding boxes

The bounding boxes technique in video annotation is similar to the one described for image annotation, with one additional difference: bounding boxes continuously bind the objects in all frames till the object is in the visual frame.

Polygon annotation

Polygon is a more detailed technique of video annotation in which the image is detected and tracked with a polygon to cover multiple corners and edges of an object. This is a more accurate method of video annotation than the bounding boxes approach.

3D cuboid

The cuboid video annotation measures and marks the object in a three-dimensional cube to provide data about the length, width, and depth of an object that is detected and tracked through the 3D-cuboid technique.

Semantic segmentation

All components appearing in a video frame are continuously marked with their respective categories, such as person, dogs, cats, cars, bicycles, trees, and other objects commonly encountered in the videos.

Key-points and landmarks annotation

The key-points video annotation is used to mark the landmarks or components of a video through bounds that form an accurate landmark. While the landmarks annotation is the same as key-points annotation, it includes additional information through a label that points out the object with a name or identity of that particular landmark in the video.

AUDIO ANNOTATION

Audio annotation is another important form of data annotation in which the recorded voice file is tagged with the metadata and other relevant information, such as the type of format, time, date, and year of recording; name of the recorder; the type of data, such as music, animal sound, human speech, and others of similar kinds.

Audio annotation is very useful for machine learning applications for managing the audio files for better searchability and efficient use of the audio files. Audio annotation is used with additional manual labor or work on the audio file to make it understandable for machine learning models in natural language processing (NLP) projects. Audio annotations are very common in the following applications and fields:[133]

- Speech recognition apps.
- Speech-to-text transcription.
- Virtual assistants.
- Chatbots.
- Security systems.

TYPES OF AUDIO ANNOTATION

Audio annotation is done through different tools to label different landmarks and data in the audio file. Different tools use various types of audio annotations that are mentioned below.[134]

Audio classification

In this type of annotation, the details about the category or class of an audio file are added to the file. That information may include the type of voice, language, background source, number of speakers, intention, and others.

Audio event tracking

In this type of audio annotation, a particular event of a voice file, such as speech, a particular background sound, or a targeted instrument voice, is detected and marked with the details so that natural language processing algorithms can easily learn from it.

Audio labeling

This method is commonly adopted in chatbot applications powered by NLP or machine learning models. The identification and proper labeling of certain audio events in an audio file are done in such a way that the ML model understands through repetitive training and predicts in test mode in a real-world environment.

Speech-to-text transcription

In this method, the speech or voice file is converted into text through natural language processing algorithms. The labeling of speech for the NLP models to learn from is done through different audio annotations in such a way that the machine can easily convert any speech data that it encounters in real-world applications. In this type of annotation or labeling technique, the spoken words in different accents are labeled with correct spelling in the text format so that the NLP models can understand pronunciation in different accents of the English language. As we know, a word in a speech file can be in different accents, such as the US, UK, African, Asian, and other accents. Understanding those accents by the machine learning model can be improved by providing the correct spelling of the text against the spoken voice for a particular word or phrase.

Audio multi-labeling

Multi-label audio annotation is mostly used in music files to differentiate between different instrument sounds, beats, rhythms, and other related sounds. This technique of annotation for an audio file also deals with the separation of different musical instruments or genres of music for better management of files in automated machine learning algorithms. In this type of audio annotation, a music or sound file is labeled with multiple tags or marks to make the file easier to understand for the machine learning or artificial intelligence models.[135]

Chapter 5

Data analytics

DOI: 10.1201/9781003688327-5

WHAT IS DATA ANALYTICS?

Data analytics is the science of processing and analyzing raw data to understand the hidden, valuable information that can be used for the betterment of the business and social activities in our real-world environment. Data analytics starts with the development of modern civilization, in which people started learning from the environment by analyzing and evaluating the hidden values through practical experience. Initially, the data analytics was purely based on brain thought or intuitiveness, but with the passage of time, it started becoming a major domain of science to analyze the recorded raw and unstructured data to generate valuable information desired for the improvement in the performance of business and other day-to-day life processes and activities, respectively.[136]

A question is, "*Why do we use the term 'Data Analytics' instead of using 'Data Analysis'?*" The answer is simple. Data analytics is basically a generic term that refers to the entire management of data and the methods and instruments employed. On the other hand, data analysis could be defined as the process of dissecting a given (specific) dataset into its component pieces and analyzing each one separately, as well as finding out how the parts relate to one another.

The main objectives and features of the data analytics field are:

- Analysis and evaluation of unstructured/raw data to skim the value from it.
- Make data-driven decisions based on the information achieved from the analytic process.
- Enhance the business processes and profit margins, reduce costs, and streamline product features to meet customer needs and increase user experience.
- A large number of software tools and applications are very common in the modern world for accomplishing the data analytics process perfectly.
- Automated processes powered by machine learning (ML), artificial intelligence (AI), and deep learning (DL) have opened up a new scope of data analytics in all fields of business and industries.
- Data analytics is one of the most fundamental domains that paved the way for the advanced versions of machine learning and artificial intelligence.
- The main target of data analytics is to find out valuable information in the shape of customer behaviors, interests, likes, dislikes, demands, and other such factors, and also in the form of certain metrics and patterns of information that can be helpful for the improvement of the business processes. Without data analytics, those metrics, behavior patterns, and other information in different forms and patterns would be lost in the pile of unstructured raw data without getting anything from it.

- Data analytics has also become highly important in the modern cyber-security field to track the normal and abnormal behaviors and activities on the networks and systems to avert any kind of cyberattack on businesses.

Short history of data analytics

In general assumptions, the history of data analytics starts with the start of human civilization thousands of years ago. The formal history of data, databases, and data analytics can be traced back to the era of Sumerian civilization (Ancient Iraq) in 2044 BC, when the tables imprinted on clay tablets were used for calculating the wages of laborers in terms of their work hours. The summary from that point of recorded history of data analytics is shown in the following chronicle of milestones with descriptions of data analytics work.[137,138]

- **2044 BCE** – This is the beginning of the databases and formal data analytics era. The first recorded tablet was found on a clay surface used in the Sumerian civilization in Ancient Iraq.
- **2044 BCE–1950 AD–** Fast forward from 2044 till 1950; the formats and structures of the databases and data analytic techniques remain almost the same without any major breakthrough for innovation in the data analytics field. The advent of computer systems or machines in the 1950s led the way for innovation in the data analytics approach.
- **1960 AD–1990 AD** – The canned reports and structured data evolved during these years. Since then, larger amounts of data could be processed with the help of computers and calculators with advanced approaches and formulas. The relational databases (RDMS) were discovered in this era, which led to the creation of advanced-level databases through SQL.
- **1990 AD–2010 AD** – The advent of the concept of business intelligence from the available data occurred. The creation of NoSQL was associated with this era. The concept of data mining was the creation of this era of data analytics. The personal computers emerged in the marketplace. Those computers started replacing the former mainframes. Thus, the power of computing got distributed to the common people, which was restricted to the large companies and corporations earlier. The new methods and approaches to data analytics that emerged in the digital world mainly focused on the business intelligence and profit margin improvement areas.
- **2010 AD–2020 AD** – This era is known as the data science and big data era. In this new era, cloud-based as well as on-premises tools have become the most common things. The huge amounts of data started piling up through different modern digital sources such as web surfing, social media, online communication, telephones, video calls, e-commerce,

and many other modern domains of business. The virtualization of databases and data analytics processes has taken root. Machine learning is playing a stronger role in data science, and modern machine learning models are continuously changing the shape of data science, especially the data analytics and automated predictions and projections of results based on the existing data that is fed to the ML systems to learn from the experience and observations of huge amounts of data available through different sources.

- **2020–Beyond** – This is the most advanced and modern era, powered by machine learning (ML), artificial intelligence (AI), big data analytics, and numerous other emerging technologies related to data science and data analytics. The name of this era is yet to be given, but it is clear that the importance of this era, in everyone's minds, will be unprecedented. This era is also sometimes referred to as infinity and beyond.

IMPORTANCE OF DATA ANALYTICS IN CYBERSECURITY

With the expansion of connected networks across the globe powered by the Internet of Things (IoT) and the creation of gigantic volumes of data through different sources such as networking devices, mobile applications, web applications, websites, voice systems, video platforms, sensor systems, and many others, it has become very critical to analyze the huge data and find out the most useful data to strengthen the cybersecurity of such gigantic networks. Cybersecurity is heavily influenced by two major factors in the modern era. They include:

- Analysis of huge data.
- Management of huge networks and systems.

Both of the above issues are interlinked through the expanding amount of data. The large volumes of data are created by the large network and systems. To maintain robust cybersecurity on such a huge landscape is very difficult without analyzing the data created by both the systems and users that are using the networks and systems simultaneously to find out the patterns and loopholes in the system security, as well as the overall anomalies or vulnerabilities of the systems. This cannot be accomplished without huge support from data analytics and its tools integrated into the cybersecurity systems and networks.

The most important factors of data analytics that directly impact the domain of cybersecurity are mentioned below:[139,140]

- A cybersecurity professional would use it to manage the security of a system by implementing different types of access control lists, firewalls, traffic types, and other traditional methods. The other thing that a professional would do in traditional cybersecurity is check for vulnerabilities in the systems so that those loopholes can be patched to avert any exploitation of the vulnerability, resulting in a cyberattack. Both of those approaches are still valid, but the two things have expanded so unprecedentedly that manual analysis of those factors – data and number of connected – is not possible. You need support from the most advanced data science approaches, such as big data, artificial intelligence (AI), deep learning (DL) models, and machine learning (ML) approaches to understand, analyze, and respond accurately as fast as possible; otherwise, the cybersecurity defense can be easily jeopardized.

- Statistical analytics and machine learning techniques are two of the most common data science approaches that are extensively used in the detection of fraud in a real-time environment on almost all online platforms.
- The detection of patterns of user behaviors in the vast landscape of network devices, software infrastructure, and applications is very difficult without the support of data analytics to cope with the emerging cybersecurity threats.
- Finding out the activities, processes, and performance of the devices as well as software systems in the digital space is an uphill task without the support of powerful data analytics tools to provide the detailed information about the behaviors and events on the systems as well as on the software applications in a real-time environment.
- The cost of a cybersecurity breach is significantly huge in the modern marketplace. Therefore, the approach of corrective measures in cybersecurity is an undesirable approach. The most desirable approach toward robust cybersecurity is the preventive approach, in which the emerging threats should be detected earlier before they materialize with the help of real-time data analytics, pattern detection, penetration checks, and behavior monitoring of both users and the systems simultaneously. If there is any abnormal situation emerging, the proper response should be triggered to stop the emerging threat before it can hit the system to breach your security systems and data.
- Time series analysis is another very crucial field that is one of the core components used in modern cybersecurity. This is the analysis of time-dependent data to scan the hidden patterns and information for activating the suitable and pre-defined response automatically through a comprehensive cybersecurity platform.
- The calculation or analysis of different parameters in modern businesses, systems, processes, and IT infrastructures and software applications, such as simple statistical parameters, probability distributions, models, user profiles, time series, anomaly detection algorithm outputs, and many other patterns, cannot be accomplished without the support of the most advanced data analytic applications and approaches in the modern systems of cybersecurity to deal with both preventive and corrective security.

- Data analytics is also the core component in modern artificial intelligence or machine learning models adopted in modern cybersecurity for automated cyber threat detection and initiating a suitable response against the emerging threat.
- Big data analytics made the following domains of cybersecurity more robust and reliable through automated responses.
  - Security intelligence.
  - Fraud detection.
  - Faster vulnerability detection.
  - Calculation of statistical parameters.
  - Easier classification and clustering.
  - And much more.

MODERN TYPES OF DATA USED IN MACHINE LEARNING

Machine learning models ingest numerous types of data in different forms and formats, such as text, audio, video, images, and sensor signals. Normally, all those formats of data are available in unstructured form, created from a wide range of modern sources such as social media, surveillance systems, video systems, audio systems, mobiles, computers, websites, and many others. The most common types of data used in modern machine learning, deep learning, and artificial intelligence projects are mentioned below.

Machine data

Machine data is one of the most important types of data that is used for data science or data analytics to make informed decisions. These are about all types of data generated by the modern IT machines such as computers, mobiles, communication systems, internet networks, servers, data storage systems, and many others in the form of voice recordings, video records, call detail records (CDRs), automated voice response (ACR), event logs, system logs, internet click streams, online transactions, e-commerce campaigns, and many others.

The most important sources from which the machine data is generated are mentioned in the following list:[141]

- Internet of Things (IoT) devices.
- Process monitoring services.
- Radio frequency identification (RFID).
- Big data management platforms.
- Internet click streams.
- Video and audio call records.
- Natural disaster warning systems.
- Satellite communication systems.
- Energy management systems.
- Traffic management systems.

Real-time data

The real-time data is a very critical type of data that is extensively used in modern data analytics and machine learning models to enhance not only the performance and efficiency of the modern business processes but also to make them highly secure in cyberspace ecosystems. The real-time data is that data which is directly presented to the end-users without any intermediary storage or any intolerable delays or lagging. Normally, the data is created by different sources of data, and that data is stored in the storage system, and then it is accessed for the presentation to the desired end-users, who can be automated systems, monitoring professionals, or data analysts. But the real-time data is presented as soon as it is generated by the sources of data to be fed to the data analytic systems, machine learning models, or even the data analyst professionals individually or simultaneously.[142]

Big data

Big data is about the generation and storage of data in huge volumes and complex formats or structures that cannot possibly be managed through traditional data management systems and need special tools and applications to manage. Such a huge amount of data would be continuously expanding. Big data is a relatively recent concept in the field of data analytics that deals with enormous volumes of data in different formats, such as structured, unstructured, and semi-structured. The main characteristics of big data are:[143]

- **Volume** – The most fundamental characteristic of big data is that it is of huge volume and continuously expanding.
- **Variety** – Big data consists of different types of data in different formats, such as structured, unstructured, and semi-structured.
- **Velocity** – The generation speed of big data is too high to handle through normal approaches. This is another important characteristic of big data.
- **Variability** – The fourth and last feature of big data is the variability of its speed, generation time, and other factors. It is not consistently the same at any point in time or in any conditions. The volumes, speeds, loads, and types vary with time and many other factors.

The most important examples of big data sources include social media websites such as Facebook, YouTube, Twitter (renamed as "X"), Instagram, and others. Other examples include online stock exchanges, civil aviation monitoring systems, and many others.

The processing and management of big data is known as big data analytics. There are numerous benefits of big data analytics, such as:

- Preemptive management of security threats.
- Earlier detection of fraud and malicious activities.
- Enhanced business process efficiency.

- Effective use of business intelligence.
- Improved return on investment (ROI).
- And much more.

Metadata

Metadata is a type of data that is the summary or prefix of the main data in any digital file. For instance, there is a text file that contains an article regarding the Internet of Things (IoT). Metadata of this file will be the following information:[144]

- Name of the author of the file
- Time of creation of the file.
- Format or extension of the file.
- Description of the file.
- Modification date.
- Size of the file.
- Keywords in the file.
- And other similar kinds of information.

Metadata can be created either manually or through automated software tools. The former is extensively used in the traditional business processes because it is more accurate and reliable as compared to creating through automated tools. Nowadays, the machine learning models ingest the data files with manual metadata for learning purposes. The automated systems will understand the data through labeled datasets with metadata. The metadata tagging can be done on numerous types of files, such as images, computer files, audio/video files, HTML files, spreadsheets, relational databases, and many others.

Usually, the types of metadata are classified based on the functions that the data serves in the information management systems. There are numerous types of metadata; a few very important ones of them are mentioned below.

- **Administrative metadata** – It pertains to the rules and restrictions for access, processing, and other management activities on the original data.
- **Descriptive metadata** – Provides the details of the main data in the form of a description.
- **Process metadata** – The details of the source, processing apps, and other information related to processing of the main data are tagged in this type of data.
- **Legal metadata** – This type of metadata denotes the information about the legal status, copyright tags, and other information related to legal matters for intellectual property management systems.
- **And many others** – The other forms include reference metadata, statistical metadata, preservation metadata, provenance metadata, structural metadata, use metadata, and so on.

MAJOR TYPES OF DATA ANALYTICS

Data analytics is a field of data processing to find out the meaningful or valuable patterns that could be used for effective decision-making in different business processes or our day-to-day social life. The importance of data analytics is very high in the modern era, fully powered by the latest technologies such as artificial intelligence (AI), machine learning (ML), deep learning (DL), Internet of Things (IoT), cybersecurity, big data, and many others.[145]

Traditionally, data analytics is divided into four major categories based on the unique characteristics as mentioned below.

- Prescriptive data analytics.
- Predictive data analytics.
- Descriptive data analytics.
- Diagnostic data analytics.

The details of all the important types of data analytics are described at length in the following subsections.

Prescriptive data analytics

Prescriptive data analysis is a very useful type of analytics in which the final takeaways of the analytic process are taken. In other words, it deals with the question, "*What to do next?*" This analysis considers all possible scenarios and factors them into the analysis and comes up with the most suitable information for making data-driven decisions. This can help you take full advantage of the predictions made through different models, such as machine learning, mathematical science, big data, and business rules used for finding out valuable information based on the input data through an automatic or manual data analysis process.[146]

Predictive data analytics

This type of data analytics handles the forecasting or prediction of the values based on the analysis of the previous data fed into the analytic models as training datasets or input data. The input data in huge volumes is analyzed to skim the most actionable information. The input data is used for forecasting the most likely possibility of an outcome or event in a certain situation. This type of data analytics can be applied in numerous statistical methods, such as machine learning, game theory, data mining, and others, that are capable of analyzing the existing patterns and predicting the future outcome of possible results based on the previous patterns. Three main phases of predictive data analytics include the following:[146]

- Predictive modeling phase.
- Analysis of the decision and optimization phase.
- Profiling of transactions.

Descriptive data analytics

Descriptive data analytics deals with the details of the past patterns, such as what happened in certain conditions or criteria. It is considered the most basic type of data analytics, which helps you have a look into the past activities in terms of certain variables such as time, groups, market segments, or any other factor that is required to be analyzed for certain events in the past. For example, it analyzes the past data of your marketing campaign and describes the details of the activities, such as failures, successes, or reasons for success, and others that occurred in the past.

It is the most suitable for finding out the answer to the question, "*What happened in the past?*" in a certain scenario, based on the raw data analysis of the past. The reporting of the past can be in the form of charts, maps, and graphs for a clear understanding of the factors that caused the events in the past, to find out valuable information to make future decisions.[145]

Diagnostic data analytics

Diagnostic data analytics deals with the reasons that caused a certain happening or event. It diagnoses the causes to find out the answer to the question, "*Why did it happen?*" In this type of data analysis, the historical data is taken into the process of analysis to find out the reasons for a certain problem or a question under consideration. The relationship between two variable factors is considered based on the relevant dependencies or any other patterns for the cause of the outcome of an activity. The most common techniques used in diagnostic analytics include correlations, data discovery, and data mining.[146]

DATA ANALYTICS METHODS

Data analytics is a broader field that deals with three major sciences and their different subdomains for establishing inter-relationships. The major fields of science that directly fall under the definition of data analytics or data science include:

- Computer science.
- Mathematics.

STATISTICS

Each field uses different methods and derived techniques from other related fields to carry out the data analysis in the data science field. The individual methods of every field of science mentioned in the above list fall under two major categories of data analysis:[147]

- Qualitative analysis.
- Quantitative analysis.

In the qualitative analysis, numerous submethods are used for deriving the data in the form of observations, words, pictures, symbols, and other such types of content description that cannot be specifically quantified into statistical descriptions or mathematical expressions. The most important subtechniques under this category include:

- **Content analysis** – Mostly deals with the content in the form of verbal data or behavioral data.
- **Narrative analysis** – Under this type of analysis, the data taken for analysis is in the form of surveys, interviews, diaries, and others.
- **Grounding theory** – This type of qualitative analysis deals with the study and analysis of past research and extrapolates the outcome from those past studies.

On the other hand, the category of quantitative analysis deals with the statistical analysis methods by collecting raw data in the form of figures and processing it in numerical formats to find out the statistical outcomes or results. The most common types of techniques adopted in this category of data analysis include the following.

- **Averaging or means analysis** – In this technique, the average or the mean of the numerical raw data is taken by combining all values and dividing by the number of entities that were summed up for averaging.
- **Hypothesis testing analysis** – A supposed condition or theory is considered to be proven with the help of available raw data to analyze and deduce the results.
- **Sample size determination analysis** – This is another technique used in quantitative analysis in which a small portion of the data, known as the sample size, is studied to draw a generalized outcome of a larger body of the study.

Moreover, the data analytics can also be categorized in terms of the field of study or sciences. There are three major fields that are directly dealt with by data science or data analytics. As mentioned before, the fields include computer science, statistics, and mathematics. If we merge the statistics and computer in one domain for data analytics and computer science in the other domain, we can categorize them into two major domains. The computer science techniques are commonly used in artificial intelligence and machine learning applications.

STATISTICS AND MATHEMATICS TECHNIQUES

There are numerous statistical and mathematical methods used for data analytics for finding out the most valuable information to make data-driven decisions. Some of the most important mathematical analysis techniques are used independently for calculating the mathematical solutions, and they are not used in relation to other common techniques of statistics. The most common techniques used for statistical analysis are those four major groups or types that have already been discussed in this chapter. Other than those four major analysis types, the remaining ones include inferential analysis, exploratory data analysis (EDA), causal analysis, mechanistic analysis, and a few others.[148]

Again, the most common types of analysis techniques used in the mathematical domains independently include real analysis, functional analysis, tensor analysis, scalar analysis, harmonic analysis, complex analysis, differential theory, vector analysis, and a few others.[149] The most common types of data analysis related to both statistics and mathematics used in modern computing systems are described below.

Factor analysis

It is a data analysis technique, precisely known as FA. In this technique, a huge number of variables is shortened into a few factors. The most common variances in all variables are pulled out and are inserted into a common score for effective simplification. The other features of the factor analysis technique include:[150]

- FA technique is a part of the general linear model (GLM).
- A certain number of assumptions are taken in this model.
- The most relevant variables are considered in the analysis.
- It uses numerous types of factoring, such as principal component factor (PCA), image factoring, maximum likelihood factoring, common factor analysis, and others.
- The most common types of concepts used in factor analysis include:
  - Confirmatory factor analysis.
  - Explanatory factor analysis.
  - Structural equation modeling.

Regression analysis

Regression analysis is a very efficient and popular statistical technique, which is used for establishing the relationship between two or more variables. It helps the data scientists identify the most relevant factors and their accurate relationships with the other variables under consideration. The regression analysis is extensively used in modern machine learning models for establishing the relationships among different variables or data points. This analysis also helps you identify the most relevant factors to choose and the irrelevant ones to discard. There are numerous types of regression analysis. A few that are commonly used in the machine learning field have already been discussed in the previous chapters of this book.

Time series analysis

The evaluation or assessment of the data points collected in a sequence of time intervals is referred to as time series analysis. It is a statistical method that is used to analyze how different parameters or variables change with the change in time interval. A large number of time series samples of parameters are taken to deduce the pattern of changes in a sequence. The time series analysis helps the data scientist discover the possible patterns in the past and project the future patterns in terms of the upcoming time. It is the best for forecasting and projections of future demands, trends, risks, and many other factors.[151]

Monte Carlo simulation

It is a mathematical data analysis technique that is used for obtaining the estimated possible outcomes of an uncertain event. This technique is widely adopted in different types of artificial neural networks that deal with deep learning (DL). This technique is also referred to as the Monte Carlo Method. In this method, the random and repeated samples are collected and analyzed to figure out the possible or estimated results of an uncertain event. It is highly effective in determining the risk impact in numerous types of real-life scenarios, such as stock exchange prices, product pricing, sales forecasting and projections, and many others.[152]

ARTIFICIAL INTELLIGENCE AND MACHINE LEARNING TECHNIQUES

A range of machine learning and artificial intelligence techniques have already been described in previous chapters, such as classification, regression, dimensionality reduction, ensemble methods, natural language processing (NLP), transfer learning, and others. The data analysis techniques that act as the most fundamental components in those systems are data analytics in different formats, as mentioned below.[153]

Cluster analysis

Cluster analysis is a data analysis method that is the most fundamental component of the clustering process in unsupervised machine learning. This type of data analysis is extensively used in machine learning models for grouping the data points based on the analysis of their similarities and dissimilarities of features and characteristics. The entire process of analyzing the features of the data points for machine learning models is called cluster analysis. The clustering analysis is used for finding out the market segments, product positioning, choosing the test markets, and other tasks.

Sentiment analysis

Sentiment analysis is an important technique to gauge the performance, mood, and outlook of any market or organization. It is also the most fundamental component in natural language processing (NLP) projects used for machine learning applications in modern business processes. The sentiment analysis considers the views, opinions, feelings, excitement, and other abstracts regarding any conversation, experience, review, or other.

DATA ANALYTICS IN MACHINE LEARNING

Data analytics sits at the core of machine learning, or artificial intelligence. Similarly, modern data analytics is hugely influenced by machine learning algorithms for the automation of business processes in all domains of industry. Thus, it can be said that both fields – data analytics and machine learning – are indispensable for each other. All machine learning algorithms use the power of data analytics to find patterns or predict values. The understanding or learning of the machines is purely dependent upon the ML models that utilize data analytics for performing a wide range of activities, such as classification, categorization, predictions, regularization, dimensionality reduction, and many others.

It is important to note that the process automation activities in all fields of modern businesses are fully dependent on machine learning or artificial intelligence, especially in information technology-oriented businesses. Moreover, machine learning cannot be thought of without the availability and processing of data in bulk. The availability of huge data to feed into data analytics made machine learning (ML) possible. The process automation through explicit computer programming is not an intelligent process. It is just a repetitive activity performed with the help of pre-programmed automated code, and no huge amount of data is required for data analysis to maintain the process of repetitive tasks. But machine learning tasks are not only automated but also have a certain level of intelligence to cope with the emerging situation or conditions automatically without any intervention of human resources. With the advent of big data, the machine learning domain has sustained huge growth and emerged as one of the most prominent technologies in the world. The main driver behind the unprecedented growth of machine learning is the availability of huge volumes of data in our modern business ecosystems. Meanwhile, the data analytics, which was fully dependent upon the intuition and intellectuality of human resources a few decades back, is now heavily influenced by computer programming and artificial intelligence, or machine learning. Almost all data analytics processes are automated through machine learning.[154,155]

Chapter 6

Deep learning and neural networks

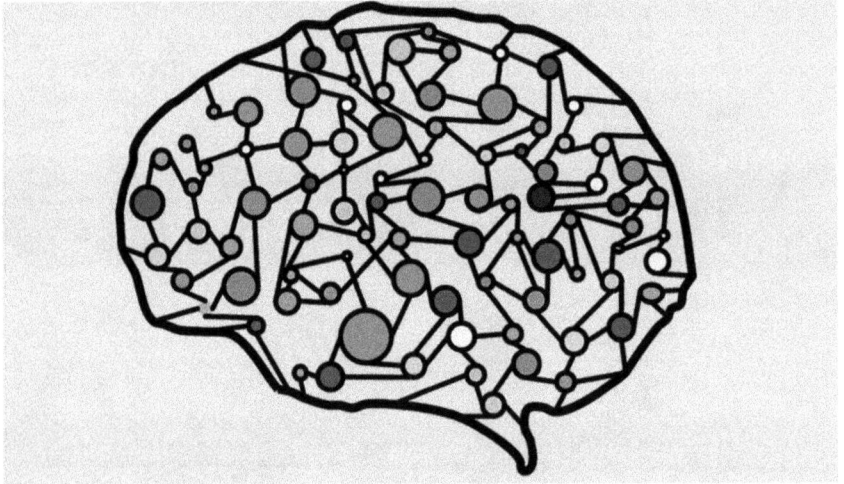

DOI: 10.1201/9781003688327-6

DEEP LEARNING (DL)

Deep learning, precisely DL, is a subdomain of machine learning. It is inspired by the functionality, capability, and natural structure of the human brain. The main objective of this domain is to make the machines capable of self-learning and making suitable decisions based on the conditions they encounter in the real-world environment, somewhat in the same way as the human brain does. Structure-wise, the human brain consists of a network of natural neurons that run in tandem in the sequence of layers. Deep learning is accomplished by an artificial neural network that also consists of artificial neurons structured in layers. They also process the input signal or data the same way as our natural brain does. Thus, we can say that deep learning is the (kind of) mimicry of our natural brain to learn about the environment through observations and experiences.

The most important features and characteristics of the deep learning (DL) field are summarized in the following list:[156,157]

- Deep learning is based on an artificial neural network that consists of at least three layers known as the input layer, the hidden layer, and the output layer.
- Deep learning is not possible without a huge amount of data to be ingested into the machine learning models.
- The more hidden layers in an artificial neural network, the more accuracy and efficiency it produces in predictions.
- The most common real-world applications powered by deep learning include virtual assistants, chatbots, credit card fraud detection, driverless cars, and others.
- Deep learning can make predictions without any human intervention by ingesting huge volumes of data to scan and determine different parameters and features of unstructured data. The unstructured data cannot be fed into the machine learning systems without any explicit tagging of data or compiling the data into structured formats.
- Deep learning uses two main types of data flow mechanisms, known as forward propagation and backward propagation.
- There are two most important types of neural networks and many other subversions of those major types. The main types are listed below.
  - Convolutional neural networks (CNN).
  - Recurrent neural networks (RNN).
- Major industries that use deep learning or neural networks in their respective activities and business processes include the following.
  - Cybersecurity and law enforcement agencies.
  - Banking and financial services.
  - Healthcare and customer care services.
  - And many others.

- Deep learning systems require huge amounts of processing power, such as graphical processing units (GPUs), to handle extremely large amounts of data for learning and predictions.
- Deep learning is a subset of representation learning that deals with numerous abstract features to make predictions through a deeper path consisting of numerous nodes in different hidden layers.

HOW DOES IT WORK?

As mentioned in the introduction, the concept of deep learning is based on the processing of input data through multiple nodes and calculating the weightage of the signal created from the input data in multiple layers of artificial neural networks. This entire workflow of deep learning is similar to human brain functionality. The human brain consists of a network of natural neurons that is called a natural neural network. In this network, millions of neurons are interconnected to participate in calculating the input data received through the ear, touch, smell, vision, taste, and other gut feelings. The final decision is made by processing through those neurons.

Similarly, the working principle of deep learning is based on an artificial neural network that consists of multiple layers of neurons classified into three major categories: input layer, hidden layer(s), and output layer. The number of input and output layers in any neural network is one each, while the number of hidden layers can be at least one or more than one, depending upon the complexity and power of the neural network to process the data for a deeper understanding of the data it receives through the input layer.

Each layer consists of nodes and branches. Each node of any layer is connected to each node of the next layer and vice versa through branches. There is a threshold value for each neuron to be activated, which is calculated through different mathematical functions. All links or arms have a specific value assigned based on the value of the input neuron to that particular link or arm. In other words, each neuron has a value that is activated when the threshold value of the input signal is achieved. When the input value crosses the threshold value of the neuron processed through mathematical functions, the neuron gets activated, and the output link or arm gets activated and sends the signal to the neuron in the next layer. If the threshold value does not cross due to the input signal to the neuron, the neuron does not get activated and does not share the value with the neurons of the next layer. The change in the value of activation can be done through a technique known as gradient descent. Thus, the signals keep passing through the hidden layers of the neural network and reach the output network layer.[158,159]

MAJOR TYPES OF NEURAL NETWORKS USED IN DEEP LEARNING

Neural networks are the artificial schematic structures built through computing algorithms. The neural networks consist of three major parts as far as the structural entities are concerned. Those parts are referred to as layers. They are the input layer, hidden layer(s), and output layer. This layered structure is also known as a neuron. If there are a few input data fed to a node of the layer, the second step that takes place in the hidden node is the summation of all input values received from the nodes of the input layer. The summed values are processed through function activation, which produces the result or output. The output is sent to the node of the output layer. This logical flow is also known as the single neuron working flow in our modern neural networks.

Neural networks are very powerful as well as very useful models extensively used in the solutions of non-linear and complex problems that the normal machine learning models and algorithms are not able to solve. The neural networks are highly effective in detecting a huge number of parameters of an object or data point and applying the most efficient methods to regularize the expanded volume of parameters without losing crucial parameters. The most important reasons for choosing deep learning models in the modern artificial intelligence (AI) fields, such as natural language processing (NLP), computer vision (CV), speech recognition (SR), robotics, and other domains of automation, include the following:

- Highly effective decision boundary.
- Extremely efficient feature engineering.

Neural networks offer greater accuracy and solutions to the most complex and non-linear problems for classification and predictions based on the effective decision boundary capability. In neural networks, data points with a huge number of features and a non-linear data point space can be classified easily through powerful non-linear and complex relationships among the data points through a highly capable decision boundary.

The second most important aspect of artificial intelligence, or AI-based model building, is feature engineering, which consists of two main functions:

- Feature extraction.
- Feature selection.

The capability of neural networks to extract features and choose the most relevant and crucial features for generating the best results is huge compared to the normal machine learning systems that we learned in the previous chapters. Deep learning models based on neural networks can extract thousands of features from just a small image at a time and can also summarize that huge number of features through effective and efficient regularization in such a way that the most important features remain and the irrelevant features are discarded easily. Doing these two activities manually through machine learning models would lead to the consumption of huge manpower, time, and modifications in computing models simultaneously.

Different types of neural networks are used in the use of modern solutions to problems pertaining to computer vision (CV), natural language processing (NLP), and many of the latest domains, such as robotics, self-driving vehicles, facial recognition, voice detection, and many others. Neural networks can be broadly classified into two categories based on the flow of data processing or the direction of the data propagation. The two categories include:[160]

- Feed-forward neural networks.
- Feedback neural networks.

The most important types of neural networks that fall in the feed-forward neural network category include the following.

- Artificial neural networks (ANN).
- Convolutional neural networks (CNN).

On the other hand, the most important type of neural network that falls in the feedback neural network category includes:

- Recurrent neural network (RNN)

The details of each neural network falling under the above-mentioned categories are described in the following topics.

Artificial neural network (ANN)

An artificial neural network is a type of feed-forward neural network in which the data processing flow is directed in the forward direction, starting from the input layer to hidden layers and to the output layer without any feedback or recurrent data flow in the backward direction. An artificial neural network is also commonly known as a multi-layer perceptron (MLP) network because it consists of multiple layers of neurons, which are also referred to as perceptrons.

The most fundamental features and characteristics of an artificial neural network, or multi-layer perceptron neural network, are:[161,162]

- It is the most fundamental or basic type of neural network that is used for the solution of basic problems in artificial intelligence, such as tabular data, image data, and text data in the most basic structures.

- Each layer of this neural network, which consists of a set of non-linear functions of weights equal to the sum of all outputs, is fully connected with the prior layer.
- It is capable of learning any non-linear functions; that is why they are also referred to as universal function approximators by learning different weights that can map any input data to an output data or outcome.
- Logically speaking, the artificial neural network perceptron consists of input weights, summation, bias, activation function, and output.
- The activation function is the main component that helps computers learn and estimate the complex and non-linear relationships between two parameters.
- The working flow of an image with the artificial neural network is that it converts the *two-dimensional* into single dimension vector, which leads to the increased number of training parameters with the small increase in the size of image.
- The spatial features of an image in this method are lost due to the conversion of the image into vectors.
- One of the most common problems with all other neural networks, known as vanishing and exploding gradients, also exists in this type of neural network.
- The updating of the weights of the neural networks is done through backpropagation algorithms in neural networks by calculating the gradients. If the number of hidden layers increases, then the updating through backpropagation may lead to the vanishing and exploding of the calculated gradient in all types of neural networks.
- This type of neural network is not capable of recording the sequential data in any type of problem in which the sequence of the data is critical to consider. Thus, the inability to record sequential data makes it unsuitable for many natural language and video data learning solutions in modern automated applications.

Convolutional neural network (CNN)

Convolutional neural network, precisely referred to as CNN, is the most popular neural network used in all domains, applications, and communities of deep learning at present. It is a type of feed-forward neural network. The CNN is extensively used for deep learning applications for video and image processing. The most fundamental component of a convolutional neural network is the kernel, which is also known as the basic building block of this neural network. The kernel uses the convolution operation for processing the images and video data. The convolution function applied to an image or video results in feature extraction.[163]

The most important features and characteristics of convolutional neural networks are mentioned in the following list:[160,161,162,163]

- The basic structure of CNN is divided into two components, as mentioned here:
  - **Convolution layers** – This part is designed to extract features of the input data.
  - **Fully connected or dense layers** – This component of CNN deals with creating output from the feature extraction accomplished by the first component.
- Like an artificial neural network, the learning process of this neural network also consists of two main activities or processes, such as:
  - **Forward propagation** – This process consists of receiving input data, processing it, and generating an output.
  - **Backward propagation** – The most important functions of this process include comparing the output generated by the forward propagation process with the actual value of the input to create an error value or deviation and updating the parameters of the network to run another entire learning process of the neural network.
- The image is converted into a vector, and then the pixel values of the entire image are calculated through a convolution layer of the CNN network through a convolution filter, which is a small patch of an image.
- These data or feature extraction results are sent forward to the fully connected layer of the CNN.
- The dense or fully connected layer generates the results from the data received from the convolution layer.
- Like other types of neural networks, the neuron of CNN is also characterized by three characteristics: weight, bias, and activation function.
- The result of the input data is generated through weights and biases. Once the result is generated, the activation function is applied to it.
- The activation function is a mathematical operation used to learn about the non-linear functionality or non-linearity of the input dataset. There are numerous types of activation functions used in CNN networks, such as linear activation functions, binary steps, Rectified Linear Unit (ReLU), parameterized ReLU, Sigmoid, and many others.
- After applying the activation function, the data is subjected to the linear transformation for comparing the output with the original values to find out the error value so that the network may be reset for another learning process through backward propagation.
- After finding out the error, the entire network process is reset by updating the parameters with the help of the gradient descent technique.
- The main applications that deploy the convolutional neural networks include computer vision, facial recognition, traffic management, recommendation engines, digital product and file classification, and others.
- It uses a single filter for scanning and capturing the spatial features of an image or video.

Recurrent neural network (RNN)

A recurrent neural network, precisely known as RNN, is the major type of feedback neural network category. In this type of neural network, the output achieved through the hidden layers is fed back to the hidden layers through recurrent connections or loops. This looping constraint allows the RNN to take the sequential data through input nodes. The recurrent neural network is used for three solutions to the following main problems.

- Text data processing.
- Time series data processing.
- Audio data processing.

The most important features, capabilities, and characteristics of a recurrent neural network are mentioned in the following list:[164]

- It is very useful for NLP applications because of the ability to process time series and sequential data of sentences in spoken and written languages.
- The RNN is known for its capability of parameter sharing across a range of time steps, which decreases the computational cost and number of parameters to process simultaneously.
- The most basic unit of a recurrent neural network is known as a "cell", which consists of processing layers and a series of cells that help the network in processing the sequential data or time series data in deep learning.
- Very effective in applications that use handwriting recognition, speech recognition, and other similar kinds of functions.
- Normally, it uses the backpropagation through time, or BPTT (Backpropagation Through Time), algorithm for the learning process. This algorithm is based on the gradient.
- They support the mapping of varying types or lengths of input and output data.
- It is used to combine the output of hidden layers through a loopback constraint.

Deep learning regularization

Before diving deeper into the concept of deep learning regularization, it is very important to recap the definition of regularization that we already covered in this book. Regularization is a technique that is used to avoid overfitting in machine learning models or algorithms. Overfitting is the inability of the ML model to recognize the problem in spite of very deep learning of problems with a large number of irrelevant features known as noise. To avoid the overfitting problem, different regularization techniques are used in machine learning. For example, dimensionality reduction was one of the most important techniques used in linear machine learning algorithms. Similarly, different techniques of regularization are used in deep learning (DL) through neural networks that are mentioned in the following list:[164,165]

- L1 regularization.
- L2 regularization.
- Dropout regularization.

L1 regularization

L1 regularization is also referred to as Lasso regression. It uses another regularization term (Ω) for calculating the L1 regularization loss function. The loss function in L1 regularization is equal to the sum of the gradients of the old loss function and the sign of a weight value times ALPHA. In this type of regularization, the weight values are forced to become zero. There are different mathematical derivations used in the calculation of L1 regularization to reduce the overfitting problem in deep learning models. Those equations are beyond the scope of this book.

L2 regularization

L2, or Level-2, regularization is one of the most commonly used techniques in modern deep learning through neural networks to reduce overfitting in ML models. It is also referred to as "weight decay" and "ridge regression" alternatively. This regularization uses lengthy mathematical derivations to calculate the loss function of L2 regularization. It is very important to recall that loss functions refer to the method of assessing the efficiency or effectiveness of the machine learning model, that is, how well the ML model understands or learns from the training. The loss function is determined by extending the regularization term (Ω), which is equal to a mathematical expression.

The regularization L2 is also known as the Euclidean Norm (L2 Norm) of weight matrices. Thus, the L2 weight matrix is the sum of all squared weight values of the weight matrix. The loss function is then calculated through a formula, and finally, the gradient is found to update the model. Thus, the L2 regularization reduces the overfitting. In other words, the L2 regularization multiplies the regularization term (Ω) by ALPHA and adds the entire expression to the loss function. In this type of regularization, the weight parameters are decreased but not made equal to zero. The curve showing this phenomenon becomes almost flat at near zero. The derivations of those mathematical equations are beyond the scope of this book.

Dropout regularization

This type of regularization is known to produce highly reliable results as compared to the other regularization techniques used in deep learning models. This is the reason that it is one of the most commonly used techniques in all types of modern ML projects powered by deep learning or neural networks. In this technique, a few randomized nodes are dropped out of the deep learning layers at each iteration of updating the parameters. The result of each iteration of the process helps learn the model more effectively by reducing the overfitting problem. The dropout technique is applied to two types of layers – hidden layers and input layers. By turning off the neurons, the network becomes simpler with fewer variables or features; thus, it provides a clearer picture of the environments for the machines to learn. The selection of neurons is done on the basis of random probability.

Deep feed-forward neural networks

Deep Feed-Forward, precisely referred to as Deep feed-forward (DFF), is a type of feed-forward neural network (FFNN) characterized by the flow of data processing. There are two main types of feed-forward neural networks:[166]

- Multi-layer perceptron (MLP).
- Deep feed-forward (DFF).

The DFF is a simple form of neural network without any loopback for any kind of feedback to the hidden layers. The main difference between simple feed-forward or MLP and deep feed-forward is the number of hidden layers. In simple feed-forward neural networks, there is only one hidden layer. On the other hand, there are multiple (i.e., more than 2) hidden layers in a deep feed-forward neural network. The DFF networks perform much better than shallow neural networks or simple feed-forward networks. It is highly suitable for complex problem solving that involves multiple features, such as image or video data mapping. The most common activation function used in this type of neural network is known as the Rectified Linear Unit (ReLU). It produces fewer issues related to vanishing gradients.

Training optimization of deep learning models

Training optimization is a process to reduce the loss function through different techniques in deep learning models. The reduction in the loss function is accomplished by adapting or modifying the features or attributes of a neural network, such as weights and learning rate, with a new iteration of processing. By doing this, the accuracy and performance of neural network-based machine learning models improve, and the loss function or cost function decreases.

There are many techniques that are used for optimizing the training of deep learning models. Those training optimization techniques are known as training optimizers in general terminology. A few of the most fundamental training techniques extensively used in all types of neural networks are mentioned in the following list:[167]

- Gradient Descent (GD).
- Stochastic Gradient Descent (SGD).
- Mini-Batch Gradient Descent (BM GD).
- Momentum Based Gradient Descent (MB GD).
- Nesterov Accelerated Gradient Descent (NAGD).
- Adaptive Gradient Algorithm (AdaGrad).
- Root Mean Square Propagation (RMSprop).
- Adaptive Moment Estimation (Adam).

The selection of the most suitable optimizer for any neural network-based deep learning model depends on the type, objectives, data, and problems to be solved. Data scientists can decide which training optimization technique will be useful for which model.

Recurrent sequential modeling network

Recurrent sequential modeling networks are those neural networks that can process the sequential data, time series, text, and images to make the models learn about the data that are affected by the time and sequence of other events or parameters. The most common recurrent sequential modeling networks are known as recurrent neural networks, or RNNs. There are three more types of recurrent neural networks that are capable of working as recurrent sequential modeling networks for deep learning applications, as mentioned below:[168]

- Simple Recurrent Neural Network (SR NN).
- Long Short-Term Memory Neural Network (LSTM NN).
- Gated Recurrent Unit Neural Network (GRU NN).

The simple neural networks are those that have a simple loopback in the hidden layers to feed back the output of a neuron. In this type of node, the nodes or neurons are not modified, but they just send the feedback to the other neurons of the layer.

On the other hand, the Long Short-Term Memory Neural Networks (LSTMs) are formed by modifying the neurons or nodes with an additional three gates. Those gates are named the input gate, output gate, and forget gate. This addition or modification enables the model to become more sophisticated in deciding whether to feed back the output to the other neurons or not. This model is more suitable for applications using non-formal sequence data like words, images, and videos in deep learning processes. This type of network offers greater accuracy in anomaly detection, video data, and audio data applications. It is also effective in resolving the issue of vanishing gradient in all major deep learning applications powered by LSTM neural networks.

The third type of recurrent neural network is the gated recurrent unit, or GRU. It is also based on cell type or neuron type, similar to the LSTM. In this type of neural network, the output gate is not available as it is in the LSTM model. GRU has three times fewer parameters than the normal or simple recurrent neural networks. Meanwhile, the LSTM has four times (greater) the number of parameters as compared to the simple RNN.

Recursive sequential modeling network

Recursive sequential modeling neural networks are based on the structural flow of data processing. All other neural networks that have been discussed in this book are based on either a feed-forward neural network (FFNN) or a feedback neural network structure. The recursive sequential model is based on the structure of hierarchical processing. In this model, the data flows from the sequence of parent to child nodes in the neural networks. This type of neural network (denoted by the RvNN model) is created by putting the same weights recursively.[169,170]

Chapter 7

Modern cybersecurity tools

DOI: 10.1201/9781003688327-7

INTRODUCTION TO MODERN CYBERSECURITY

Today, cybersecurity is a very commonly used word in the field of computer science and information and telecommunication technologies. It is the combination of two words – Cyber and Security. The word "Cyber" is meant for all things related to computer machines and their applications. "Security" is meant to protect the entire cyber ecosystem. Initially, the concept of cybersecurity was much simpler than the present-day or modern concept of cybersecurity due to the emergence of advanced technologies in all associated fields, such as software, hardware, information, connectivity, web environments, cloud environments, and many others.

Modern cybersecurity is a comprehensive field of protecting all types of digital resources, such as hardware, software apps, information, and their associated stakeholders, from all types of cyber threats. In the earlier days, computer applications, data storage, and networks were smaller and confined to certain segments of users; therefore, the domain of cybersecurity was also very limited. With the enhancement and evolution of different technologies, which materialized the digital transformation in almost all types of business processes as well as all other societal activities across the strata of nations worldwide, the landscape of modern cybersecurity has also changed drastically. The modern definition of cybersecurity encompasses numerous processes within the field of cybersecurity, as mentioned in the following list:[171,172,173]

- Identification of emerging threats in light of ecosystem weaknesses.
- Detection of malicious or abnormal activities prior to their materialization in the cyberspace ecosystem.
- Protection of the entire cyberspace components, such as computer machines, software applications, connecting networks, information storage or digital data, and all stakeholders and associated components that get affected.
- Provision of proper response to the emerging threats before they materialize so that any potential risk or damage to the cyber environment is averted.
- Recovery and restoration of the entire cyber ecosystem to normalcy in the worst-case scenario when the data breach or cyberattack is successful in inflicting damage to the cyberspace environment (deliberate attempts by the cyber criminals or hackers).

Thus, the modern jurisdiction of cybersecurity is huge. It incorporates numerous technologies, platforms, mechanisms, and agents to accomplish the security of an expanded environment of a large number of applications, software platforms, hardware tools, a combination of networks, types of data storage, and advanced integrated automated processes to maintain robust cybersecurity.

TYPES OF MODERN CYBERSECURITY

Modern cybersecurity is very sophisticated as well as very complex, consisting of numerous platforms, processes, applications, tools, techniques, and hardware systems. It has to deal with a range of components that form a complex cyber environment. With the advent of the Internet of Things (IoT), artificial intelligence (AI), machine learning (ML), Bring Your Own Device (BYOD), and other platforms and technologies, modern cybersecurity has also been divided into different categories, types, and domains to deal with their respective domains. The most important types and domains of modern cybersecurity systems are mentioned in the following list:[172,173]

- Application security.
- Network security.
- Data/information security.
- Cloud security.
- Endpoint security.
- Mobile security.
- IoT security.
- Operational security.
- Physical access security (Zero Trust Security).
- Critical infrastructure security.
- Disaster recovery.

All of the above-mentioned domains or types of cybersecurity are accomplished through an integrated cybersecurity system that consists of a wide range of modern tools, platforms, applications, and mechanisms. Those components of cybersecurity play their respective roles not in isolation but in an integrated and coordinated ecosystem so that the emerging threats can be detected earlier and a suitable response to those emerging threats can be initiated automatically with the help of predefined security response programs. The most important tools, platforms, applications, or systems involved in modern cybersecurity include the following:[172]

- Security firewalls (FW).
- Identity and access management (IAM).
- Antivirus and anti-malware programs.
- Data loss prevention (DLP).
- Intrusion detection and prevention systems (IDS/IPS).
- Endpoint protection systems.
- Virtual private networks (VPNs).
- Cloud access security broker (CASB).
- Encryption tools.
- Cloud workload protection platform (CWPP).
- Vulnerability scanners.
- Endpoint detection and response systems.

The details of a few very important platforms, tools, and systems used in modern cybersecurity will be discussed in the last chapter of this book. The introduction of different types of modern cybersecurity is given in the following subtitles.

Application security

In modern business environments, the role of process-specific applications to deliver different types of services is very critical. The security of those applications to run smoothly without any access or data breach is called application security. The application security may include code-level implementation of security features, encryption, firewalls, and other steps at the application development and operational levels. Application security deals with both the software and hardware level securities in on-premises as well as in cloud environments. Regular scanning for vulnerabilities and patching those weaknesses is also a major part of this type of security.[171]

Network security

Securing all components of a single network or a combination of different networks in terms of their operational continuity, performance, access, and authorization is known as network security. The main activities involved in network security include:

- Protecting the integrity, sustainability, and safety of network users.
- Continual monitoring of network performance and efficiency.
- Access control of the network users.
- Analyzing traffic destination and types.
- And many more.

These processes can be accomplished through network operational and maintenance systems, firewalls, access control systems, virtual private networks, encrypted communication, and other functions deployed at the network layer.

Data/information security

Data or information security is a type of cybersecurity that safeguards data from corruption, theft, and unauthorized access. It deals with the entire lifecycle of digital data or information. The data security may include encrypted storage and transmission, authorized access systems, security policy development and implementation, data masking, automated auditing and reporting to the concerned personnel, and redaction of sensitive files in case of highly sensitive data residing in those files on the computer storage devices. Data security, or information security, is accomplished through software and hardware tools simultaneously.[174]

Cloud security

Cloud security is a domain of security similar to traditional on-premises security in a cyber environment. After the advent of cloud ecosystems, traditional security and cloud security have become two separate domains. Cloud security deals with the overall security of data, applications, and servers residing in the cloud environment. The security of the entire cloud infrastructure is also a part of cloud security. All components that deal with general cybersecurity are also parts of cloud security and a few additional components are added in this system.

Endpoint security

As the name suggests, it is a type of security that deals with the endpoints or end-users of a network or a connected environment to avoid any kinds of malicious attacks or campaigns that can lead to direct impact on the end-users as well as the networks in which the users are located. The main devices used as endpoints include mobiles, laptops, desktops, tablets, and other gadgets. The most important techniques used for maintaining endpoint security include firewalls, access control lists, data sniffers, intrusion detection systems, antiviruses, anti-malware, and others.[175]

Mobile security

The security of mobile devices such as mobile phones, tablets, laptops, and other mobile gadgets connected to the Internet or any other networks through wireless connectivity is known as mobile security. The main components of mobile security include facial recognition, mobile device security features, strong passwords, secure network selection, and authorized data access in all networks the mobile devices travel through.

IoT security

IoT security deals with a new emerging field of the connected world known as the Internet of Things, precisely IoT. In this new world of connected devices, all physical devices used in our day-to-day lives, whether they are fixed or movable, are given an identity in the shape of an IP address, and they communicate with other devices and software applications through a centralized control system. The maintenance of robust security of the entire IoT ecosystem is known as IoT security.[176]

Operational security

Operational security is also referred to as procedural security and is mostly deployed in a wide range of business and technological processes in modern industries. This is a five-phase (or step) security that is designed from the perspective of adversaries so that the operation of a process is maintained with full or robust security. The five steps of operational security include:[177]

- Identification of critical data.
- Identification of possible threats.
- Assessment of system vulnerabilities.
- Analysis of associated risks.
- Designing, developing, and deploying counter security measures.

Physical access security (zero trust security)

The physical access security deals with the secure admission or access granted to the authorized users to a wide range of physical resources such as buildings, servers, control rooms, air-conditioning and heating systems, and other infrastructures. Traditionally, this type of security was handled by human guards. Modern physical access security is extensively handled by physical access control systems (PACS).[178]

Critical infrastructure security

Critical infrastructure security is a kind of security that deals with the smooth operation under a secure environment for all critical components of a business ecosystem. The critical infrastructure is that of assets, hardware, software, data, or any other installation that would be deemed as the most crucial or critical for the operation as well as the existence of the business. The critical infrastructure in national security includes the garrisons, powerhouses, grids, water supply systems, financial hubs, and so on. In modern businesses in cyberspace, the critical infrastructures are those without which the business cannot run smoothly, and any compromise with them will lead to disastrous outcomes, such as business data, customers' personal and financial data, policy data, and others.[179]

Disaster recovery

Disaster recovery, precisely written as DR, is a part of cybersecurity that comes into play after a disaster strikes cyberspace or systems. Disaster recovery is a comprehensive plan to restore and get control of the IT operations or services, infrastructure, and data servers after any kind of disaster, such as cyberattacks, natural disasters, and man-made disasters like war and terrorism. The disaster recovery is governed by a comprehensive disaster recovery policy, plan, and procedure. The most important components of disaster recovery include the identification of business-critical components, devising automated backups, assessment of potential threats, continual performance testing and optimization, and so on.[180]

A BRIEF HISTORY OF CYBERSECURITY

The history of modern cybersecurity originates from the traditional security of computer machines and their operations when they were first developed in 1943. Initially, the security of the computers was very limited because only a few people knew how to operate or deal with the big computer machines. Those machines were standalone machines and were not connected; therefore, the security would mean the physical access and then some modification or alteration to the machine operations or software operating at the backend. The concept of modern cybersecurity was first introduced by the pioneer of modern computers, John Von Neumann, in 1949. He pointed out the concept and possibility of computer viruses.

The later chronicle of computer cybersecurity – both in standalone and connected ecosystems history – is shown below:[181]

- **1950s** – The start of phone phreaking. Phreaking is a type of hacking that involves manipulating the telephone system to make free or unauthorized calls. Though this continued until 1980, new cybersecurity problems arose during that period.
- **1960s** – Early physical access-based intrusion into the computer machines and environments started in this decade.
- **1967** – IBM computer system components were accessed by the students who were given training on those computers. It was a standalone cybersecurity issue at that time.
- **1970s** – With the birth of Advanced Research Projects Agency Network (ARPANET), the advent of the connected world started with enormous probabilities of computer hacking or intrusions.
- **1971** – The invention of the Creeper program, known as the first virus, made by Bob Thomas.
- **1980s** – The emergence of different types of viruses and malware was noticed during the initial years of this decade.
- **1986** – The brain virus for IBM PCs was released.
- **1987** – The first concept of cybersecurity emerged.
- **1987** – The first antivirus programs known as Anti4us and Flushot Plus were introduced.
- **1990s** – The entire world goes online with a huge spread of viruses and the fast emergence of a new industry known as cybersecurity. Numerous cybersecurity systems, encryption, antivirus, anti-malware, and other systems emerged.
- **2000 and onward** – An explosive growth of the cybersecurity industry is continuing with exponential growth across all domains of cybersecurity.

TRADITIONAL CYBERSECURITY TOOLS

Traditional cybersecurity relates to the most fundamental components used in the start of cybersecurity systems. The early threats that emerged in the field of cybersecurity a few decades back were mostly focused around antiviruses, anti-spyware, anti-malware, and firewalls because the threats were limited to viruses, malware, and spyware. The details of the traditional tools are mentioned below separately.

Antiviruses

Antiviruses are the software programs designed to catch and remove viruses from your computer machines. Those viruses are short malicious programs designed to harm your computer and data on your computers and laptops.

Antispyware

Antispyware is another important tool traditionally used to find and remove any malicious software installed unknowingly on computers by hackers or to detect it at the time of installation or downloading on the computer. Spyware is a malicious program designed to spy on your activities and steal personal data from your computers.

Anti-malware

Anti-malware is another important tool that was used in old cybersecurity systems to protect your computers from a wide range of malware programs designed for stealing data, personal information, damaging your computer data storage, and other activities through a malicious program. The computer programs that can inflict the above-mentioned damages are known as malware in the field of cybersecurity. A computer program developed against malware programs to prevent them from installing on computers or downloading for installation on your data is known as anti-malware.

Hardware firewalls

A hardware firewall was one of the most powerful components used in traditional cybersecurity in the initial decades of cybersecurity. At present, numerous types of powerful software applications simulating the old hardware firewalls have been developed. The hardware firewall was installed at the face of a business or private network to prevent any unwanted and malicious traffic coming from other networks and also prevent any malicious traffic from within the organizational network through certain firewall rules.[182]

MODERN CYBERSECURITY TOOLS

The present-day hackers, or malicious users, have become so advanced and skilled; they use an innovative approach and the most sophisticated tools to unleash cyberattacks on the modern IT infrastructures. To cope with those advanced threats, the traditional methods or tools are not sufficient. The most advanced and integrated cybersecurity platforms are required to face the security challenges posed by modern hackers. Those modern cybersecurity tools are powered by numerous modern technologies such as machine learning (ML), artificial intelligence (AI), and advanced data analytics (DA). A few very important modern cybersecurity tools are mentioned below.[183]

Security information and event management (SIEM)

Security information and event management, precisely written as SIEM, is a comprehensively integrated modern cybersecurity tool that merges the capabilities of software computer security and event analysis into one platform. It is a comprehensive software-based security platform that is used to analyze the events generated by all software as well as hardware equipment involved in the web or connected environment in real-time to preempt any emerging threats based on the results of the analysis of the events. The alerts or other events generated by all components of a modern IT environment are collectively analyzed to generate a suitable response to the emerging threats. The term SIEM was coined by Amrit Williams and Mark Nicolett in 2005.[184]

The most salient features and capabilities of modern security information and event management systems include:

- It is a combination of two subdomains of management, such as:
  - Security information management (SIM).
  - Security event management (SEM).
- The main functionalities of a professional-grade SIEM solution include the following:
  - Detection of the indicators or parameters of potential attacks based on the security policy defined by the organization to achieve their respective desired business objectives and goals.
  - Detection of unauthorized intrusion of local, remote, or network events and activities to alert the system for further analysis.
  - Identification of unauthorized use of the network or web environment or any other system that falls under the jurisdiction of the SIEM system by using different techniques, such as organization-defined rules or methods, and assignment of authorization as per the criteria of the company.
  - Invoking the internal monitoring capabilities of the SIEM system or deploying additional systems or devices for the monitoring of the

events to collect organization-defined information and tracing specific kinds of transactions from different ad hoc locations within the system that are of the organization's interest.

- Analysis of the anomalies and events of the entire system and network of an organization.
- Adjustment in the levels of the system monitoring process when some changes in different categories initiate, such as risk to operations or IT assets, individuals, or other business organizations within the ecosystem.
- Establishing the capabilities for threat hunting within the organization's ecosystem.
- The other focus of an SIEM system is maintenance of managed security services (MSS) as well as security as a service (SECaaS).

- Aggregation of data related to events and information from multiple sources within as well as from outside sources such as servers, databases, networks, applications, and other devices such as endpoint users.
- Establishment of correlation among the data collected from different sources to bundle them into groups or categories.
- Generation of alerts and informative charts from the analysis of the events or correlated data collected from multiple sources.
- Retention of data and information required for the compliance of any industrial and regulatory standards for a certain time duration.
- Provisioning of forensic analytical capabilities to scan through long piles of logs and events and other information to develop valuable sets of information that are proficiently used in developing suitable security responses.
- The components of an SIEM may vary from vendor to vendor, but the most fundamental components of a professional-grade SIEM may include:
  - **Data collector** – This component collects the data related to events and other system information from the sources and sends it to the aggregation part of the system.
  - **Indexing or aggregating point** – This part of the system takes the data from the collector and performs different activities such as parsing, data normalization, developing data correlations, and others.
  - **Search node** – The search node is used for different activities such as queries, reports, alerts, visualization, and others.

Threat intelligence tools

Threat intelligence tools are extensively named as a threat intelligence platform (TIP) in cybersecurity. These tools are used by the security personnel to collect, aggregate, and organize the threat intelligence in any existing IT infrastructure. This can collect vulnerabilities, weaknesses, possible threats, and other parameters of a network to analyze the health of that particular network so that any emerging threats can be countered properly.

The most common features and characteristics of cyber threat intelligence (CTI) tools are:

- A comprehensive tool designed to detect intelligence about the adversary networks and preparedness that can create a serious cybersecurity threat to the organization's infrastructure and services.
- Normally, a threat intelligence platform (TIP) checks a few very important components in IT communication, such as domain names, IP addresses, malicious endpoints, hash checksum of malware software, phishing email headers, and others.
- A threat detection tool is capable of performing cybersecurity threat detection, which is one of the core components of a cybersecurity system, along with two additional components, such as prevention and providing a suitable response.
- The entire process of threat detection can be classified into four major categories, as mentioned in the following list:[186]
  - **Configuration** – In this category, the tool scans and analyzes the configurations of the network and other elements working in an IT environment.
  - **Modeling** – In this functional category, the threat detecting tool uses model environments for hackers (with their capabilities) to attack the system and check the response.
  - **Indicator** – The indicators of the system are analyzed to detect the possibilities of threats that may affect the system.
  - **Threat behavior** – In this method, the threat codes, behavior of threat actors, and the methods that they can use to unleash a cyberattack are analyzed to detect the entire landscape of behavior of the adversary.
- There are four more important and most commonly used approaches to threat detection applications in almost all types of tools, such as:
  - Investigation of all relevant functions and activities in any cyberspace.
  - Discovering the never-happened-before activities related to cyberattacks.
  - Discovering and analyzing similar kinds of activities that have already occurred in similar types of cyberattacks.
  - Scoping is the fourth important approach to assess the depth of the security incidents that can impact the systems at a certain level.

Vulnerability scanning tools

Vulnerability scanning tools, or vulnerability scanners, are automated platforms that scan the entire corporate network and its elements and make a digital inventory. All components of the network, such as servers, computers, desktops, laptops, virtual machines, containers, routers, printers, switches, and any other network elements, are also scanned for their configurations, default settings, operating systems, updates, and all other attributes that are critical for cybersecurity. Vulnerability scanners are classified into five major categories based on their segment of the IT environment, such as:[185]

- Application-based scanners.
- Wireless-based (Wi-Fi) scanners.
- Network-based scanners.
- Host-based scanners.
- Database-based scanners.

The other major characteristics and capabilities of a professional-level vulnerability scanner tool may include the following:

- It is used for detecting the known vulnerabilities and weaknesses in a computer, application, or computer network of a given IT ecosystem.
- The major criteria used to detect vulnerabilities in the environment include the misconfiguration of the devices and flawed development of computer code used in applications or services of an organization.
- Numerous modern vulnerability scanners are available in both on-premises services and SaaS services in the cloud to use.
- Modern vulnerability scanners are also equipped with additional features to conduct a few preventive activities, such as customization of reports, installation of software patches or full tools, opening ports, installing certificates, and others.
- Modern vulnerability scanners can support two major types of scanning, as mentioned in the following list:[187]
  - **Authenticated Scanning** – This is a type of scanning that is the most reliable and generates the authenticated information report about the system because it has been initiated through an authenticated way by using the authorization protocols via remote administrative protocols such as remote desktop protocol (RDP) and secure shell (SSL) protocol for scanning the connected assets through system-authenticated information provided to the network and related assets. By authenticated scan, the vulnerability scanner can get information regarding low-level data like configuration details, specific services enabled on different devices and applications, information about the operating systems of hosts and other network devices connected within a network, and others.
  - **Unauthenticated Scanning** – This is an unreliable type of scanning mostly performed by hackers and malicious users on the target networks to detect flaws. This type of scanning generates a large number of false positives and the report can be so confusing and unreliable. This scan mostly focuses on finding the operating systems and applications installed on the devices in the network.

Packet sniffers

Packet sniffers are also referred to as packet analyzers, network analyzers, or protocol analyzers. The main purpose of these advanced tools is to intercept the traffic packets and system logs at different protocol levels and analyze the traffic to find any threats in it. These tools assist security professionals in preempting any emerging threats.

The most important features, characteristics, and capabilities of packet sniffers used in the IT field include the following:[188]

- A packet sniffer can be either a dedicated hardware-based software or a computer program (software-based) application installed on certain network elements.
- Sniffers intercept the packets of communication based on different communication protocols at different levels to check the content of those packets so that any kind of threat can be detected on the basis of the information in those packets.
- The packets can be intercepted between two computers within a network, two separate networks, or even from the Internet-connected traffic.
- There are six most important parts of a modern sniffer, as mentioned below:
  - **Hardware** – This is a type of network adapter installed on the network.
  - **Capture filter** – This is one of the most important components of the entire packet sniffer assembly. It performs multiple functions, such as capturing the network traffic directly from the connected wire, filtering it for the traffic that security personnel are interested in, and finally storing the filtered data into the buffer for further processing.
  - **Buffers** – Buffers are the storage of the packet sniffer to keep until further processing is done on the filtered data.
  - **Real-time analyzer** – The main function of this component is to sift through the traffic and analysis of it so that real-time data can be done.
  - **Decoder** – This component is used for decoding the protocol type by performing protocol analysis activity.
  - **Packet transmission and editing** – This is one of the most advanced components or features added to the packet sniffer. This allows the security personnel to edit their own packets and transmit them over the network.

Public key infrastructure (PKI) services

Public key infrastructure, or PKI, is an advanced cybersecurity framework that is used to maintain the security of the communication between two entities over the network. It is the combination of both software and encryption technologies to generate certificates and other security measures that can help the two end-users remain within the predefined communication security policy.

The most important characteristics, features, and capabilities of public key infrastructure are mentioned in the following list:[189]

- It is a comprehensive security system that is used for maintaining digital certificates with asymmetric encryption. Asymmetric encryption involves both public and private encryption security keys.
- A comprehensive platform for providing encryption and digital signature services to large-scale users, network elements, and web environments.
- This system is also responsible for delivering the components that are highly required for a secure and reliable business environment in major fields such as the Internet of Things (IoT) and e-commerce.
- With the help of PKI service, all users, network elements, and other entities working in a digital environment for materializing the modern business processes are provided with identification so that trustworthy interactions and communication can be established.
- All entities within a web environment connected through the Internet and other networks are assigned digital keys and certificates. Those certificates are issued by designated authorities, which are commonly known as Certificate Authorities (CAs).
- CAs are always the main target of hackers and malicious users who hack legitimate identities to unleash illegal activities.
- The most common encryption technologies used in public key infrastructure services include Transport Layer Security (TLS) and Secure Sockets Layer (SSL).
- PKI service is capable enough to cater to a huge number of entities simultaneously and manage them perfectly without any confusion in a complex Internet ecosystem.
- The most pivotal component of information integrity, data confidentiality, data access control systems, and authentication processes is PKI in modern digital communication and business ecosystems.
- PKI can be classified into major components. The most important components of a PKI system may include the following:
  - Certificate authority (CA).
  - Digital certificates.
  - Hardware Security Module (HSM).
  - Public encryption key.
  - Private encryption key.
  - Certificate store.
  - Certificate revocation list.
- It is a fundamental tool that enables trust between the entities over an untrusted network through certificate verification.

Web vulnerability scanning tools

Web vulnerability scanning tools are specialized types of vulnerability scanners that are used to scan the vulnerabilities in software applications in an online web environment to detect any kinds of security-related weaknesses or vulnerabilities. The most important vulnerabilities it can detect include the following:

- SQL injection issues.
- Cross-site scripting (XSS).
- Cross-site request forgery (CSRF).

The major features, characteristics, and capabilities of web vulnerability scanning tools are mentioned below.[190]

- An automated software program that can scan and dive deeper into the parameters and development weaknesses of a software application that can be exploited by hackers to unleash an attack.
- These tools use the patterns of known as well as possibly emerging threats to simulate hacker attacks on the software loopholes and check them. The software is able to withstand the simulated test.
- The web vulnerability scanner sends crawlers to the web applications or other online software platforms to check the content, default configurations, and vulnerabilities in the system by using the most advanced security technologies.
- Normally, there are two types of approaches in web vulnerability scanning:
  - Active scanning.
  - Passive scanning.
- The passive scanning is a very simple approach in which all required characteristics or features are just scanned or listed without testing them. For example, if there is a loophole in the software or there is an unnecessary port open, it will just note that status and move on without testing the vulnerabilities with any other activities.
- On the contrary, the active scanning is like a simulated cyberattack on the vulnerabilities to check if they can sustain the possible or emerging threats. It checks the level of damage or risk on the applications.
- The entire application is mapped with the help of a spider or crawler to check all the weaknesses and other issues in the software application.
- Some of the most important issues that are detected by web vulnerability scanners include directory traverse, straightforward directory listings, open redirections, reflected cross-site scripting (XSS), SQL injection, and command injection vulnerabilities.
- The protocol scanners are also another type of web vulnerability scanner that scans for ports, network services, and protocol vulnerabilities.

- Most of the vulnerabilities found in web applications relate to:
  - Web-based application system faults.
  - Form inputs without sanitization or validation.
  - Misconfigurations of servers.
  - Application design flaws.

Endpoint detection and response (EDR) systems

Endpoint detection and response system, precisely known as EDR, is also referred to as endpoint threat detection and response system (ETDR). It is a fully consolidated and automated endpoint security system that is capable of continuously monitoring and analyzing the endpoint data. It can provide a suitable response to any emerging threat. The response is mostly based on predefined rules to counter an emerging security threat.

Main features and characteristics of an endpoint detection and response system (EDR) are mentioned below:[192]

- It is an initial automated security system designed for continuous monitoring and rule-based automated response on the endpoints of a network or web environment. The endpoints may include tablets, end-users, desktops, laptops, Wi-Fi routers, and other types of hosts in the network.
- The main focus of EDR has been on finding the threat profile based on malware such as viruses, spyware, adware, and other malicious codes on the end devices and providing a rule-based response to remove them.
- The term EDR was coined by Anton Chuvakin, a researcher at Gartner.
- The most fundamental functions conducted by an EDR include:
  - Threat indicating data collection from endpoints and hosts.
  - Analyzing the data and recognizing the pattern of threats.
  - Providing a rule-based response to the emerging threat to avert any bigger damage.
  - Working as a forensic and analysis tool for the investigation of the incidents.
- An EDR consists of three fundamental components such as:
  - Data collection agents (Endpoint)
  - Automated response module
  - Forensic and analysis module
- The main focus of EDR remains on the analysis and protection of endpoint data, while the advanced version of EDR focuses on the larger canvas of the network elements, endpoints, and also the web environments.
- The advanced version of EDR is XDR, with additional capabilities to be discussed next.

Extended detection and response (XDR) systems

Extended detection and response, precisely known as XDR, is a unified system for detecting any events or abnormalities, analyzing them properly, and generating a suitable response automatically. It is used to provide deeper insight, analysis, and response across all types of IT users and components used in the enterprise network, such as endpoints, networks, elements, and workloads. With the help of an XDR system, the security personnel become capable of devising an automated, faster response by detecting and analyzing emerging threats within the cyber environments.

The most salient features, capabilities, and characteristics of the extended detection and response systems are mentioned below.[191]

- An automated system that is used to provide you with a deeper insight and visibility into all major components of a web or information technology ecosystem, such as clouds, endpoints, data storage, network connectivity, configuration, and applications, by finding out the weaknesses and performance of those components. It is designed not only to provide insight into the performance, security, and other status of the network elements but also to provide a suitable automated response to the emerging threats or system vulnerabilities that may lead to disastrous cyberattacks.
- It is an effective tool used for preempting any emerging threats to your network or web environments properly.
- XDR is an advanced version of its predecessor, called endpoint detection and response, precisely known as EDR, which had lesser capabilities and features, mostly focusing on the detection of viruses and other malware on the endpoints and initiation of predefined remedial responses for those viruses.
- XDRs can provide deeper visibility into the entire network and web environment by providing security teams with:
  - Detecting advanced levels of emerging threats before they strike the networks.
  - Providing the most critical information to the security teams to take faster actions.
  - Helping build strong resilience and agility in the entire network and web ecosystem.
- Supports a wide range of automated security tasks that can be scheduled under certain conditions and criteria to activate automatically.
- Integrated with the most advanced machine learning and artificial intelligence capabilities, the XDRs can act as informed systems that can provide highly robust preemptive and corrective security issues.
- XDRs are based on the proactive approach of cybersecurity to react and respond in a real-time environment.
- It can dive deeper across multiple layers of communication and network structures simultaneously to provide you with deeper and comprehensive insight.

- Top benefits of using an XDR include the following:
  - Catching threats proactively before they strike.
  - Effective and faster incident investigation.
  - Reduces mean-time-to-respond (MTTR) and mean-time-to-detect (MTTD) significantly.
  - Comprehensive threat detection solution.
  - Improves organization productivity, security, and efficiency.

Penetration testing tools

Penetration testing tools are also known as pen test tools. These are advanced cybersecurity testing tools that are designed to unleash a cyber-attack-type software attack to check the sustainability of a network or any web environment. A penetration test is a software program that is used to check the network security threats by exploiting all available vulnerabilities and security weaknesses in the computer systems and web applications.

The main objective of using penetration testing tools in any business environment is to check the capabilities and strengths of the information technology infrastructure and organizational structure of the business to cope with real-world hacking attacks and provide a suitable response to restore the services to normalcy. This tool is extensively used as a preventive measure building tool for averting any cyberattack before it materializes in the network. Penetration testing tools use different types of tests to check the strength of a system. A few of the most important tests conducted through penetration testing tools are listed below. Meanwhile, the categories of penetration testing tools are also classified based on those tests, such as:

- Black-box assessment test.
- White-box assessment test.
- Gray-box assessment test.

All of the above-mentioned tests attack the networks by exploiting the vulnerabilities and weaknesses to prepare an organization for better security mechanisms to put in place to avert any emerging cybersecurity threats perfectly. The most important features, capabilities, and characteristics of penetration testing tools are summarized in the following list:[193]

- A penetration test is a simulated type of cyberattack test code that runs on computers, networks, and web applications to check the vulnerabilities and the countering ability of those entities to cope with that threat.
- The prime objective of these testing tools is to identify the vulnerabilities that can be exploited by real-world hackers or attackers.
- Penetration testing tools can support both manual and automated testing.
- The entire process of penetration testing may consist of three main phases or steps, such as:

- Collection of information about the targets.
- Exploiting the vulnerabilities found in the first step to breach into the systems.
- Compilation of a detailed report of vulnerabilities and respective solutions.
- Penetration testing uses two approaches of scanning applications, such as:
  - Static scanning.
  - Dynamic scanning.
- The most critical domains of penetration testing based on the network or environment partitions can be categorized into:
  - **Penetration testing of network services** – This is also referred to as infrastructure penetration testing. The core objective of this testing is to intrude and analyze the weaknesses of the network to safeguard it from the most common types of network attacks, such as Distributed Denial of Service (DDoS) attacks and others. This test is normally conducted on routers, firewalls, hosts, switches, and security appliances.
  - **Penetration testing of web applications** – This type of testing is based on three basic steps – Reconnaissance, Discovery, and Exploitation. It is performed on web applications and their respective components, such as databases, source code, APIs (Application Programming Interfaces), and other backend resources.
  - **Penetration testing of physical access** – The modern physical access is extensively monitored by the automated lock systems and other digital keys. It is a type of testing in which all possibilities are tested for any kind of unauthorized physical intrusion into the server or other network rooms.
  - **Penetration testing on client side** – In this type of penetration testing, the client-side tools, such as web browsers, workstations, mobile devices, and others, are targeted to check if they are free from any vulnerabilities that the attackers can exploit to launch attacks such as XSS, HTML, SQL injections, and others.
  - **Penetration testing based on social engineering** – In this penetration testing, the employees and stakeholders of the company or an organization are targeted to deal with the social engineering attacks. The results are analyzed, and weaknesses are addressed for the final solution.
  - **Penetration testing of mobile applications** – The main focus of mobile application penetration is on the mobile applications, not on the servers or mobile APIs. The core objective of this type of pen testing is to find out the vulnerabilities in mobile applications through both static and dynamic analysis.

Chapter 8

Machine learning in cybersecurity

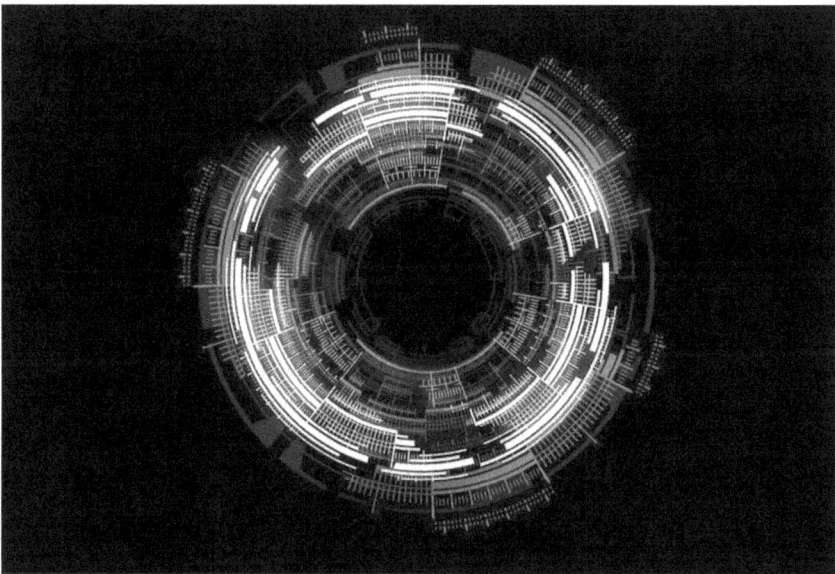

DOI: 10.1201/9781003688327-8

INTRODUCTION TO ML IN MODERN CYBERSECURITY

Before we dive into the importance, roles, use cases, and other aspects of machine learning in the field of modern cybersecurity, let us have a deeper look at modern cybersecurity and its features, components, and other characteristics. Modern cybersecurity has transformed significantly from traditional cybersecurity, principally from rule-based security to automated security algorithms. Traditional cybersecurity was based on a few fixed software applications that would detect the known cyber threats, such as viruses, malware, spyware, and other similar kinds of activities. The preventive measures were also powered by the precalculated or designed formulas, such as access control lists, rule-based firewalls, port-based restrictions, and similar types of other functions. Those functions are not so agile as to cope with the most advanced cyberattacks unleashed by the most sophisticated and learned hackers of the modern world. To cope with the most innovative and sophisticated attacks by the most advanced attackers, the use of machine learning comes as a savior.

Modern cybersecurity system

Any cybersecurity system powered by advanced machine learning capabilities is known as a comprehensive modern cybersecurity system. Modern cybersecurity systems are more agile, proactive, fast, deep, diligent, and intelligent as compared to traditional cybersecurity systems. Different standard and regulatory authorities define a comprehensive framework of modern cybersecurity that consists of modular structures to interact with each other. One of the most acceptable frameworks standardized by the National Institute of Standard and Technology (NIST) consists of five functional elements. Those most fundamental components or elements of modern cybersecurity systems powered by the modern machine learning capabilities include:[194]

- **Identify** – The identification function or element of a modern cybersecurity system that deals with figuring out a range of hardware and software infrastructures and elements, such as:
  - Discovering physical infrastructure.
  - Identification of software assets.
  - Carrying out supply chain assessment.
  - Deploying risk management strategy.
  - Discovering security vulnerabilities.
  - Defining security policies.
- **Protect** – This is the second major component of a modern cybersecurity system and is the functionality known as protect. The main activities under the protective functionality of modern cybersecurity include:
  - Identity management and access control protection.
  - Staff awareness and training initiatives.

- Data security protection in line with risk strategy.
- Deployment of protective procedures and processes.
- Thorough system management for continual operations.
- Adopting a system and security resilience policy.
- **Detect** – This is the third element of a modern cybersecurity system defined by NIST. The most important activities and functions under this component of modern cybersecurity include the following:
  - Timely detection of system anomalies and events.
  - Deploying continual security monitoring capability.
  - Continuous verification of the efficacy of protective methods.
  - Implementing continuous training for awareness.
- **Respond** – Automatic response is one of the most fundamental parts of a modern cybersecurity system. In this category, various functional procedures or activities are considered, such as:
  - Proactive and automated response generation.
  - Restricting the effect of the potential threat.
  - Response planning procedure and policy implementation.
  - Analysis of response and recovery policies.
- **Recover** – A comprehensive cybersecurity system is not complete until the capabilities of disaster recovery are implemented properly. This is known as the last component of a modern cybersecurity system powered by machine learning technology. The most important functionalities of this element are:
  - Restoration plans for services and capabilities of the systems.
  - Implementation of recovery planning procedure for the affected systems.
  - Deployment of continual improvements to enhance the robustness of the systems.
  - Management and analysis of internal communication for devising future recovery policies more effectively.

Other than the above-mentioned five major components of a modern cybersecurity system, there are a few other characteristics that play a vital role in the definition of the comprehensiveness of a modern cybersecurity system. One such characteristic is its operational compass across all elements of an information system environment. A unified modern cybersecurity system will cover all of the following elements of a network system, such as:

- Multiple clouds such as public, private, and hybrid clouds.
- Hyper-converged infrastructures and servers.
- All networking elements.
- Entire data protection and recovery systems.
- All types of data storage systems.
- All kinds of endpoints connected to the system.
- And any other software or hardware part of the network or system.

Role of machine learning

A modern cybersecurity system is a holistic security environment for the entire network that can accomplish numerous activities in collaboration with all components, infrastructure, hardware, software, and the network in a real-time environment. Such a comprehensive, energetic, proactive, fast, analytical, and intelligent system is not possible to develop without the major role of machine learning (ML) technology. Machine learning technology enables the cybersecurity system to undertake a range of functionalities to make it more capable, such as:[195]

- Analysis of activity patterns.
- Understand from patterns.
- Prevention from threats of previous patterns.
- Learning the changing behaviors of stakeholders/users.
- Real-time events and activities analysis.
- Automating routine security tasks faster.
- Monitoring all types of real-time online activities proactively, such as gaming, e-commerce transactions, shopping, financial activities, social media, and others.
- Providing deeper insight into the vulnerabilities and weaknesses of the system.
- Triggering an automated response based on previous experience and understanding.
- Automated decision-making for threat response and recovery activities.

All of the above-mentioned activities influenced by machine learning make the modern cybersecurity systems highly efficient, responsive, fast, reliable, and cost-efficient. Almost all organizations in web environments are benefiting from the power of machine learning deployed in their cybersecurity systems. A few very important benefits of using machine learning technology in modern cybersecurity systems are listed below:[197]

- Prevention of cyberattacks similar to those that happened in the past.
- Higher reliability and peace of mind for both entrepreneurs and clients/users.
- Scanning and understanding valuable information from previously successful cyberattacks.
- Faster threat detection or almost real-time threat detection capabilities.
- Instant response to any emerging threats without any delays.
- Effective preventive security plans.
- Perfect security authentication mechanism to avert any unauthorized intrusion.

- Continual improvement of the security system based on learning from network and user behaviors over time.
- Effective management of the security of large volumes of data and a huge number of system entities and endpoints.
- Future prospects of developing an ultra-secure environment for cybersecurity by learning through experience and observations.

Based on these capabilities of machine learning in the field of cybersecurity, a large number of use cases have already been implemented in cybersecurity applications. And many future applications are also under study to be implemented in the near future. The most salient use cases of machine learning in the modern field of cybersecurity are mentioned below:[196]

- Protection against mobile SMS scams through the ML-powered Mobile Threat Defense System (MTDS), Unified Endpoint Management (UEM), and other tools.
- Development of AI-based threat mitigation systems through different systems powered by artificial intelligence and machine learning technologies.
- Network threat detection through ML technology-powered security systems to monitor incoming and outgoing calls and requests in a diverse environment of network topologies and network boundaries.
- Security of mobile endpoints through ML-powered systems such as Google security in mobiles, Apple Siri and Amazon Alexa (and others), to name a few.
- Human behavior analysis through an AI2 machine learning-powered platform is another major use case that enhances the analysis power of security systems to learn human behavior and human nature to avert any human error and malicious activities.
- Monitoring of emails and other text-based communication through the most advanced machine learning technologies, such as natural language processing (NLP) and its other subcategories, to safeguard users from spamming, viruses, social engineering, malware, spyware, and other similar kinds of activities.
- Safeguarding users and systems against bots is another very crucial use case of machine learning technology in modern cybersecurity. It is estimated that more than 25% of the Internet traffic consists of bots.
- Detection of viruses and malware programs in an integrated and consolidated cybersecurity system is an important use case of machine learning in cybersecurity. ML-powered antiviruses and anti-malware programs detect any anomaly by tracking the behavior of a file or a software program. It can automatically flag the suspicious programs and can also take a proper response to block them effectively.

The future of machine learning technology in cybersecurity is very bright. A large number of future applications powered by machine learning are anticipated in the modern field of cybersecurity. A few of those futuristic functionalities of machine learning are mentioned below:[197,198]

- Complete eradication of zero-day attack risk. The term "zero-day" is about taking advantage of an unknown or unaddressed security flaw in computer software, hardware, or firmware (which can cause an attack). In this case, the victim has zero days to fix the vulnerability before the attacker exploits it.
- Advanced preemptive and predictive threat intelligence before the attack materialization.
- Development of autonomous threat responding systems and integrated forensic capabilities.
- Realization of automated industrial compliance and governance.
- Utilization of machine learning in blockchain to build new generation AI-driven ecosystems.
- Automated and machine learning enabled security operations centers without human intervention.
- Instant and real-time automation of insights for a huge number of endpoint devices.
- Automated identification and profiling of all devices connecting to any network in a real-time ecosystem.
- Suggesting the security policies for all devices, especially firewalls and other cybersecurity-related equipment or software systems, without any human intervention.
- Automated detection and prevention of system anomalies in an enterprise environment or a network system.

MAJOR MACHINE LEARNING ACTIVITIES IN CYBERSECURITY

The modern cybersecurity field is using the capabilities of machine learning extensively in numerous activities related to different domains of cybersecurity. A large number of use cases have evolved in modern security that use the major characteristics and competencies of machine learning to provide a reliable, automated, preemptive, and effective security solution. The main characteristics that are extensively used in cybersecurity activities include the following:[199,200]

- Regression or prediction capability.
- Classification or categorization ability.
- Clustering or grouping feature.
- Dimensionality reduction or generalization characteristic.
- Association rule learning capability.
- Generation modeling feature.

The above-mentioned capabilities of machine learning are tapped to utilize different activities performed in cybersecurity to make those activities more robust, accurate, effective, and reliable. Among such major types of activities that utilize the features and characteristics of machine learning technology to enhance their outcomes include:[199,200]

- Identification of vulnerabilities and weaknesses.
- Prediction of potential threats emerging from different sources.
- Detection of any kind of anomaly or incident before it strikes.
- Generation of response to any emerging threat preemptively.
- Continual monitoring of performance, activities, logs, events, and incidents.
- Analysis of data or forensics for policy and reporting activities.
- And many others.

Now, a question is, *"How are all these activities effectively utilized in different types of securities in an integrated IT environment?"* Let us have a look at different sections or domains of cybersecurity and how they use the characteristics of machine learning in their respective fields.

Network security

The protection of complex networks is one of the most important domains of cybersecurity, where the use of machine learning capabilities is huge. A network is not just a simple set of connected devices; it may consist of numerous different types of devices and connections, such as wireless connectivity, wired connectivity, on-premises devices, cloud-based devices, storage devices, and many more. Maintaining the security of a heterogeneous network is a very cumbersome task.

In the traditional method of network security, the use of intrusion detection systems would be used, which would work on the basis of signature-based approaches. Those signature-based approaches are not so efficient due to numerous downsides. The modern network security activity is performed by the modern network security system powered by machine learning by using the Network Traffic Analytics (NTA) approach. This approach analyzes the network traffic at multiple layers of the network to detect any kinds of anomalies or threats. The main features of machine learning used in modern network security include:

- **Regression** – To predict the parameters of a network packet and compare with the normal ones in network communication.
- **Classification** – To identify different categories of network attacks or threats that may emerge.
- **Clustering** – It is used for the forensic analysis of the traffic.

By using all major characteristics of machine learning, a highly robust network cybersecurity system can be achieved (somewhat) perfectly in the modern security field.

Endpoint security

The endpoint security of a modern cybersecurity system includes the safety of all computers, tablets, laptops, servers, containers, IoT gadgets, mobile phones, and other devices from viruses, spam, malware, and other malicious programs. The traditional antivirus would use the definition of viruses to protect the devices, which has become very easy to break for hackers. The modern endpoint security powered by machine learning capabilities is known as Endpoint Detection and Response (EDR), which is a next-generation antivirus platform to protect all types of endpoints.

This security solution also uses all three major characteristics of machine learning, such as regression, classification, and clustering. The regression capability is used for predicting the next system call for an executable process and comparing that with the real processes to predict any abnormality in the system execution call. On the other hand, the classification feature of machine learning separates different categories of programs, such as viruses, ransomware, spyware, malware, or any other types of threats. The use of clustering is normally done for the protection of email gateways for protecting from any malicious files attached to the emails.

Application security

Application security is one of the major as well as bigger domains in the area of modern cybersecurity systems powered by machine learning and artificial intelligence. The requirements and mechanisms of application security vary from class to class of applications. Applications can be classified into different major categories, such as:

- Database applications.
- Web applications.
- Mobile applications.
- Enterprise resource planning (ERP) applications.
- Microservices applications.
- Software as a service (SaaS) applications.

All those applications need different capabilities and security features to cope with the emerging modern cybersecurity threats. It is not possible to build a comprehensive or all-in-one application security platform to cater to the needs of all those domains of applications. Thus, different types of security platforms powered by machine learning are developed to meet the requirements of those different domains of applications. The most important aspect of machine learning in application security platforms is to analyze:

- Web application firewalls (WAF).
- Application source codes.

These two activities, powered by machine learning capabilities, are able to detect and provide a proper response to the following types of attacks:

- XML External Entity (XXE) attacks.
- Server-Side Request Forgery (SSRF) attacks.
- Structured Query Language (SQL) injection attacks.
- Cross-site scripting (XSS) attacks.
- Remote Code Execution (RCE) attacks.
- Distributed denial of services (DDoS) attacks.
- Mass exploitation attacks.
- And similar other attacks.

The regression capability of machine learning technology is used to detect HTTP (Hypertext Transfer Protocol) request abnormalities that result in Server-Side Request Forgery (SSRF) and XXE vulnerability attacks. Bypassing the authentication attacks is also handled by the use of the regression capability of machine learning in application security platforms used in modern security systems. Moreover, the use of classification characteristics of machine learning is adopted in detecting different types of injection attacks, such as Structured Query Language (SQL) injection, Remote Code Execution (RCE), and Cross-site scripting (XSS) attacks. The threat of mass exploitation and different types of DoS attacks is detected and responded to by the application security systems with the help of the clustering capability of machine learning technology.

Process security

The security of any business process is a completely new domain of security because it does not necessarily resemble application security. The application security systems are built by considering the generic activities dealing with authentication, request processing, responding to queries with generic information, and other such types of activities. But the process application is completely a new system because it requires a huge knowledge of the domain in which the process is dealing. Each process has different criteria and standards. For example, a process application dealing with banking transactions is completely different from an e-commerce retail app or even a manufacturing process handling application. Thus, you need specific domain expertise to develop a security system to deal with the emerging threats at process levels in an advanced and proactive environment.

Different process platforms have different cybersecurity threats; two of the generalized threats commonly encountered in process security are:

- Fraudulent activities.
- User data theft.

The machine learning characteristics, such as regression, classification, and clustering, are extensively used in process security systems for protecting the processes from fraudulent activities, which are the most important threats in this domain. The regression capability is perfect for predicting the next user action and also detecting outliers like credit card fraud and similar types of other activities. The classification capability of machine learning technology helps the system detect previously known fraudulent patterns and activities. Any fraudulent business process is detected by comparing it with other legitimate business process parts to detect the outliers.

User behavior security

The user security is accomplished by the analysis of user behaviors. User behavior analysis is one of the most complex matters in the field of cybersecurity. There are numerous types of users, which cannot be categorized into one broader class because they have different behaviors and requirements for analytics. The most common types of users encountered in the field of cybersecurity include:

- Software as a service users.
- Application users.
- Domain users.
- Messengers.
- Social network users.

In the traditional (old) security systems, security information and event management (SIEM) was the most advanced system for maintaining an advanced level of cybersecurity for users in a specific domain. The SIEM also uses machine learning and artificial intelligence capabilities to a certain level. But, having a broader area of application, the SIEM is not fully sufficient to provide the most advanced user behavior analysis and predictive response in modern cybersecurity environments. The continuously changing behaviors and new behaviors that were the basic foundation for unleashing new attacks were not within the capabilities of SIEM to detect and respond properly.

The modern user behavior analysis is accomplished with the help of an advanced system referred to as user and entity behavior analytics, also known as UEBA. Although they are a bit advanced, the comprehensive behavior analysis is not fully covered by this advanced cybersecurity system either. The most important activities performed with the help of modern machine learning capabilities include:

- User login and other action anomalies are detected with the help of regression characteristics in this advanced system powered by machine learning.
- The analysis of the user behavior of peer groups in terms of class of users is accomplished with the help of the classification capability of machine learning.
- Different groups are separated with the help of clustering characteristics of machine learning to detect the outliers.

Additional activities of cybersecurity

Other than the above-mentioned different types of use cases of machine learning in cybersecurity fields, there are a few other major domains that hold significant importance in cybersecurity. The main objective of all types of use cases is to safeguard hardware and software resources working in an ICT or IT environment. A few additional key domains may include:[202]

- Comprehensive ICT security.
- Information security.
- Internet security.

All domains of cybersecurity or use cases are accomplished through a few very important and fundamental activities. Those activities or subdomains can be further classified into the following main categories:[201]

- **Static file analysis** – Used to analyze the features of a data file to detect any kind of maliciousness or threat in it.
- **The detection of anomaly** – Scanning and assessing any kinds of abnormality or risk score in data or events for threat investigation.
- **Management of vulnerability** – In this subdomain, ML and AI technology help find out the vulnerabilities and weaknesses in the entire system for generating a priority of criticalities of the emerging threats.
- **Analysis of behaviors** – In the entire cyber kill chain, the analysis of adversary patterns, models, and other routines is done at runtime.
- **Sandbox analysis of malware** – Analysis of source and other code samples running in the IT environment in an isolated ecosystem to detect any malicious behavior and then map them to already known adversaries.
- **Forensic analysis** – In this category, a counterintelligence scheme is run to analyze attack progression as well as to find out vulnerabilities in the systems.

To accomplish all those subfunctions, machine learning is used to carry out a few technical processes, as mentioned below in separate topics.

Differentiating legitimate/illegitimate URLs

Numerous types of cyberattacks are spread through malicious or illegitimate links or Uniform Resource Locators (URLs). Those URLs may be either enclosed within spamming emails or other types of ads on social media or other online surfing sources. The traditional/old systems were not efficient enough to differentiate between legitimate and illegitimate links or URLs. With the help of modern technology such as machine learning and artificial intelligence, it has become relatively easier to detect the legitimacy of the URLs instantly by modern security systems powered by ML technologies. Modern cybersecurity systems accomplish the following activities to differentiate between the legitimate and illegitimate Uniform Resource Locators:

- Checking and verification of the SSL certificate.
- Any HTTP request anomalies.
- Checks if any one of the two conditions is met – either the Uniform Resource Identifier (URI) reference is valid or the Uniform Resource Locator's Internationalized Resource Identifier (URL's IRI) reference is valid without any additional query components.
- Learning from the experience and past decisions.
- And other related ML activities.

Breaking CAPTCHA

Completely Automated Public Turing test to tell Computers and Humans Apart, precisely referred to as CAPTCHA, is a process of recognizing or selecting distorted texts or images that only humans can easily recognize but computers find it very difficult to recognize. This technique is very useful to differentiate between a bot and human users in a modern web environment. The distorted texts are further added with additional noises such as cross-lines and blobs on the text and image so that they become very difficult for computers to recognize without any human-level cognition.

By using the power of modern machine learning, the CAPTCHA test can be broken to a certain level. Numerous techniques such as support vector machine (SVM), K-means clustering, convolution neural network (CNN), moving window algorithm, and multi-CNN algorithm are used to break different types of CAPTCHA. The results of convolutional neural networks have proven more robust in breaking the CAPTCHA as compared to many other algorithms used in this field.[203]

From this discussion, it is very clear that hackers can utilize the power of breaking CAPTCHA and intrude into the networks and web environments unknowingly. Meanwhile, the addition of pictures with certain images in the blocks is more complicated as compared to text CAPTCHA. The work for machine learning technology remains to develop countermeasures to avoid hackers that can bypass the CAPTCHA test.

Catching spam and fraudulent mail

Spam and fraudulent emails are one of the major sources of phishing attacks and other fraudulent activities on the Internet. According to the latest research, on average, about 48.63% of the emails generated in the digital world were spam in 2022. The ratio was about 3.7% higher than the previous year's ratio. Detecting spamming and other types of fraudulent emails is a mammoth task, which requires high-power computing and advanced technologies. Machine learning is one of the best solutions for this menace.[204]

To catch the fraudulent and spam emails, numerous detection techniques are deployed in modern security systems. The most prominent techniques used by the machine learning technology are listed below:[205]

- Neural networks.
- Naïve Bayes.
- Random forest.
- Decision tree.

All these techniques or models are used to filter the spamming or fraudulent emails based on different types of parameter analyses and learning from past experience by the ML-powered program. Filtering technique is considered the most effective and efficient in detecting the emails based on their two types, such as ham emails (i.e., those that are generally wanted and desired by the recipient) and spam emails. Machine learning technology adopts two major types of filtering approaches as listed below:

- Behavior pattern-based filtering.
- Semantic pattern-based filtering.

The other types of techniques that are also used for identifying or filtering the spam or fraudulent emails with hidden links or URLs include the following:

- Whitelisting and blacklisting scheme.
- Keyword.
- Analysis or detection technique.
- Mail header analysis or detection.
- Message feature extraction.
- And others.

The learning-based technique is commonly used in machine learning for the detection of spam and fraudulent emails. One of the examples of learning-based techniques of machine learning is the Extreme Learning Machine (ELM). The process of spam email filtering is classified into multiple categories based on the location and process. A few important processes of spam email filtering categories used in the modern cybersecurity field include:

- Enterprise-level spam filtering.
- Client-side spam filtering.
- Case-based spam filtering.
- Standard spam filtering.

In the modern applications powered by the advanced machine learning technologies, more powerful techniques of email filtering are used as compared to previously used techniques mentioned in the above list. Those techniques powered by machine learning are listed below:[205]

- Decision tree classifier.
- Supervised machine learning.
- Support vector machine.
- Naïve Bayes classifier.
- Artificial neural networks.
- And many other unsupervised machine learning approaches.

Network anomaly detection

Network anomaly detection is a technique through which the abnormal behavior of a network, or even incidents, traffic volumes, and other parameters that stand out from the routine parameters, is detected as suspicious behavior of an IT network. Normally, this technique is materialized with the help of modern technologies such as machine learning and artificial intelligence. The most common technique used in machine learning for detecting network anomalies is known as network behavior anomaly detection, precisely referred to as NBAD.[206]

This technique is used to provide security to the network from any external intrusion for malicious activities. The NBAD continually monitors the network behavior, traffic, performance, and other attributes and compares them with the normal behaviors that it has already learned through numerous machine learning techniques, rule-based decision-making, or a combination of both techniques. If any kind of abnormality is detected, the system alerts the security personnel and also generates a suitable response based on its findings automatically. The most important anomalies detected by the network behavior analysis (NBA) include the following:[206]

- Medium Access Control (MAC) and IP spoofing (Internet Protocol address spoofing).
- Payload anomaly.
- Duplicate MAC or IP address.
- Virus detection in the network.
- Connection bandwidth and data rate anomalies.
- IP, Transmission Control Protocol (TCP), or User Datagram Protocol (UDP) fan-out.

In machine learning terminology, the anomalies are classified into three major categories as mentioned below:

- **Change in events** – Sudden or gradual changes from previous normal events.
- **Outliers** – Non-systematic small or short changes in data patterns are called outliers.
- **Drifts** – A continual, long-term, and slow change in a particular direction is called drift.

The most commonly used machine learning algorithms to detect network anomalies are mentioned below:[207]

- Isolation forest based on the random forest algorithm.
- Local outlier factor technique.
- Robust covariance technique.
- One-class SVM method.
- Stochastic Gradient Descent (SGD) One-class SVM.

Context-based malicious activity detection

Another very important activity performed by the advanced capabilities of machine learning is the detection of malicious programs or activities based on the context of other related parameters. This is one of the most crucial and complex activities that can handle anomaly detection in real-time environments. Traditionally, different types of approaches were used for detecting malicious activities or programs on a network or a host. Among such major approaches, some are mentioned here:[109]

- Signature-based anomaly detection.
- Application-based anomaly detection.
- Anomaly based anomaly detection.
- Network-based anomaly detection.
- Host-based anomaly detection.

All those approaches would use different types of macro-level resources and parameter measurements, but all of them missed one very common discipline of parameters, which are the low-level resources of a system, such as CPU usage, memory consumption, bandwidth utilization, and similar types of other low-level parameters. The context-based anomaly detection uses the low-level parameters or resources to monitor in a real-time environment to detect any kind of abnormal activities occurring in the process. It is powered by semi-supervised machine learning, in which the machines are primarily trained with tagged data and then trained through untagged datasets to learn about the entire system by scanning and understanding the vast datasets of the environment.

Other most salient features and characteristics of the context-based anomaly detection systems powered by ML technology include:[208]

- The parameters considered in this type of approach are subsemantic parameters because they are of low-level and do not rely upon the semantic models.
- The subsemantic parameters, such as CPU temperature, CPU usage, memory usage, and similar types of low-level parameters, are used to establish an abnormal activity.
- A context-based system is a real-time, adaptive, and dynamic type of approach that uses ontological engineering and ontologies.
- This approach can accomplish the following objectives:
  - Analysis of the effect on numerous low-level heterogeneous indicators, as mentioned earlier in this topic.
  - Identification of abnormalities by using time-series analysis and semi-supervised machine learning technologies.

Catching hackers/impersonators in real time

- Catching hackers or impersonators is a very uphill task, not only in a real-time environment but also in an offline environment. Normally, hackers disguise themselves in the name of other people or roles to intrude into the thoughts and minds of online users to make them believe (as a legitimate entity) and get trapped in a data breach. The entire process of disguising hackers from their legitimate identities is known as impersonation. Hackers are normally impersonators because they hide their identities to carry out social engineering and phishing activities.[209]

Fortunately, machine learning offers the capability to catch such hackers in a real-time environment. It is very important to note that hackers are also very advanced technologists, and they can use machine learning in their favor. To cope with the malicious intentions of hackers, the following tips should be followed:

- Datasets should have accurate data labels for training ML models.
- Introduction and testing of numerous adversarial ML-powered techniques and approaches.
- Security teams and systems must always remain updated.

Chapter 9

ML-powered top platforms

DOI: 10.1201/9781003688327-9

ML-POWERED CYBERSECURITY PLATFORMS

The cybersecurity field has been expanding exponentially for the last few decades and has become a gigantic multi-billion-dollar industry. The threat surface of cyberattacks is expanding with the introduction of advanced technologies such as the Internet of Things (IoT) and an extensively connected world of billions of devices and entities into a colossal network. In fact, billions of transactions and events occur on just one single host in a day. Thus, billions of devices interconnected in a collaborative and interactive manner must be producing billions of events and digital transactions between the connected devices. Processing all those events and activities is necessary to have deeper insight into the probabilities of emerging threats in a digital world. The reality is, processing such huge volumes of transactions, events, activities, and messages is not possible with traditional methods of data analytics or with just human intervention through customized data analysis tools to skim any valuable information from those huge volumes of data.[210]

Artificial intelligence, precisely machine learning, is the answer to this problem of processing huge volumes of data consisting of billions of events, activities, transactions, and communication messages. The platforms that are built by utilizing the power of machine learning technology are known as ML-powered unified cybersecurity platforms. These platforms can detect any emerging threats preemptively in the real-time environment. The involvement of machine learning technology enables the computer models to learn from experience with the passage of time by analyzing different situations, outcomes, reasons, and many other parameters recorded in the past. It can also predict a possible threat based on the findings it gets from the analysis of data and compare the past learning with the new outcomes. Thus, a large number of modern tools powered by machine learning technology have emerged in the modern field of cybersecurity.

The main features and characteristics of cybersecurity platforms powered by machine learning technology are mentioned below:[209,211,212]

- The capability of processing billions of time-varying signals in a real-time environment.
- Faster analysis of huge incidents, activities, signals, and other parameters, and identification of any emerging threat based on the outcome of the analysis of those signals.
- Historical learning through machine learning builds the profiles of networks, assets, and users to detect any abnormality instantly.
- It uses the information hidden in the heaps of unstructured data to increase its capabilities and smartness with the passage of time.
- Handles hundreds of attack vectors, millions of devices, big data, monitoring a vast attack surface, and real-time analytics.
- It is able to provide numerous functionalities such as asset inventory, control effectiveness, threat exposure, breach risk predictions, incident response, and others.

- Capable of dealing with ever-expanding risk surface and data volumes.
- ML-enabled tools are able to use the power of data analytics, deep learning, statistical analysis, regression predictions, and many more.
- Usually, the ML-powered tools are referred to as user and entity behavior analytics (UEBA) tools in the cybersecurity field.
- Offers extensive automation of routine tasks as well as the automated response to any emerging threats in real-time, as well as in the predicted future.
- Huge process automation of cybersecurity operations and maintenance to minimize the requirement of human resources.
- Offers a wide range of features such as detailed analysis, comprehensive operations, automated prediction and response, faster alerts, reduced false positives, and many more.
- A greater level of accuracy and speed can increase the organization's productivity significantly.
- Ability to conduct multi-layer analysis of traffic, protocols, and other communication transactions simultaneously.

TYPES OF CYBERSECURITY TOOLS

The cybersecurity field is a very vast field. It consists of numerous types of devices, connectivity, software, infrastructure, hardware, and other elements. Protecting all those components of a gigantic IT field is called cybersecurity. Broadly speaking, cybersecurity can be classified into five major categories as listed below:[213]

- Cloud cybersecurity.
- Critical infrastructure cybersecurity.
- Network cybersecurity.
- Internet of Things (IoT) cybersecurity.
- Application cybersecurity.

Each category of cybersecurity has different requirements for maintaining high-level security of the components falling in that particular class. The requirements of cybersecurity are devised based on the potential threats that may affect the devices, factors, or services running under that category. Those requirements are named according to their functionalities and features. The most common cybersecurity functionalities, capabilities, and features that give a name or type to the security tools are mentioned in the following list:

- Endpoint detection and response (EDR).
- Anti-ransomware.
- Antivirus.
- Extended detection and response (XDR).
- Managed detection and response (MDR).

- Exploit prevention.
- Active adversary mitigation.
- Zero trust network access (ZTNA).
- Public key infrastructure (PKI).
- Firewalls.
- Communication packet sniffers.
- Intrusion detection systems.
- Penetration testing.
- And others.

Based on the above main functionalities and types of security tools, a few very advanced cybersecurity tools that are powered by machine learning and artificial intelligence capabilities are described in the next section of this chapter.

TOP FIVE PROFESSIONAL CYBERSECURITY PLATFORMS POWERED BY MACHINE LEARNING

According to one of the latest research studies (at the time of writing this book), the global damages due to breaches in cybersecurity would be approximately US $10 trillion, which would be the third largest economy in the world after the USA and China by 2025.[214] Thus, the demand for highly advanced cybersecurity tools and platforms, especially those powered by cutting-edge technologies like machine learning (ML) and artificial intelligence (AI), will continue increasing exponentially. To cope with this huge economic menace triggered by security breaches in the field of cybersecurity, numerous cybersecurity organizations are building the most sophisticated and advanced cybersecurity platforms and tools. A few very important ones of those cybersecurity tools powered by machine learning and advanced artificial intelligence technologies are mentioned with specific details in the following topics.

CrowdStrike Falcon

CrowdStrike Falcon is a comprehensive cybersecurity solution to safeguard all endpoints, network devices, and applications under one single roof. A large number of big organizations, especially in the financial sector, rely on the capabilities of this cybersecurity platform. This platform uses advanced machine learning and artificial intelligence technologies to develop a unified cybersecurity solution for an enterprise (see Figure 9.1).

The most important features, capabilities, and characteristics of this advanced cybersecurity solution are mentioned below:[215,216]

- Reliable capabilities of extended detection and response (XDR).
- All features of professional endpoint security software are designed to detect all types of advanced malicious software attacks on endpoints.

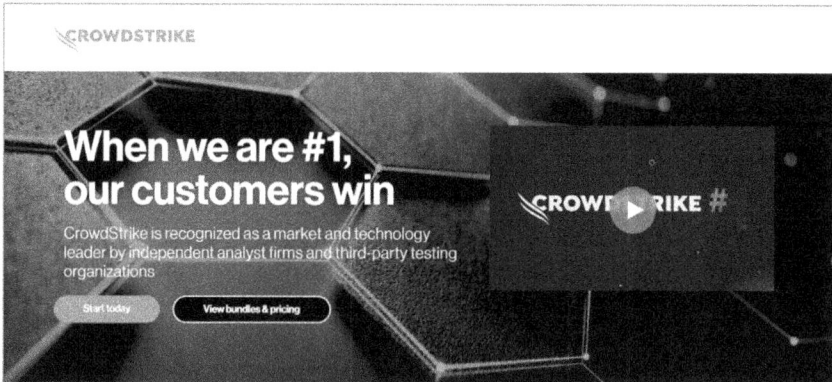

Figure 9.1 CrowdStrike cybersecurity (screenshot).

- Capabilities of the endpoint detection and response (EDR) platform.
- It can be compared with the advanced features and capabilities of Microsoft Defender for endpoints and similar types of other high-level endpoint solutions.
- It embeds next-generation antivirus, endpoint protection, and fully managed services.
- It is an agent-based application with a very lightweight and agile design.
- A robust device control system is an integrated part of this platform.
- Support integrated threat intelligence and comprehensive threat hunting capabilities.
- Robust firewall management and support for the IT hygiene standard.
- Available in multiple plans and schemes for varying uses.
- Supports identity protection and advanced security and IT operations processes.
- Deeper insight and visibility into your entire enterprise network and cloud infrastructure for better security, resilience, and productivity.
- Different levels of penetration testing and network monitoring.
- CrowdStrike Falcon tool is powered by AI technologies and 100% cloud-native capabilities.
- Capable of providing both rapid and surgical remediation very fast.
- Unified security of cloud workloads.
- Embedded executive dashboard, message analyst, and message center capabilities for secure communication and responsibility tracing.

IBM QRadar advisor

IBM QRadar is a modern cybersecurity tool that deals with security information and event management, precisely referred to as security information and event management (SIEM). It uses advanced technologies such as

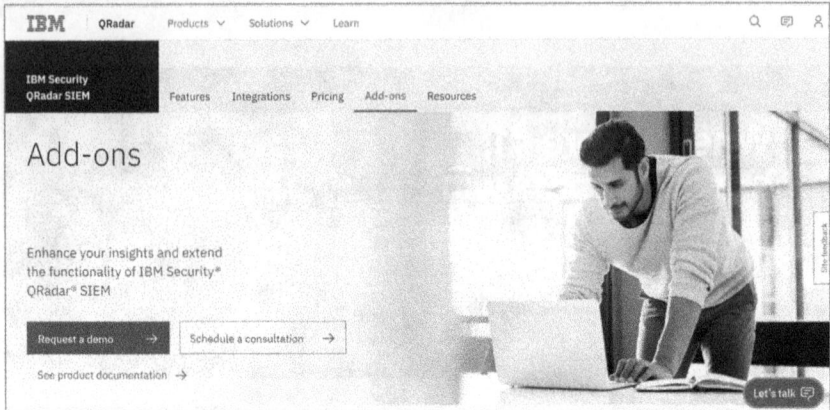

Figure 9.2 IBM QRadar SIEM (screenshot).

machine learning and artificial intelligence to provide the most robust and reliable cybersecurity capabilities (see the screenshot in Figure 9.2). This platform uses the power of the IBM Watson platform, which is considered one of the most powerful artificial intelligence applications in the modern world of information technology. It provides comprehensive automation of security operations in building highly advanced and cutting-edge security operation centers (SOCs). The forensic capabilities of QRadar are the most fundamental feature of this application to investigate and triage a range of incidents in a complex IT environment.

There are numerous features and capabilities of this platform. A few very important ones are mentioned in the following list:[217,218,219]

- With the help of IBM cognitive artificial intelligence under the umbrella of the IBM Watson application, it helps the security personnel investigate, triage, analyze, and respond preemptively to the emerging threats and any security events that may cause damage to the system continuously.
- Supports a wide range of add-ons and extensions to install to increase the productivity and profile of cybersecurity systems significantly.
- Easy to configure with X-Force without installing a license key. You just need to configure QRadar in the Watson Configuration Wizard.
- Supports major web browsers such as Google Chrome, Mozilla Firefox, Microsoft Edge, and others.
- Very fast in catching the threats through abnormal incident monitoring and higher priority of high-fidelity alerts.
- It is capable of analyzing threat intelligence, user behavior, and network and application-level anomalies instantly.

- This platform is also able to correlate, trace, track, and identify related activities across the entire kill chain automatically without any human intervention at all.
- Features of security orchestration, automation, and response, precisely known as SOAR, automate the suitable responses based on the best security practices.
- IBM security information and event management (SIEM) supports the integration with other identity and access management platforms or tools smoothly.
- Professional correlation capabilities with customizable dashboards and workspaces are other key features of this platform.
- Specialized features of reporting and compliance management to stand out in the field of cybersecurity industry standards.
- Ability of baselining and behavioral analytics.
- Supports multiple environmental configurations such as on-premises, on-cloud, and software as a service (SaaS) platforms.
- Offers greater visibility and a unified platform for centralized and correlated security operations by removing silos within different security processes.
- Supports centralized event and log data gathering, correlation, deployment flexibility, and event and log management and normalization.
- Ability to detect network as well as host-based intrusion into the environment.
- The capability of searching and indexing incidents.
- Supports both rule-based and algorithmic detection of threshold parameter values and incidents with greater accuracy.
- Efficiency of collecting, parsing, and storing heaps of data related to cybersecurity and other related IT operations data.
- Ability to provide unified features for a network detection and response (NDR) tool through professional integration.
- Support for automated threat intelligence and STIX/TAXII (Structured Threat Information eXpression/Trusted Automated eXchange of Intelligence Information) standards.
- It can collect logs and events from hundreds of sources integrated into this machine learning-powered cybersecurity platform.
- More than 700 supported integrations through professional APIs. A few of them include Randori, ReaQta, QRadar SOAR, NDR, and others.
- IBM QRadar SIEM supports Device Support Module (DSM), which is a plug-in file that allows this system to collect event and log data from third-party platforms related to cybersecurity smoothly without any conformability issues.
- The types of integration this platform can support include event log sources, threat intelligence feeds, vulnerability scanners, network behavior collection devices, customized integrations, and many other modern security environments.

Sophos intercept X endpoint

Sophos Intercept X Endpoint is a unified endpoint cybersecurity solution with advanced security features and capabilities powered by the use of modern technologies such as machine learning (ML) and artificial intelligence (AI). It is developed by the Sophos Cybersecurity Company to provide advanced cybersecurity solutions for all types of users and organizations across the verticals of modern industries and sectors. A screenshot of Sophos is shown in Figure 9.3.

The main features, characteristics, and capabilities of the Sophos Intercept X Endpoint platform are mentioned in the following list:[220,221]

- It consists of all main features and capabilities that are required for providing full security to the endpoint devices, such as hosts, mobiles, workstations, and other network devices that act as the endpoints in the systems.
- The capability of endpoint detection and response (EDR) to detect emerging threats, prioritize them, and develop a suitable response well before the target endpoint or device is affected by the emerging threat.
- Highly advanced and efficient XDR, or Extended Detection and Response, capabilities to provide you with deeper insight into endpoint security.
- With the help of next-generation anti-ransomware, it preemptively protects the files, automates the file recovery if compromised, and analyzes the behaviors of users and threat actors before they can inflict substantial damage.
- Uses the most advanced machine learning, referred to as deep learning (DL) neural network models, for learning advanced malware and viruses without relying on traditional technologies such as signatures and others.
- Supports the managed detection and response (MDR) services too.

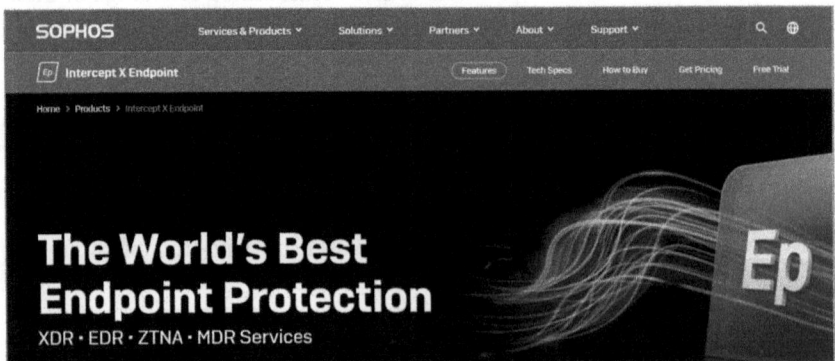

Figure 9.3 Sophos intercept X endpoint tool (screenshot).

- Ability to prevent exploits by blocking vulnerabilities, exploits, and other virus-distribution techniques used by hackers.
- All modules and domains of endpoint security are managed from the unified central dashboard or SOC console by breaking the silos.
- Supports the active adversary mitigation feature, which offers robust prevention of machine persistence and support for malicious traffic detection and credential theft detection simultaneously.
- Allows the remote work secure access through the most modern technique known as Zero Trust Network Access, also known as ZTNA.
- The ability of Sophos Intercept X Endpoint to detect suspected devices or unprotected devices by using the advanced capabilities, such as intrusion protection system (IPS) and advanced threat prevention (ATP) from active firewalls.
- Ability to identify a wide range of IoT devices and other elements that are unguarded or unprotected instantly and make necessary security arrangements for them automatically to avert any emerging threat.
- Supports both on-premises and cloud-based endpoints and network elements in your enterprise estate simultaneously.
- Stops the unhealthy devices from using the network or systems that can make the entire system vulnerable to threats.
- It is a single-vendor, single-agent, and single-console cybersecurity endpoint solution.
- Allows additional features such as app control, behavior detection, fileless attack prevention, and much more.

SentinelOne

SentinelOne is another very professional cybersecurity company based in California, USA. It offers a comprehensive cybersecurity solution that removes the traditional complexities, such as multi-agent, multi-vendor, multi-platform, and multi-alert systems, and merges the entire environment of modern cybersecurity under one umbrella. It is an endpoint security solution that has features of extended detection and response (XDR) in all major environments, such as on-premises and on-clouds simultaneously. The company terms this product Singularity XDR. The SentinelOne cybersecurity product is a unified platform to offer high speed, faster detection, quicker responses, infinite scaling, and a completely autonomous security solution. Autonomous security is considered the future of cybersecurity. This platform uses advanced technologies such as machine learning and artificial intelligence to boost the capabilities, features, and productivity of this product. It has also integrated the capability of protecting against identity theft and other issues on the endpoint devices of an enterprise network or environment (see Figure 9.4).

The most salient features, capabilities, and characteristics of the SentinelOne Cybersecurity endpoint tool are mentioned below:[222,223,224]

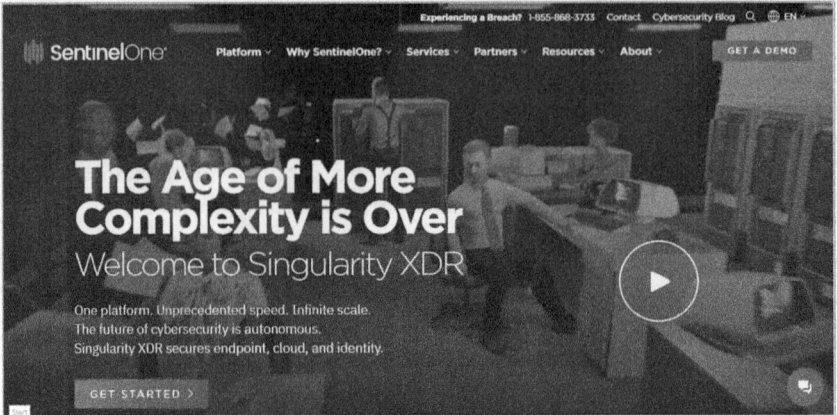

Figure 9.4 SentinelOne endpoint security tool (screenshot).

- SentinelOne is an autonomous tool with numerous singularity modules used as an integrated platform that can effectively work in detecting and responding to threats in real-time and a highly dynamic attack surface environment with cross-platform connectivity.
- A comprehensive platform to work in the cloud and on-premises to safeguard endpoints, identity management, and any other data.
- Supports the detection of insider threats and deception, endpoint threats, and any other data breaches simultaneously.
- Integrated endpoint protection, security data analytics, attack surface management, identity detection and response, and other features.
- SentinelOne endpoint solution consists of a flexible, modular structure and all-in-one end-device security with the full capabilities of MDR, EDR, and others.
- SentinelOne is a very well-known name in the energy, finance, health-care, and education industries for comprehensive endpoint security solutions.
- Highly capable in finding any kinds of threats on all endpoint devices connected in a networked environment, such as mobiles, laptops, tablets, workstations, IoT devices, and many others.
- It is capable of preempting a proper response to any emerging cyberse-curity threat from within the network or externally.
- Capable of restoring the systems very quickly in case the systems have been compromised through any cyberattack.
- A unified tool to counter any kind of viruses, malware, spyware, ransomware, and other types of malicious codes and activities on the end devices.
- Capable of performing deep file inspection, attack anticipation, anti-virus replacement, automating immunization, and others.

- SentinelOne is able to detect threats at all levels, layers, and stages.
- Uses the most powerful artificial intelligence (AI) and machine learning (ML) technologies to boost the robustness of the tool.
- Uses a holistic agent with a lightweight program that does not overload your endpoint devices, servers, and other network resources.
- Supports dynamic blacklisting and whitelisting capabilities.
- A wide range of other integrations can be deployed through APIs to provide a centralized security management platform.
- If SentinelOne anticipates any kind of danger or dangerous activities, it starts inspecting all files, credentials, emails, memory storage, documents, payloads, and other content and resources deeply.
- It could be the best option for major organizations to replace their antivirus software platforms with this next-generation endpoint security tool.
- Supports a wide range of devices using operating systems such as Windows, iOS, Android, Linux, and others. It can also provide support to the web-based devices.
- The main modules of SentinelOne Singularity security include the following for domain-specific security. They can be integrated into one unified platform, too.
  - SentinelOne Singularity XDR.
  - SentinelOne Singularity XDR App.
  - SentinelOne Rangers.
  - SentinelOne Active EDR.
  - SentinelOne Singularity Mobile.
  - SentinelOne Singularity Cloud.

Symantec enterprise cloud

Symantec Enterprise Cloud, precisely referred to as SEC (see Figure 9.5), is a unified cybersecurity platform for finding, fixing, and responding to any emerging threat in the modern dynamic field of cybersecurity. This platform consists of multiple modules, which are integrated into one unified cybersecurity platform through smooth and seamless integration. The most important modules that form this unified security platform for enterprise include:[225]

- Endpoint security.
- Information security.
- Network security.
- Email security.

Symantec Enterprise Cloud is a data-centric hybrid security tool that is designed for all types of enterprises, especially for large organizations in numerous industries ranging from healthcare, education, finance and banking, information technology, and others. It works perfectly on all types

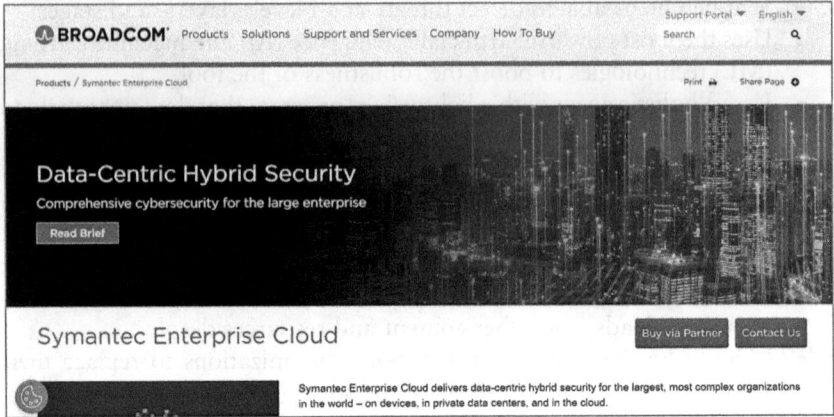

Figure 9.5 Symantec enterprise cloud (screenshot).

of on-premises devices, in the cloud, and in private data centers. It helps an organization achieve the following main objectives:

- **Secure remote network** – It allows all employees or other users of the network to access it from anywhere in the world with perfect security, without any compromise on security or exposure to risks on the Internet.
- **Compliance consistency** – Helps the organization maintain a high level of consistency in the industrial and regulatory compliance management.
- **Data threat protection anywhere** – Enables the enterprise to scan, detect, identify, block, and remediate any kind of emerging threats or targeted attacks on endpoint devices, network devices, or backend servers simultaneously.

The most important characteristics, features, and capabilities of the Symantec Enterprise Cloud cybersecurity platform are mentioned below:[226,227,228]

- Highly innovative solution achieved through the creation, acquisition, integration, and extension of advanced technologies such as artificial intelligence (AI) and machine learning (ML) into the unified platform.
- This platform anticipates and aligns the Secure Access Service Edge (SASE) and Zero Trust frameworks to provide extremely robust security in the most dynamic cybersecurity environment.
- A unified and single-vendor solution of the SEC enhances the cybersecurity management capabilities of an organization.
- Supports both on-premises and cloud-based deployments of a comprehensive SEC cybersecurity platform.

- Offers the capability of cross-platform and cross-control point security and management under one single hood.
- A competitive platform to protect both managed and unmanaged endpoints and network elements perfectly.
- Provides the capability of smooth migration of the security policies from an on-premises environment to the cloud-based environment without any exposure to cyber threats or risks at all.
- Being an integral part of the largest civilian threat intelligence network in the world, referred to as the Global Intelligence Network, it helps organizations preempt any emerging threat from anywhere in the world with great accuracy.
- Provides the support of over 11 trillion elements of telemetry, which play a vital role in global threat intelligence, to provide enterprises with comprehensive network security.
- Inherited support from three main cybersecurity resources to keep your security ahead of the hackers' thoughts, such as the Security Center, Global Intelligence Network, and Threat Intelligence Blogs platforms.
- It works great for the futuristic bring your own device (BYOD) ecosystem, which is based on unmanaged devices.
- The endpoint module or portfolio of SEC consists of three main sub-portfolios, such as:
  - **Endpoint security** – For workstations, mobiles, laptops, tablets, and others.
  - **Server security** – For all types of main machines running as servers of different types of services in the network.
  - **Endpoint management** – It is a perfect portfolio to manage the endpoints, both managed and unmanaged, seamlessly.
- Highly effective endpoint security throughout the entire attack chain to provide organizations with attack prevention, threat detection and response, attack surface reduction, and breach prevention comprehensively.
- Capable of providing on-premises, on-cloud, and hybrid cybersecurity protection for all types of endpoint devices in all those environments.
- The endpoint security solution is further divided into two commercial packages based on the requirements of the domain-specific organizations, such as:
  - Endpoint security complete.
  - Endpoint security enterprise.
- The server security portfolio can offer a range of security capabilities, such as:
  - Security of private and public clouds.
  - Comprehensive vulnerability reduction in storage servers.
  - Security of critical data center infrastructure.
  - Cloud workload protection and data center security.
  - Protection engine for cloud services.

- SharePoint server protection and NAS storage.
- And others.
- The endpoint management module of the SEC security platform offers the additional feature of managing endpoint devices with perfect security. It can deal with both managed and unmanaged devices perfectly.
- The endpoint management portfolio has further sub-domains or modules to deal with different types of endpoint devices, such as:
  - **Client management suite** – For the automation of routine and redundant tasks.
  - **Asset management suite** – For controlling assets and implementing compliance.
  - **Ghost solutions suite** – For migration and deployment of OS and other platforms.
  - **Server management suite** – For monitoring and controlling virtual as well as physical servers simultaneously.
- The network security portfolio of Symantec Enterprise Cloud offers numerous sub-modules and functionalities to manage the network security perfectly. A few of the most important capabilities of a network security portfolio include:
  - Secure web gateway.
  - Advanced threat protection for networks.
  - Encrypted traffic management.
  - Messaging security.
- The major features of the network security module also include Zero Trust Network Access (ZTNA) that uses the advanced software-defined perimeter (SDP) technology, web isolation for the protection of viruses and other malware programs, and the sandboxing technique used in emulation and virtualization to catch the advanced malicious behaviors and threats.
- Symantec Secure Web Gateway (SWG) runs on a secure proxy server architecture for monitoring, controlling, and securing traffic in a safe web environment.
- There are different modules designed and integrated into the SEC security system pertaining to the secure web gateway services or solutions. A few of the most important capabilities of them are mentioned below:
  - Symantec Cloud Secure Web Gateway.
  - Symantec Web Isolation.
  - Symantec Edge Secure Web Gateway.
  - Symantec Content Analysis and Sandboxing.
  - Symantec Intelligence Services.

All those features of secure web gateway security enable the organizations to detect threats well before they materialize into an inevitable threat and provide proper preemptive response to avoid any kind of risk to the network and web environment. There are many other cybersecurity tools available in the market that are powered by machine learning and artificial intelligence technologies. Choosing the right tool depends on the requirements of an organization and the criticality of the processes it wants to safeguard. Also, this depends on the budget allocated and the availability of the supporting resources and infrastructure on the organization's premises.

References

1. https://www.techtarget.com/whatis/definition/Confidentiality-integrity-and-availability-CIA
2. https://www.forbes.com/sites/chuckbrooks/2022/06/03/alarming-cyber-statistics-for-mid-year-2022-that-you-need-to-know/?sh=5e29964e7864
3. https://www.statista.com/statistics/273575/us-average-cost-incurred-by-a-data-breach/
4. https://www.embroker.com/blog/cyber-attack-statistics/
5. https://link.springer.com/article/10.1186/s40537-020-00318-5
6. https://link.springer.com/article/10.1186/s40537-020-00318-5/tables/4
7. https://www.statista.com/statistics/1307426/number-of-data-breaches-worldwide/
8. https://iot-analytics.com/number-connected-iot-devices/
9. https://www.precedenceresearch.com/machine-learning-as-a-service-market
10. https://www.sailpoint.com/identity-library/how-ai-and-machine-learning-are-improving-cybersecurity/
11. https://www.techtarget.com/searchenterpriseai/definition/machine-learning-ML
12. https://www.mygreatlearning.com/blog/difference-data-science-machine-learning-ai/
13. https://www.techtarget.com/searchbusinessanalytics/feature/Data-science-vs-machine-learning-vs-AI-How-they-work-together
14. https://www.fortunebusinessinsights.com/big-data-analytics-market-106179
15. https://www.edureka.co/blog/types-of-artificial-intelligence/
16. https://mitsloan.mit.edu/ideas-made-to-matter/machine-learning-explained
17. https://www.forbes.com/sites/bernardmarr/2016/02/19/a-short-history-of-machine-learning-every-manager-should-read/?sh=4ffddccd15e7
18. https://www.techtarget.com/whatis/A-Timeline-of-Machine-Learning-History
19. https://en.wikipedia.org/wiki/Timeline_of_machine_learning
20. https://www.techtarget.com/searchenterpriseai/tip/9-top-AI-and-machine-learning-trends
21. https://www.techtarget.com/searchenterpriseai/definition/natural-language-processing-NLP
22. https://www.ibm.com/cloud/learn/natural-language-processing
23. https://en.wikipedia.org/wiki/Natural_language_processing
24. https://www.precedenceresearch.com/natural-language-processing-market
25. https://www.techtarget.com/searchenterpriseai/definition/deep-learning-deep-neural-network
26. https://www.coursera.org/articles/what-is-deep-learning
27. https://www.ibm.com/cloud/learn/neural-networks
28. https://aws.amazon.com/what-is/neural-network/
29. https://www.javatpoint.com/basic-concepts-in-machine-learning

30. https://www.javatpoint.com/supervised-machine-learning
31. https://www.techtarget.com/searchenterpriseai/definition/supervised-learning
32. https://en.wikipedia.org/wiki/Unsupervised_learning
33. https://www.ibm.com/cloud/learn/unsupervised-learning
34. https://www.geeksforgeeks.org/ml-semi-supervised-learning/
35. https://www.javatpoint.com/semi-supervised-learning
36. https://www.techtarget.com/searchenterpriseai/definition/reinforcement-learning
37. https://www.geeksforgeeks.org/what-is-reinforcement-learning/
38. https://www.linkedin.com/pulse/difference-between-algorithm-model-machine-learning-yahya-abi-haidar
39. https://docs.aws.amazon.com/machine-learning/latest/dg/types-of-ml-models.html
40. https://machinelearningmastery.com/types-of-classification-in-machine-learning/
41. https://www.javatpoint.com/machine-learning-models
42. https://towardsdatascience.com/all-machine-learning-models-explained-in-6-minutes-9fe30ff6776a
43. https://en.wikipedia.org/wiki/Decision_tree
44. https://levelup.gitconnected.com/random-forest-regression-209c0f354c84
45. https://www.ibm.com/docs/en/spss-modeler/18.0.0?topic=networks-neural-model
46. https://www.javatpoint.com/k-means-clustering-algorithm-in-machine-learning
47. https://towardsdatascience.com/understanding-k-means-clustering-in-machine-learning-6a6e67336aa1
48. https://analyticsindiamag.com/hands-on-tutorial-on-mean-shift-clustering-algorithm/
49. https://www.geeksforgeeks.org/ml-mean-shift-clustering/
50. https://pro.arcgis.com/en/pro-app/latest/tool-reference/spatial-statistics/how-density-based-clustering-works.htm
51. https://elutins.medium.com/dbscan-what-is-it-when-to-use-it-how-to-use-it-8bd 506293818
52. https://pberba.github.io/stats/2020/07/08/intro-hdbscan/
53. https://www.geeksforgeeks.org/ml-optics-clustering-explanation/
54. https://www.javatpoint.com/hierarchical-clustering-in-machine-learning
55. https://www.w3schools.com/python/python_ml_hierarchial_clustering.asp
56. https://www.javatpoint.com/dimensionality-reduction-technique
57. https://www.geeksforgeeks.org/dimensionality-reduction/
58. https://royalsocietypublishing.org/doi/10.1098/rsta.2015.0202
59. https://hub.knime.com/knime/extensions/org.knime.features.base/latest/org.knime.base.node.preproc.lowvarfilter2.LowVarFilter2NodeFactory
60. https://www.analyticsvidhya.com/blog/2021/04/beginners-guide-to-missing-value-ratio-and-its-implementation/
61. https://towardsdatascience.com/factor-analysis-my-ml-oreo-detector-2e02abc 2bb30
62. https://www.analyticsvidhya.com/blog/2018/08/dimensionality-reduction-techniques-python/
63. https://www.jeremyjordan.me/autoencoders/
64. https://www.techtarget.com/searchbusinessanalytics/definition/Ensemble-modeling
65. https://www.intellspot.com/anomaly-detection-algorithms/
66. https://www.seldon.io/transfer-learning
67. https://www.sciencedirect.com/topics/engineering/classification-algorithm
68. https://www.simplilearn.com/tutorials/machine-learning-tutorial/random-forest-algorithm
69. https://www.ibm.com/topics/decision-trees
70. https://www.javatpoint.com/machine-learning-naive-bayes-classifier

71. https://www.simplilearn.com/tutorials/machine-learning-tutorial/naive-bayes-classifier
72. https://towardsdatascience.com/machine-learning-basics-with-the-k-nearest-neighbors-algorithm-6a6e71d01761
73. https://www.ibm.com/topics/knn
74. https://www.techtarget.com/whatis/definition/support-vector-machine-SVM
75. https://www.javatpoint.com/machine-learning-support-vector-machine-algorithm
76. https://www.analyticsvidhya.com/blog/2021/09/gradient-boosting-algorithm-a-complete-guide-for-beginners/
77. https://machinelearningmastery.com/gentle-introduction-gradient-boosting-algorithm-machine-learning/
78. https://www.seldon.io/machine-learning-regression-explained
79. https://www.analyticsvidhya.com/blog/2021/05/all-you-need-to-know-about-your-first-machine-learning-model-linear-regression
80. https://www.javatpoint.com/linear-regression-in-machine-learning
81. https://towardsdatascience.com/multiple-regression-as-a-machine-learning-algorithm-a98a6b9f307b
82. https://www.simplilearn.com/what-is-multiple-linear-regression-in-machine-learning-article
83. https://www.mygreatlearning.com/blog/understanding-of-lasso-regression/
84. https://www.jigsawacademy.com/blogs/ai-ml/lasso-regression
85. https://www.techtarget.com/searchbusinessanalytics/definition/logistic-regression
86. https://www.ibm.com/topics/logistic-regression
87. https://www.upgrad.com/blog/introduction-to-multivariate-regression-in-machine-learning/
88. https://www.freecodecamp.org/news/8-clustering-algorithms-in-machine-learning-that-all-data-scientists-should-know/
89. https://www.geeksforgeeks.org/ml-expectation-maximization-algorithm/
90. https://www.javatpoint.com/em-algorithm-in-machine-learning
91. https://towardsdatascience.com/machine-learning-algorithms-part-12-hierarchical-agglomerative-clustering-example-in-python-1e18e0075019
92. https://www.datanovia.com/en/lessons/agglomerative-hierarchical-clustering/
93. https://towardsdatascience.com/hierarchical-clustering-agglomerative-and-divisive-explained-342e6b20d710
94. https://www.simplilearn.com/tutorials/machine-learning-tutorial/k-means-clustering-algorithm
95. https://towardsdatascience.com/k-means-clustering-algorithm-applications-evaluation-methods-and-drawbacks-aa03e644b48a
96. https://medium.com/geekculture/fuzzy-c-means-clustering-fcm-algorithm-in-machine-learning-c2e51e586fff
97. https://en.wikipedia.org/wiki/Fuzzy_clustering
98. https://www.mathworks.com/help/fuzzy/fuzzy-c-means-clustering.html
99. https://www.techtarget.com/searchenterpriseai/definition/machine-teaching
100. https://oden.io/glossary/model-training/
101. https://www.javatpoint.com/train-and-test-datasets-in-machine-learning
102. https://en.wikipedia.org/wiki/Training,_validation,_and_test_data_sets
103. https://research.aimultiple.com/datasets-for-ml/
104. https://pub.towardsai.net/types-of-data-in-machine-learning-6c1f262a17e7
105. https://www.tibco.com/reference-center/what-is-structured-data
106. https://www.geeksforgeeks.org/what-is-unstructured-data/
107. https://www.lexalytics.com/blog/text-analytics-functions-explained/
108. https://towardsdatascience.com/machine-learning-text-processing-1d5a2d638958
109. https://summalinguae.com/data/where-to-find-speech-data/

110. https://summalinguae.com/data/types-of-speech-recognition-data/
111. https://www.ridgerun.com/video-based-ai
112. https://www.taskus.com/insights/video-data-collection-for-machine-learning-a-guide/
113. https://nanonets.com/blog/machine-learning-image-processing/
114. https://kili-technology.com/data-labeling/computer-vision/image-annotation/image-recognition-with-machine-learning-how-and-why
115. https://www.javatpoint.com/how-to-get-datasets-for-machine-learning
116. https://wearablesinpractice.com/wp-content/uploads/2018/12/wearables_symposium_mark_hoogendoorn.pdf
117. https://www.mdpi.com/1424-8220/20/21/6019
118. https://www.usgs.gov/faqs/what-are-differences-between-data-dataset-and-database
119. https://www.clickworker.com/customer-blog/machine-learning-datasets
120. https://www.section.io/engineering-education/how-to-create-a-dataset-for-machine-learning/
121. https://www.techtarget.com/searchbusinessanalytics/feature/Data-preparation-in-machine-learning-6-key-steps
122. https://monkeylearn.com/blog/data-classification
123. https://www.ibm.com/topics/data-labeling
124. https://www.shaip.com/blog/the-a-to-z-of-data-annotation
125. https://kili-technology.com/data-labeling/nlp/what-is-text-annotation-in-machine-learning
126. https://www.simplilearn.com/what-is-image-annotation-and-its-importance-in-machine-learning-article
127. https://www.v7labs.com/blog/image-annotation-guide
128. https://sunix.in/lines-splines/
129. https://labellerr.medium.com/keypoint-detection-what-when-and-how-labellerr-labelling-made-easy-blog-5c7650adaa58
130. https://www.anolytics.ai/polyline-annotation-services/
131. https://kili-technology.com/data-labeling/computer-vision/video-annotation
132. https://www.superannotate.com/blog/video-annotation-for-machine-learning
133. https://www.clickworker.com/ai-glossary/audio-annotation/
134. https://www.taskus.com/insights/guide-to-audio-annotation-services-for-machine-learning
135. https://ieeexplore.ieee.org/document/9053065
136. https://www.investopedia.com/terms/d/data-analytics.asp
137. https://www.dataversity.net/brief-history-analytics/#
138. https://www.linkedin.com/pulse/brief-history-data-analytics-deryck-brailsford-%E5%AD%99%E5%BE%B7%E7%91%9E
139. https://www.analyticssteps.com/blogs/big-data-analytics-cybersecurity-role-and-applications
140. https://www.ijert.org/big-data-analytics-in-cyber-security
141. https://www.techtarget.com/iotagenda/definition/machine-data
142. https://www.splunk.com/en_us/data-insider/what-is-real-time-data.html
143. https://www.guru99.com/what-is-big-data.html#1
144. https://www.techtarget.com/whatis/definition/metadata
145. https://online.hbs.edu/blog/post/types-of-data-analysis
146. https://www.geeksforgeeks.org/data-analytics-and-its-type/
147. https://www.simplilearn.com/data-analysis-methods-process-types-article
148. https://www.analyticssteps.com/blogs/7-types-statistical-analysis-definition-explanation
149. https://en.wikipedia.org/wiki/Mathematical_analysis

150. https://www.statisticssolutions.com/free-resources/directory-of-statistical-analyses/factor-analysis/
151. https://www.tableau.com/learn/articles/time-series-analysis
152. https://www.ibm.com/topics/monte-carlo-simulation
153. https://towardsdatascience.com/10-machine-learning-methods-that-every-data-scientist-should-know-3cc96e0eeee9
154. https://www.udacity.com/blog/2020/08/machine-learning-for-data-analysis.html
155. https://www.simplilearn.com/data-science-vs-data-analytics-vs-machine-learning-article
156. https://www.ibm.com/topics/deep-learning
157. https://www.deeplearningbook.org/
158. https://www.simplilearn.com/tutorials/deep-learning-tutorial/what-is-deep-learning#how_does_deep_learning_work
159. https://www.freecodecamp.org/news/want-to-know-how-deep-learning-works-heres-a-quick-guide-for-everyone-1aedeca88076/
160. https://blog.paperspace.com/feed-forward-vs-feedback-neural-networks/
161. https://viso.ai/deep-learning/deep-neural-network-three-popular-types/
162. https://www.analyticsvidhya.com/blog/2020/02/cnn-vs-rnn-vs-mlp-analyzing-3-types-of-neural-networks-in-deep-learning/
163. https://www.analyticsvidhya.com/blog/2020/02/mathematics-behind-convolutional-neural-network/
164. https://www.analyticsvidhya.com/blog/2017/12/introduction-to-recurrent-neural-networks/
165. https://towardsdatascience.com/regularization-in-deep-learning-l1-l2-and-dropout-377e75acc036
166. https://towardsdatascience.com/deep-feed-forward-neural-networks-and-the-advantage-of-relu-activation-function-ff881e58a635
167. https://www.upgrad.com/blog/types-of-optimizers-in-deep-learning/
168. https://pub.towardsai.net/three-types-of-recurrent-neural-networks-567b4e9c4261
169. https://en.wikipedia.org/wiki/Recursive_neural_network
170. https://www.simplilearn.com/recursive-neural-network-in-deep-learning-article
171. https://digitalskills.engin.umich.edu/cybersecurity/introduction-to-cybersecurity/
172. https://www.techtarget.com/searchsecurity/definition/cybersecurity
173. https://www.checkpoint.com/cyber-hub/cyber-security/what-is-cybersecurity
174. https://www.ibm.com/topics/data-security
175. https://www.trellix.com/security-awareness/endpoint/what-is-endpoint-security/
176. https://www.proofpoint.com/us/threat-reference/iot-security
177. https://www.digitalguardian.com/blog/what-operational-security-five-step-process-best-practices-and-more
178. https://www.techtarget.com/searchsecurity/definition/physical-security
179. https://www.techtarget.com/whatis/definition/critical-infrastructure-security
180. https://www.vmware.com/topics/glossary/content/disaster-recovery.html
181. https://www.knowledgehut.com/blog/security/history-of-cyber-security
182. https://www.checkpoint.com/cyber-hub/network-security/what-is-firewall/what-is-a-hardware-firewall/
183. https://brainstation.io/career-guides/what-tools-do-cybersecurity-analysts-use
184. https://en.wikipedia.org/wiki/Security_information_and_event_management
185. https://www.balbix.com/insights/what-to-know-about-vulnerability-scanning-and-tools/
186. https://www.dragos.com/wp-content/uploads/The_Four_Types-of_Threat_Detection.pdf
187. https://en.wikipedia.org/wiki/Vulnerability_scanner
188. https://www.just.edu.jo/~tawalbeh/cpe542/lab/sniffers.pdf

189. https://cpl.thalesgroup.com/faq/public-key-infrastructure-pki/what-public-key-infrastructure-pki
190. https://portswigger.net/burp/vulnerability-scanner/guide-to-vulnerability-scanning
191. https://www.cisco.com/site/us/en/solutions/security/extended-detection-response-xdr/index.html
192. https://www.trellix.com/security-awareness/endpoint/what-is-endpoint-detection-and-response/
193. https://brightsec.com/blog/penetration-testing/
194. https://www.techtarget.com/searchsecurity/CyberResiliency/5-Key-Elements-of-a-Modern-Cybersecurity-Framework
195. https://www.securityroundtable.org/the-growing-role-of-machine-learning-in-cybersecurity/
196. https://www.hitechnectar.com/blogs/machine-learning-in-cybersecurity/
197. https://cloudinfrastructureservices.co.uk/how-machine-learning-is-used-in-cybersecurity/
198. https://www.analyticsvidhya.com/blog/2023/02/future-of-ai-and-machine-learning-in-cybersecurity/
199. https://www.geeksforgeeks.org/top-5-applications-of-machine-learning-in-cyber-security/
200. https://towardsdatascience.com/machine-learning-for-cybersecurity-101-7822b802790b
201. https://www.crowdstrike.com/cybersecurity-101/machine-learning-cybersecurity/
202. https://publisher.uthm.edu.my/ojs/index.php/jscdm/article/view/8798/4556
203. http://cs229.stanford.edu/proj2017/final-reports/5239112.pdf
204. https://securelist.com/spam-phishing-scam-report-2022/108692/
205. https://www.hindawi.com/journals/scn/2022/1862888/
206. https://en.wikipedia.org/wiki/Network_behavior_anomaly_detection
207. https://towardsdatascience.com/5-anomaly-detection-algorithms-every-data-scientist-should-know-b36c3605ea16
208. https://www.thinkmind.org/articles/securware_2017_1_20_30078.pdf
209. https://www.techtarget.com/searchsecurity/tip/How-hackers-use-AI-and-machine-learning-to-target-enterprises
210. https://www.balbix.com/insights/artificial-intelligence-in-cybersecurity/
211. https://www.xenonstack.com/blog/machine-learning-cybersecurity
212. https://www.cybereason.com/blog/ai/ml-powered-automation-the-future-of-cybersecurity-at-scale
213. https://www.marktechpost.com/2022/08/11/top-artificial-intelligence-based-tools-for-cyber-security/
214. https://cybersecurityventures.com/top-5-cybersecurity-facts-figures-predictions-and-statistics-for-2021-to-2025/
215. https://www.peerspot.com/products/crowdstrike-falcon-reviews
216. https://www.crowdstrike.com/services/managed-services/falcon-complete/
217. https://www.trustradius.com/products/ibm-security-qradar/reviews#product-details
218. https://www.ibm.com/products/qradar-siem/addons
219. https://www.ibm.com/docs/en/qradar-common?topic=apps-qradar-advisor-watson-app
220. https://www.sophos.com/en-us/products/endpoint-antivirus
221. https://www.gartner.com/reviews/market/endpoint-protection-platforms/vendor/sophos/product/sophos-intercept-x
222. https://www.sentinelone.com/
223. https://comparecamp.com/sentinelone-review-pricing-pros-cons-features/
224. https://www.sentinelone.com/platform/

225. https://www.broadcom.com/products/cybersecurity
226. https://www.gartner.com/reviews/market/zero-trust-network-access/vendor/broadcom-symantec/product/symantec-enterprise-cloud
227. https://www.softwareadvice.com/encryption/symantec-endpoint-protection-profile/reviews/
228. https://www.broadcom.com/products/cybersecurity/network

Index

For Product Safety Concerns and Information please contact our EU
representative GPSR@taylorandfrancis.com
Taylor & Francis Verlag GmbH, Kaufingerstraße 24, 80331 München, Germany

www.ingramcontent.com/pod-product-compliance
Lightning Source LLC
Chambersburg PA
CBHW060352220326
41598CB00023B/2887

9 781041 171683